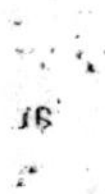

Learning to Be Chinese:
The Political Socialization
of Children in Taiwan

Learning to Be Chinese:
The Political Socialization
of Children in Taiwan

Richard W. Wilson

The M.I.T. Press
Cambridge, Massachusetts,
and London, England

Contents

List of Figures

Preface

Although interest in studies of China has increased greatly in the past decade, it is still very apparent that only a beginning has been made in the analysis of this remarkable society. Far from causing dismay or alarm, however, this condition presents one of the broadest, most exciting, and challenging prospects for scholarship to be found in the world today. As this challenge is met, we shall not only know more about China herself but also make her society less of the baffling question mark it remains for many who would like to use Chinese materials in the comparative study of societies.

Some of the more puzzling questions we face in the study of any society can be analyzed in terms of the particular style of group life common to the members of that society. When such an analysis is made with specific regard to the symbols, values, and beliefs associated with authority relationships within the group, we are justified in saying that the study deals with the "political culture" of that society. One increasingly important approach in this new and exciting field is that of "political socialization," how an individual comes to be a member of a group with particular political attitudes and distinctive political behavior patterns.

An analysis of childhood political socialization in Taiwan reveals a great emphasis during training on shaming techniques. The emotions generated through such techniques are part of a complex of attitudes associated in the Chinese language with the concept of "face." There seems to be an intimate relationship between face and values that support a predominantly vertical group structure and centralized authority pattern.

In studying Chinese children on Taiwan, I have analyzed three areas crucial to an understanding of the political culture. First, I have attempted to describe the relationship between the various social units or groups in which Chinese live. By a discussion of training techniques, many of which rely heavily on "face," I have then tried to reveal not only the type of attitudes held toward the various social units and their memberships but also the intensity of loyalty directed toward each group or level of group life. One main element of this analysis is how the educational system attempts to train children to identify with, and invest loyalty in, the state. Next, I have tried to show the relationship of these group attitudes, in the Chinese case, to the attitudes that individual group members hold toward authority figures, and in particular toward their political leaders who come to personify the political process. It has been demonstrated how children's attitudes toward the father and teacher in primary group life are paralleled, to a great extent, by similar orientations toward political leaders. Last, I have endeavored to describe how socialization techniques seem to generate considerable anxiety about proper behavior with peers and with authority figures. There are, however, limited ways to express the hostility associated with this anxiety. Hostility may be channeled with considerable emotional intensity against selected outgroups in a manner sanctioned by society. It may also be manifested in a nonsanctioned way, such as covert cynicism, often expressed concurrently with overt formalistic and "proper" manifestations of loyalty. How hostility emotions and defenses against group pressure are expressed is critical to an understanding of the stability or instability of a political system.

In carrying out my research I incurred a debt of gratitude to many, of whom, I regret, only a partial listing can be made here. Let me reverse the normal order and thank my wife first, for she not only encouraged this project but also helped me in many aspects of its undertaking. To Richard H. Solomon I am deeply indebted for his stimulation and encouragement and, more important, his creative help in pointing out many of the intricate interrelationships of the socialization process. In like manner Lawrence W. Chisholm and William W. Whitson helped in unraveling some of the less obvious facets of Chinese behavior patterns. To Lyman P. Van Slyke, Carl Leban, Alex Han, and the teaching staff at the Inter-University Program for Chinese Language Studies in Taipei, I am also indebted for encouragement and for help in carrying out my research.

At Princeton University William W. Lockwood, Frederick W. Mote, and Glenn D. Paige have been especial sources of inspiration, encouragement, and greatly appreciated criticism. They are representative of a wider group at Princeton to whom I owe a debt of great significance.

Last, I wish to give thanks to the educational authorities of the Ministry of Education of the Republic of China, to the principals and teachers of the schools where I did my research, and most of all to the "little friends" who happily, patiently, and willingly were the subject of this study.

Learning to Be Chinese:
The Political Socialization
of Children in Taiwan

Introduction

Decades of involvement in the Far East have not reduced the perplexity of many Americans in their perception of Asia. Missionaries, merchants, and, more recently, soldiers have experienced life in the Orient, and all have brought home to America their own versions of who the Chinese, Japanese, Koreans, or Vietnamese are. Sometimes the stories are romantic, sometimes sordid, sometimes terrifying, but never do they seem to comprise a complete picture. There is always something missing and unrealistic, and events, therefore, take on a make-believe quality with no beginning, no end, and no real substance in between.

Our gaps of knowledge about the Orient are too frequently filled for many by clichés and by gross stereotypes. Asians are reputed to be stoical, to care nothing about human life, and to be able to survive where others would perish quickly. At their worst they are crafty and cruel, endlessly devious and cunning, with a belief in their own superiority and the patience to persevere until one day that superiority is acknowledged by the world. For the waves of young Americans who since 1941 have lived and fought in Asia as soldiers, the faceless people surrounding them have often been seen in the least flattering of possible lights, if not as enemies then as representatives of some of the gamier aspects of human existence. The accounts of these unwilling visitors to a foreign continent have all too often reinforced an image that is both unjust and untrue.

Yet it cannot be denied that reports from more sympathetic observers (and in all fairness it should be added that many Americans are deeply sympathetic) seem often no more real than the less flattering comments. Thrift and hard work, honest friendship and great generosity—these are virtues that are difficult to place in a scene so vast, so changing, and so often violent.

Perhaps at no time is American perplexity greater than when we view the politics of Asia. Westerners are not strangers to violence and revolution, to massed crowds marching mindlessly toward some promised land. But in viewing Asia there is the haunting doubt that, in what superficially appear to be similar phenomena, something is basically different. For how could the Japanese, resisting to the death, turn overnight in defeat to meek acceptors of an alien occupation? Or again, how does a society that we are taught to believe has for millennia held filiality as the highest virtue teach its young in a few short years to denounce parents in savage criticism meetings? Punishments for political opponents seem bizarre. What is the meaning of giant meetings where men are made to confess guilt before one hundred thousand screaming onlookers? An article on China in the mass-distribution *New York Times Magazine* quotes Mao Tse-tung on the subject of punishment:

A tall paper hat is stuck on the head of one of the local tyrants or evil gentry. . . . He is led by a rope and escorted with big crowds in front and behind. Sometimes brass gongs are beaten and flags waved to attract people's attention. This form of punishment, more than any other, makes the local tyrant and evil gentry tremble. Anyone who has once been crowned with a tall paper hat loses face altogether and can never again hold up his head.[1]

Why will this form of punishment, *more than any other*, make men tremble? Surely this humiliation of enemies seems mild in comparison with the treatment often meted out to political opponents elsewhere in the world. Yet there is no reason for us not to believe that in China, at least, this type of sanction is severe indeed.

If perplexity stopped with forms of punishment alone, Americans might dismiss such actions as a quirk in an otherwise explicable pattern. Unfortunately such is not the case. Unbelievingly we read of ping-pong teams claiming victory on the basis of the political thought of Mao Tse-tung, and that the ping-pong ball itself symbolizes the head of Chiang Kai-shek. Should one laugh at this account, or is there an attitude behind such statements and actions that must be taken seriously? On a broader plane Americans have watched in China sudden shifts from what appears to be remarkable monolithic political solidarity to anarchistic disorder. Observers and scholars of Asia with impeccable credentials have been able neither to predict such occurrences nor to pinpoint their cause. Small wonder that Americans are puzzled when even their experts are baffled. Further examples could be easily added, but the point has

---

1. Jean-Louis Vincent, "Life in Peking: Report from a Long Nose," *The New York Times Magazine*, Feb. 26, 1967, p. 91 (quoting Mao's 1927 report on the peasant movement in Hunan Province).

been made. For good or bad, Americans are involved in an area where many basic organizing principles of social life seem different (and hence inexplicable) from those intuitively thought by Westerners to be normal and immutable.

Knowledge of East Asia has increased enormously in the last two decades, but the rate of change in East Asian social patterns and the frequent disorder noted there have very probably increased our problems of understanding. It is sometimes forgotten that the aging leaders of many of the Asian governments we now deal with have encompassed in their own lives changes that took several centuries to transpire in the West. Men like Chiang Kai-shek and Mao Tse-tung were born and spent their childhoods in predominantly traditional societies. The coming of nationalism has increased diversity and widened the differences between East Asian societies, but even now, in all these countries, we still observe with remarkable clarity a common heritage of the past. For while the more formal precepts of the traditional culture are no longer consciously invoked, many patterns of traditional social interaction have been slow to change.

In China, both Communist and Nationalist, the legacy of a common outlook on life remains despite different political ideologies and different attempts to restructure social life. In *Report from a Chinese Village*, Jan Myrdal has set down the results of an interview he had with a young elementary school principal in the Communist mainland village where he lived. Several quotations are worth repeating, for in tone or substance there is little difference between them and the gist of many interview remarks made by school authorities on Nationalist Taiwan.

Because we explain to the children that the purpose of their studying is to make them fit to build up their country, our pupils now work with great enthusiasm. That was not the case in the old days. . . . We attach great weight to their moral education. We hold up various models and heroes as moral examples for them. We tell them what they should do, and what they should not do. We make it clear to them where the line runs between right and wrong.[2]

2. Jan Myrdal, *Report from a Chinese Village* (London: William Heinemann Ltd., 1965), p. 296. Morals, says one Nationalist Chinese educational source, are an integral part of group consciousness, and therefore "morals are the most important part of school educational content." Tao-te Chiao-yu Shih-shih Luen 道德教育實施論 [A Discussion of the Practical Application of Morals Education] by Kung Pao-shan 龔寶善 (Taipei, Taiwan, 1962), pp. 5–6, 29 國立教育資料館.

Hygiene and cleanliness is another difficulty. . . . We show them various posters and pictures and try to inculcate good habits of hygiene. In the lower classes, we usually go round and inspect the children to see that they are clean and newly washed.[3]

. . . in the first class there is not much discipline. There everything's more of a game. The children must think all the time that school is fun. Then gradually, as they become older, they see the necessity of work discipline, and then we require more of them.

There is a certain amount of fighting and quarreling. We try to quell this and sort it all out with discussion and persuasion. As I've said, no teacher must ever try to settle anything by striking a child. We have to check disorder by other means. And it always succeeds.[4]

[Li Shung-chen] dreams of being a Pioneer, but he hasn't been allowed to join. He is far too undisciplined, and he does not work at his studies. So he has not been accepted as a member. It's not his dull-wittedness that is the obstacle—he can't help that—but the fact that he neglects his work.[5]

The children elect a leader for each class. The leader's job is to help the teacher maintain order; and he also has to help organize the pupils when on excursions and that sort of thing. He also presides over the committee of three that the pupils of each class elect to manage the various jobs the class does jointly. The committee of three consists of the class leader, a study leader, and one who is responsible for practical matters, such as keeping the classroom clean, work in the garden, etc.[6]

There are great differences between the educational philosophies and educational systems on the Communist Mainland and on Taiwan. Yet as these few quotes quite unconsciously reveal, there are aspects of education where great similarity may exist. The emphasis on moral education and on using heroes as models, the desire for cleanliness, the suppression of aggressive behavior and the use of noncorporal means of punishment to eliminate disorder (or create order), the emphasis on work and achievement as the criteria for group membership, and the use of a graded hierarchy in group life are general aspects of child training which seem common to both political systems.

The truth is that in many ways it is easier to hypothesize similarity

3. *Ibid.*, p. 314.
4. *Ibid.*, p. 302.
5. *Ibid.*, pp. 311–312.
6. *Ibid.*, p. 306.

in Chinese child-rearing techniques than dissimilarity. While a government or party may decree or advocate changes in the ways in which people interrelate, the styles of speech that adults use with children, the daily and generally mild sanctions employed in child training, parental expectations about what constitutes good behavior, are types of attitudes and actions that are extremely resistant to radical change. Not only are child-training techniques often largely unconscious, an amalgam of expected and sanctioned ways of dealing with other people, but if changed radically they are likely to result in considerable disorientation for the individuals involved, calling into question basic motives and values by which the routines of daily lives are governed. Therefore when a once unified society has separated into antagonistic political sections, there may be enormous and crucially significant differences in particular areas of learning, especially with regard to political matters, yet there may also remain enormous and crucially significant similarities in the ways in which people generally relate to others.

Socialization

The usefulness of studying children implies a relationship between child and adult that is based on the assumption of a continuity of learning experiences "both in the home and in extrafamilial social settings, for the eliciting, shaping, and maintaining of behavior patterns that are still evident, though of course in modified forms, in later years of life."[7] Beyond this there is the assumption of social scientists that a crucial link exists between early political training and the adult political process. To some, such assumptions are used as postulates to explain the persistence of political systems, from traditional village politics to modern nation states.[8] To others, the study of the tasks of socialization leads to

7. Albert Bandura and Richard H. Walters, *Social Learning and Personality Development* (New York: Holt, Rinehart & Winston, Inc., 1963), p. vii.

8. David Easton and Jack Dennis, "The Child's Image of Government," *Annuals of the American Academy of Political and Social Science*, vol. 361 (Sept. 1965), p. 41: "But for the fact that each new generation is able to learn a body of political orientations from its predecessors, no given political system would be able to persist. Fundamentally, the theoretical significance of the study of socializing processes in political life resides in its contribution to our understanding of the way in which political systems are able to persist, even as they change, for more than one generation."

an understanding of how change in one social aspect can lead to change for the system as a whole.[9]

What is meant by the term socialization? Erik Erikson has ventured a definition in which socialization is the process whereby "Man's 'inborn instincts' are drive fragments to be assembled, given meaning, and organized during a prolonged childhood by methods of child training and schooling which vary from culture to culture and are determined by tradition."[10] Socialization involves, in the first place, an interaction between an individual's personality and the society in which he is living, and therefore a study of socialization must examine not only personality or the social system but the interaction of the two. In the second place, socialization begins in childhood, although of course it does not end there. Third, the training given the individual is organized in some way, in the home with other family members, with groups of friends, perhaps formally as in school, in work, in play, etc. Last, the content of this training is to give meaning to the habits which one is taught to acquire, the content itself being, in effect, the culture of the society. It goes beyond saying, of course, that the process of socialization is not uniform for all individuals.

Socialization goes on throughout an individual's life, and it would, therefore, be erroneous to assume a one-to-one relationship between childhood experience and adult life. When we examine the socialization process for children, therefore, it is not because we consider childhood influences to be all important but because we consider them to be important. That there is a continuity between childhood and adult life is well established in psychological theory. Erikson, again, has said in writing an explanation for his study of Luther:

---

9. See Francis X. Sutton, "Education and the Making of Modern Nations," in *Education and Political Development*, James S. Coleman, ed. (Princeton, N.J.: Princeton University Press, 1965). Sutton says (p. 51) there are three tasks of socialization:
　　1. Definition of memberships and affiliations
　　2. The inculcation of ideas, symbols, and disciplines that are part of the general culture and transcend particular relationships or affiliations
　　3. A differential instruction in the accomplishments and expectations that go with different statuses in the society.

10. Erik H. Erikson, *Childhood and Society* (New York: W. W. Norton & Co., Inc., 1950), p. 90.

Man is not organized like an archeological mound, in layers; as he grows he makes the past part of all future, and every environment, as he once experienced it, part of the present environment. Dreams and dreamlike moments, when analyzed, always reveal the myriad past experiences which are waiting outside the gates of consciousness to mingle with present impressions.[11]

Even though socialization continues throughout life, and even though we must acknowledge and take into full account the fact that important changes may take place in adulthood,[12] it is still true that most theorists believe that when such changes take place in adulthood, they are profoundly influenced by earlier events.[13] The reasons for this have been under investigation for a long time. As early as 1879 two hypotheses were formulated which came to be known, after their originator, as Jost's laws. They are that (1) "If two associations are of equal strength but of different age, a new repetition has a greater value for the older one," and (2) "If two associations are of equal strength but of different age, the older diminishes less with time."[14] Fred I. Greenstein, in one of the most brilliant books written on political socialization, has set down four hypotheses as to why such early cultural content learning is least likely to change.[15] In the first place, the child learns uncritically; second, much early learning is at an unconscious level of imitation and identification; third, parents are highly authoritative; and fourth,

11. Erik H. Erikson, *Young Man Luther* (New York: W. W. Norton & Co., Inc., 1962), pp. 117–118.

12. Daniel J. Levinson in "The Relevance of Personality for Political Participation," *Public Opinion Quarterly*, vol. 22, no. 1 (Spring 1958), p. 8, has written: "Every individual has multiple political potentials and is capable of some measure of political change. Such change may come about not only through new knowledge and external circumstances but also as a result of inner changes in ideology-relevant aspects of personality. While acknowledging the importance and durability of the personality structure established by the age of five or six, we must still allow for important new developments and partial restructurings throughout life."

13. See Nathan Leites, "Psycho-Cultural Hypotheses about Political Acts," *World Politics*, vol. 1 (Oct. 1948), p. 109, as an example.

14. Quoted in David C. McClelland, *Personality* (New York: The Dryden Press, 1951), pp. 341–342, from John A. McGeoch, *The Psychology of Human Learning* (New York: Longmans, Green, 1942), p. 140. McCelland also presents an interesting critique of these hypotheses.

15. Fred I. Greenstein, *Children and Politics* (New Haven, Conn.: Yale University Press, 1965), pp. 80–81.

personality characteristics are being formed, and political and social learning becomes part of basic psychic equipment, i.e., the child is at a very formative age.

The chaos of sensations that the newborn infant experiences are "gradually welded into a world of perceived forms on the basis of sheer frequency of stimulus pairing in experience."[16] The experiences of a child, either those that are generated by him as outputs or those that come to him from the outside as inputs, become associated by contiguity in time or type and gradually form a pattern of perceptions. One experience is likely to activate an association with another if the two are paired as inputs or outputs. When a neutral stimulus is contiguous with some significant experience, it is likely that "the neutral stimulus will acquire an increment of association."[17] By this process of associating stimuli children slowly develop a habit complex.

A major aspect of this stimulus association is a rather unconscious modeling of behavior after some other individuals. Often, of course, this model is one with whom the child has established a relationship, but very complex patterns of behavior can also be developed by emulating a model with whom no prior relationship has been established. The values, needs, perceptions, and habits that are thus slowly acquired and forged out of a welter of stimuli—stimuli it must be recalled that come to a great extent from individuals whose own values, needs, perceptions, and habits have already been largely formed—become "singularly difficult to change by conscious knowledge or rational considerations in later life."[18] When a number of people of a society share common experiences and training and manifest similar habit complexes, we can speak of a custom complex.

Studying Political Socialization

Greenstein has stated the importance of distinguishing politically "relevant" aspects of personality development from "specific" political learning. The former deals with such factors as basic dispositions, beliefs, and attitudes. Included in this category would be the building of group

16. Charles E. Osgood, "Behavior Theory and the Social Sciences," in *Approaches to the Study of Politics*, Roland Young, ed. (Evanston, Ill.: Northwestern University Press, 1958), p. 231.

17. *Ibid.*, p. 234.

18. E. E. Hagen, "How Economic Growth Begins: A General Theory Applied to Japan," *Public Opinion Quarterly*, vol. 22, no. 3 (Fall 1958), p. 378.

cohesiveness, the role of self-criticism in learning, attitudes toward primary and secondary group authority figures (including such factors as sense of intimacy, benevolence versus nonbenevolence), and acceptable and unacceptable targets for aggression.

Research dealing with "specific" political learning examines the development of attitudes about, and knowledge of, formal political life. For instance, what aspects of the adult political process are children aware of? What is the extent of awareness? What is the nature of children's orientations toward such aspects of politics as parties and public officials? What is the content of children's perceptions of politics, what do they view as approved methods, etc.?

In studying childhood political socialization, it is necessary to obtain some sense of the extent of reinforcement between politically relevant aspects of individual development and specific political learning. It is also interesting to examine how children's attitudes vary with respect to age, sex, and socioeconomic background. In addition, the relation between ideal and actual patterns of behavior and the implications toward political behavior of the differences, if any, should be noted. Questions about the role of models in learning must also be asked. Models examined in this work will be immediate ones, such as parents and teachers, as well as more distant ones, such as those models found in books and pictorial representations. One must examine not only the content of modeling but also how models are effective and why. Throughout this work I will be testing the hypothesis that "Learned patterns of response tend to generalize to situations other than those in which they were learned, the extent of generalization being a function of the degree of similarity. . . ."[19]

It should be made quite clear that this work is not oriented primarily toward hypothesis testing; rather, it is largely exploratory in terms of what in Taiwan constitutes politically specific learning and politically relevant learning, what are the major ways in which reinforcement in political learning is achieved, and who serve in the role of model in political learning, and why. However, as these factors are often highly interdependent, no attempt is made to isolate them for rigorous individual analysis. Rather, an effort is made to examine three interrelated and basic facets of childhood training that incorporate, to some degree, all of the elements mentioned and that show the interaction between them.

19. Bandura and Walters, *Social Learning*, p. 8.

The initial area of investigation covers the social environment of the child, the group or groups he is a member of. The relevant factors for analysis are the means by which group integration is achieved, the nature of the stimuli that bring such integration about, and how responses are related to these stimuli. From this analysis the nature and strength of the cohesive bond between group members and attitudes toward group membership in general can be determined. In terms of political socialization an analysis is made of the ways in which generalized group loyalty is attached to the concept of the society and, in particular, to the political system.[20]

Second, the internal authority arrangements of groups are analyzed. This is essentially an examination of the nature of hierarchy within the group, whether authority is diffuse or unitary, and the nature of power and responsibility among the levels of hierarchy. Various types of leadership at differing levels of group generalization are examined to determine the degree of congruence among groups in authority relations. The role of the leader as model is investigated. Examining aspects of specific political education with regard to authority entails an analysis of how political leaders are introduced into educational content, the role of the political leader in political learning, and how children come to perceive of the political leader vis-à-vis the political process.

Last, an analysis is made of how hostility is expressed in terms of group solidarity and in terms of ideal authority relations. The relationship of hostility to the socialization process is also discussed. An examination is made of how the political authorities, acting through the educational system, attempt to channel potential hostility into increased loyalty and solidarity for their own political system and into hatred for political enemies. The implications for the political system of certain types of unchanneled hostility are also investigated.

Although age limits are difficult to assess, particularly in cross-cultural analysis, some theorists believe that the authority inception period extends from birth to six to ten years of age. During this period concepts of legitimate and nonlegitimate behavior are learned; the child learns

20. Sidney Verba, "Comparative Political Culture," in *Political Culture and Political Development*, Lucian Pye and Sidney Verba, eds. (Princeton, N.J.: Princeton University Press, 1965), p. 535, has stated that two crucial areas are a sense of national identity (a vertical form of identification) and the sense of integration one has with one's fellow citizens (horizontal identification).

to "locate his own behavior within the realm of the legitimate"; much of this training is done by "the very act of imposing authority on the child."[21] At this time the child obtains a generalized image of authority figures and lays the foundation for future conceptions of other authority figures.

The very fact that the authority inception period takes place in the first decade of life would make that period important as a basis for understanding adult political attitudes. There is a question, however, as to which time segment within the child's first decade is most important, for as the child is developing, his widening environment puts him into contact with many new influences. With regard to general socialization, it is certainly true that parents have an enormous influence in the very early years and may indeed be the most important one. Yet as Hyman has pointed out with regard to socialization toward political orientation, parents are "only one of the many agents of such socialization and . . . their influence is not that great."[22]

In this study attention has been focused upon the training a child receives in elementary school. This does not mean, however, that the base line of this study is the first-grade class—although no children were sampled below that group—for obviously a child does not shut off the attitudes derived mainly from the home the day he first arrives in school. Indeed, far from it, for these attitudes are intensely apparent and are the foundation upon which formal school training is based. The main reasons for focusing on school training are two: (1) many children—in some societies most—are, during their most impressionable years, gathered together in school for long periods and exposed to a common set of tasks imposed and "evaluated by one agent in terms of one set of standards,"[23] and (2) political aspects of training in school in transitional societies are often more emphasized than in the West because of a desire to counter traditional training received in the home and to create a

21. Much of the argument here is derived from Elisabeth Ruch Dubin and Robert Dubin, "The Authority Inception Period in Socialization," *Child Development,* vol. 34, no. 4 (Dec. 1963), p. 895.

22. Herbert H. Hyman, *Political Socialization: A Study in Political Behavior* (Glencoe, Ill.: The Free Press, 1959), p. 72.

23. See Talcott Parsons' remarks on achievement focusing in his article "General Theory in Sociology," in *Sociology Today,* R. K. Merton, Leonard Broom, and L. S. Cottrell, Jr., eds. (New York: Basic Books, Inc., 1959), p. 31.

sense of nationality.[24] Particularly in societies where potential or actual political instability is perceived by government leaders, civics training may become a deliberate policy, and the schools may be required to carry out many of the functions ordinarily performed informally by other institutions such as the family.

One of the values of examining political socialization through the medium of schools is the opportunity to view, in a terse, direct form, the ideals of the adults of that society (or at least that particular group of adults that controls the educational system). As Richard H. Solomon has said of the Chinese children's readers he analyzed: "While we would not look to the readers for a detailed view of a culture, they do seem useful for revealing a distilled image of the values, motives and points of view which are perceived by the educational elite as being most important for training the younger generation."[25]

Caution is of course necessary in judging how representative of the culture materials such as textbooks are. Yet it must be emphasized that such readers may influence the future culture of the society through a deep and lasting effect on the total habit complexes of the children. This is only an assumption, naturally, for the readers themselves do not absolutely predict later adult behavior,[26] but their influence can be tested against the current behavior of the children.[27] Furthermore, the importance of readers as attitude formers may be enhanced in societies where exposure to other forms of communication is limited—by design,

24. James S. Coleman, "Introduction: Education and Political Development," in *Education and Political Development,* Coleman, ed., pp. 20–22. In addition to the reasons cited, there is, I think, the rather obvious point that one must judge whether the quantity of data that could be gathered within a reasonable research period from several family studies is sufficiently large to justify generalizing about the population as a whole, or whether the convenience of having many school children concentrated together, whose attitudes toward the family can certainly be tested, despite their not being in a home environment, would provide more complete and varied data. Let me make it clear that I believe doing both would be desirable and that it is a matter of research time, expense, and practicality that may force the choice.

25. Richard H. Solomon, "Educational Themes in China's Changing Culture," *The China Quarterly,* no. 22 (April–June 1965), p. 156.

26. *Ibid.*

27. In the same way, of course, one can also look at the organized and unorganized content of children's games which not only indicate interests but are a mechanism for shaping interests. Greenstein, *Children and Politics,* p. 122.

because communication facilities are scarce, because the educational pattern leaves little extra time for outside exposure, or because of a combination of such factors.[28] Certainly the question of reinforcement or the lack of it by factors outside the school is crucial. However, to cite McClelland, who was speaking of the value of studying children's readers as guides to rates of future economic growth:

> It may come as something of a shock to realize that more could have been learned . . . by reading elementary school books than by studying such presumably more relevant matters as power politics, wars and depressions, economic statistics, or governmental policies governing international trade, taxation or public finance. The reason apparently lies in the fact that the readers reflect sufficiently accurately the motives and values of key groups of men in a country which in the long run determine the general drift of economics and political decisions. . . .[29]

In short, they give the attitudes which a key group of adults feel children should approximate.

The Taiwan Case

It is not my intention to provide here an inclusive and exhaustive list of facts concerning Taiwan—these can be quite adequately and properly obtained elsewhere—but only to enumerate the points of major concern for this study and to give the reader some familiarity with the environment in which this analysis was made.

Taiwan is a small island of roughly 14,000 square miles, located about 100 miles off the coast of southern China and opposite the mainland province of Fukien. The population as of early 1966 was approximately 12,700,000, of which nearly one tenth, or 1,150,000 people, lived in the capital city of Taipei.[30] The director of the Department of Elementary

28. In the case of Taiwan, all these factors are involved.

29. David C. McClelland, *The Achieving Society* (Princeton, N.J.: D. Van Nostrand Co., Inc., 1961), p. 202.

30. *China Post,* vol. 15, no. 4973 (June 2, 1966), p. 6. Exact figures given were 12,742,755 for the island as a whole and 1,152,493 for Taipei. These figures are for April 1966 as provided by the Taiwan provincial government. They should be regarded as approximate only, since members of the armed forces are frequently not included in population counts. It should also be noted that according to the *China Post* of Nov. 25, 1964, Taipei Hsien, the county in which Taipei City is located, had a population of 993,966 as of Sept. 1964. This means that the Taipei area has roughly 15–20 percent of the total island population.

Education of the Ministry of Education has estimated that, in 1963, 45 percent of the population was below fifteen years of age.[31]

Most of the people who live in Taiwan are Chinese; only a small fraction of the population is composed of the indigenous aboriginal people who inhabited the island prior to the waves of Chinese who began to arrive in strength some three hundred years ago. The Chinese themselves, however, are composed of three major groups. Two of these are usually classed together as Taiwanese and are composed primarily of people of Fukien ancestry, and considerably less—about 20 percent—of Hakkas whose forefathers came for the most part from Kwangtung. These two groups, although referred to casually by outsiders as Taiwanese, have a long history of mutual hostility. The last major group of Chinese is made up from the roughly two million refugees who fled the Mainland on its collapse to the Communists in 1949. This last group has generally settled in the cities and does not consider itself Taiwanese, although some of the children of these people are ambivalent about this.[32]

It is estimated that in 1963 the per capita income was $134 per year (in United States dollars), giving the people on Taiwan the second highest standard of living in the Far East, behind that of Japan.[33]

Exhibit data of the Ministry of Education (winter 1965) classified the population by occupational categories as 54.5 percent in agriculture, the rest being divided between industry, commerce, the professions, etc. Land reform carried out in the last fifteen years has increased the number of owner farmers from 36 percent in 1949 to 65 percent in 1961, and reduced the number of tenant farmers from 39 percent in 1949 to 14 percent in 1961. In 1961, 90 percent of the land being cultivated was owner cultivated versus 59 percent in 1949.[34] More important has been a change in the tenure system, restricting the amount of land an owner may possess and placing a ceiling on the rents a tenant may be charged. These changes

31. Interview with Mrs. Chu-Sheng Yeh Cheng, Feb. 23, 1965.

32. Each of these groups has its own predominant dialect, although the Mainlanders have enforced a policy of using Mandarin, the "national" language. Theoretically, therefore, all young people are fluent in Mandarin, although this is undoubtedly more true of the city than the countryside.

33. "Tourism Weekly," no. 118, *China Post*, vol. 14, no. 4632 (June 22, 1965). The *Wall Street Journal*, Aug. 2, 1965, p. 1, in an article entitled "Asian Comer," put the per capita income at $150.

34. David W. Chang, "U.S. Aid and Economic Progress in Taiwan," *Asian Survey*, vol. 5 no. 3 (March 1965), p. 157.

are usually credited with being at least partly responsible for the doubling of agricultural output between 1952 and 1964 and for the prosperity one generally notes in the countryside.[35] Industrial production in the same period rose 400 percent, giving us a general picture of policy emphasis on increasing industrial output. One senior American official in Taipei has said flatly, in private conversation, that he believes economic goals have far greater precedence with government leaders than the often polemic political goals they frequently espouse in public. This emphasis on economics is one interpretation often heard for the increased productivity that has taken place.

Along with increasing economic productivity, and intimately connected with it, has been a large increase in literacy. From the same exhibit data noted before, it was shown that only 7.26 percent of the total population is still illiterate. The general level of literacy is reflected in the fact that there are 31 newspapers published on the island and more than 780 different types of periodicals. While the written word is still the primary means of communication, there are roughly 22,000 television sets tuned in to the three different TV stations, and also about one radio set per eighteen people. What this indicates, in short, is a population that has the means at its disposal to obtain information. It indicates also a widening circle of social interaction which has a very important but indirect educational component.[36]

This growth is not without some unusual aspects. There has been massive United States aid.[37] The fact that politically powerful Mainlanders had few ties with local Taiwanese landlords made the implementation of land reform easier than if landed interests had had political connections. Urbanization has proceeded rapidly—Taipei's population has doubled in the past fifteen years. Unemployment is extremely high, the greatest proportionate amount being among the poorest and least educat-

35. "Asian Comer," *The Wall Street Journal*, p. 1. All of these figures should be viewed with some skepticism. Scholarly work now going on in the countryside in Taiwan should, when published, give us a far better idea of actual changes and conditions.

36. For an interesting argument on how investment in social overhead relates to education see Bert F. Hoselitz, "Investment in Education and Its Political Impact," in *Education and Political Development,* Coleman, ed.

37. "Asian Comer," *The Wall Street Journal*, p. 20, put this aid at 1.5 billion U.S. dollars economic aid and 2.7 billion U.S. dollars military aid, or the equivalent on a per capita basis of giving India 60 billion U.S. dollars.

ed. These and many other possible examples point clearly to the fact that growth and change have not been obtained without social cost. However, people are aware of some of these imbalances, and some effort is being made to bring them to public attention and to solve them.

In looking at Taiwan it is a mistake, I believe, to view the island's present prosperity and relative stability as in any way foreordained. Instead, one should keep another time reference, that of 1949, in mind as well as present circumstances. In 1949 the island was economically impoverished and highly unstable politically, governed by a morale-shattered and bankrupt Kuomintang that had fled the Mainland and awaited hourly the next onslaught of their enemy. The Taiwanese at that time were almost totally alienated from this group, having been the victims two years before of bloody repression after generally moderate effort on their part to alleviate the abuses of a corrupt, rapacious, and highly authoritarian Kuomintang provincial government. That such rapid social change could have taken place after such an inauspicious beginning is based on many factors, not the least of which is education.

Research Procedure

Research was carried out in Taiwan from the winter of 1965 through the spring of 1966. Basically four types of research procedure were used. The first method consisted of actual classroom and school observations carried out in three different schools in the Taipei area. Approximately four months were spent at a large city public school (enrollment 8,600), one month at a city private school (enrollment 1,000), and one month at a country public school (enrollment 3,000) located some ten miles from the outskirts of Taipei. The city public school had a mixed mainland and Taiwanese student population with varied socioeconomic backgrounds; the city private school was composed to a great extent of children from relatively well-to-do mainland families; the country public school had children from Taiwanese farmer and small-town merchant families, together with a smaller percentage of mainland children whose families were in the military or were located in the area for some other reason.

Second, three types of questionnaires were given children in these three schools. The first was an open-ended series of questions given at all three schools, the second was a pictorial political symbol questionnaire, also given at all three schools, and the third was a projective questionnaire based on four pictures of authority situations, responses being written at the city private and country public schools and made orally as part of an interview conducted with a smaller number of children at the city public school.

Method three consisted of interviews with children (including those mentioned before), with educational authorities, with teachers, and with parents. Some of these interviews were structured, many were not.

Last, an intensive examination was made of educational materials, primarily textbooks, but also including other media by which children are influenced, such as movies, television, magazines, and wall posters.

A more complete explanation of methodology is given in the appendixes. Also noted there is a discussion of Taiwan's educational policy, background data on the children, and a content analysis of the textbooks used in elementary education.

Chapter 1

Group Orientation

The Group Tradition

Years ago Sun Yat-sen, pondering the problems of China's modernization, wrote: "If we are to recover our lost nationalism, we must have some kind of group unity, large group unity."[1] It is, I think, by no means accidental that Sun should have conceived of China's problems in group terms, for the sense of belonging to a group is one of the oldest and most enduring observations that Western analysts have made of the Chinese.

And yet, as Sun's remarks hint, there is also the sense of a lack of group unity, of a need for something that did not exist, for Sun speaks of large group unity and in traditional China it was not the society but the family which absorbed the most intense loyalties. Indeed, of the five ideal Confucian loyalties (subject to ruler, son to father, younger brother to elder brother, wife to husband, and friend to friend) four are on a primary group level of interaction, and three are in the family. The first, subject to ruler, while theoretically perhaps the most powerful bond, was in normal practice so vague and distant as to be almost meaningless in the daily context of mutual rights and obligations. On the other hand, family terms were widely used to describe many relationships and family loyalties seen as the model for all others. This family, of course, was not simply the natural family but often included members of one's extended family and clan as well. These people worked together, lived in the same village, and had a sense of mutual responsibility and identity reinforced by government policies which held all group members mutually responsible for the conduct of each other.[2]

1. Sun Yat-sen, *San Min Chu I* [The Three Principles of the People], (Taipei, Taiwan: China Publishing Co., n.d.), "The Principle of Nationalism," lecture 5, p. 31.

2. This concept of mutual responsibility is by no means dead. On Jan. 15, 1966 an article appeared on p. 6 of the *China Post*, vol. 15, no. 4836, entitled "New Suretyship Measure to Go into Force," describing how all business employees,

Traditions of family loyalty are still very strong, and children are exposed to a great many examples of filial piety and family cohesiveness. The book *Stories of the Early Years of Famous Chinese Children* is typical of such influences and contains many stories of this nature.[3] The pervasiveness of family orientation in childhood socialization came to light in my own findings where children revealed the internalization of such influences in their projective test answers (see Appendix 3 for a description of test instruments and procedures). Two third-grade boys at the city private school, writing about a classroom scene, both invoked family loyalties. One wrote how the children "were thinking to do good things so in the future they could pay back their parents." The other wrote of how later the children "would be grateful to their parents because the parents had spent money allowing them to go to school."

Obviously the notion of group orientation and group loyalties is not unique to China but is a phenomenon general to human social existence, if indeed it is not the definition of it.[4] What differentiates the Chinese is the singular focus of Chinese group loyalties and the intensity with which ideals of loyal behavior (such as sacrifice for the collective good) are held.[5] Closely associated with these factors is the similarity of role

---

teachers, and government workers would be required "to stand surety for each other's loyalty to the government." This was a revision of a previous measure.

3. *Chung-kuo Ming-jen Yu-nien Ku-shih* 中國名人幼年故事 [Stories of the Early Years of Famous Chinese Children] (Taipei, Taiwan 童年書店, 1964). Story 2, for instance, is of a filial child in Han times who would not run from his father's remains despite the fact that a large snake had entered the house.

4. Groups may be defined as being "composed of all individuals who occupy positions reciprocal to all other positions in the group structure and includes no individuals who do not meet this condition." F. L. Bates, "A Conceptual Analysis of Group Structure," *Social Forces*, vol. 36, no. 2 (Dec. 1957), p. 105.

5. One of the clearest expositions of these ideals is given in William Theodore de Bary, Wing-Tsit Chan, and Burton Watson, *Sources of Chinese Tradition* (Columbia University Press, New York, 1960). On p. 659 they specify the eight virtues of the Hung Society, a secret organization founded in the mid-seventeenth century. The virtues are: (1) Be absolutely loyal and dedicated to the country. (2) Be filial and obedient to parents. (3) Instruct and teach your wife and children. (4) Be harmonious with your brothers. (5) Be harmonious with your neighbors. (6) Help people in distress and save people in danger. (7) Advise your friends sincerely. (8) Protect the rich and help the poor.

The notions of group cooperation and group loyalty have been very important in Chinese thought. Hsün Tzu (about 298–238 B.C.) saw the capacity to form groups as one of the essential identifying characteristics of humans as contrasted

behavior required of individuals acting in different group contexts. The filiality, for instance, which a bureaucrat in old China owed his parents was the ideal for the loyalties he would hold toward his superiors in the government.

It is the very fact that no individual can escape being a member of some group that makes an investigation of the qualities and aspects of group life essential to an understanding of any society. The types of responsibilities group members owe each other, the strength of internal group cohesion, the attitudes held by members toward other groups, and the ways in which conformity to group norms is enforced are only some of the pertinent questions.[6] In China training for group life is so intensive and begins so early that no study should ever be undertaken without a thorough knowledge and grounding in the social framework in which Chinese live.

Yet modern Taiwan is not traditional China, for the focus of group loyalties is enlarging, and while the presence of older loyalties is still easily discernible, one can also detect a new intensity of group loyalty in areas less dominant traditionally.[7] What is happening, in fact, is something very new, the birth of that large group awareness that Sun Yat-sen perceived would be necessary for the creation of a modern society.

---

with animals. Rules of conduct, according to Hsün Tzu, derive from the need for social organization, which in itself arises from the desire to enjoy better living. See Fung Yu-lan, *A Short History of Chinese Philosophy*, Derk Bodde, ed. (The Macmillan Company, New York, 1962), p. 146. Such emphasis on the social factor, operating according to secular values and in response to human intelligence unaided by any supernatural authority, is unique in human cultural traditions. I am indebted to Frederick W. Mote for pointing this out to me.

6. The qualities of group life in America, which Almond and Verba find so important for American political behavior, point again to the importance of understanding the unique orientations held by Americans toward their group life in order to understand their political behavior. Gabriel Almond and Sidney Verba, *The Civic Culture* (Boston: Little, Brown and Company, 1965).

7. Proverbs are instructive about this. There is one, for instance, from the spring and autumn period which says, literally, "Righteousness destroys filiality" Ta-i Mieh-ch'in, 大義滅親) or, roughly, country above family. Values extolling secondary group loyalty existed and could be invoked on occasion, particularly during periods of national crisis where the law itself lent support to such injunctions. See Ch'u Tung-tsu, *Law and Society in Traditional China* (Paris and The Hague: Mouton and Co., 1961). These proverbs, however, did not normally carry the intensity of an expression such as "Don't put fertilizer on someone else's field" [Fei-shui Bu Lo Wai Jen T'ien] 肥水不落外人田, which, more to the point, means take care of your friends, look after your own first.

The Development of a Group Sense

One can see in Taiwan much that is traditional in childhood training, and nowhere is this probably more apparent than in the mechanism whereby individuals come to invest in the group. There is a term, "face," which has come into the English language and which describes this investment mechanism. The Chinese concept, however, has a richer variety of meanings than is carried in the English adaptation of the term. There are also, as would be expected, differences between the two societies in the emotional content associated with the word, the Chinese having more intense feelings with regard to this concept than are normally associated with it in English.

Face, for the Chinese, has two meanings. The first, *mien-tzu*, is the prestige and reputation achieved through material or social success, ostentation or generosity. The second, *lien*, is "the respect of the group for a man with a good moral reputation."[8] Of the two, *lien* carries far the greater emotional impact, for to have no *lien* is the worst type of insult, one which casts doubt on one's moral integrity. To have no *mien-tzu* means simply the failure to obtain worldly success. The two concepts, of course, are not entirely independent, and in some situations there are subtle overlappings. Nor do they apply equally to all people in the society: the higher the social standing, the more *mien-tzu* a person has; at the same time his *lien* is also more vulnerable to being insulted or having a request refused, particularly with people just below him in status,[9] although *lien* may also be lost to people above one in status and also to those at the same level. Childhood socialization points this out very clearly. It is true that for those very high in social status the most likely direction of loss will be to those directly below them, but this holds much less for people of more moderate status and is not the way, in fact, that children learn about face.

8. Hsien Chin Hu, "The Chinese Concepts of Face," *American Anthropologist*, vol. 46, no. 1, pt. 1 (Jan.-March 1944), p. 45. These criteria are from the same source and hold mostly, according to the author, for northern China and, to some lesser extent, for the central areas. Chinese I spoke with seemed to feel this description to be accurate for face as it operates in Taiwan.

9. Paul Hiniker, *Chinese Attitudinal Reactions to Forced Compliance: A Cross-Cultural Experiment in the Theory of Cognitive Dissonance*, Research Program on Problems of International Communication and Security, Center for International Studies, Massachusetts Institute of Technology, Cambridge, Mass., 1965, p. 13.

Not only is the complex of attitudes and actions connected with the word "face" wider for the Chinese than for Westerners, something which possibly increases the emotional ramifications of the term, but there is also another very distinct way in which the Chinese use of the word is different. Face can sometimes be an individual matter, but, far more frequently, it is a group concern. A person "almost always belongs to a closely integrated group on which is reflected some of his glory or shame. His family, the wider community of friends, and his superiors, all have an interest in his advancement or setbacks. So a person does not simply 'lose his own face.'"[10] This works in reverse as well, for if a family, for instance, has no face, then the individual family member has none either, no matter how good he himself may be. A Chinese friend, pointing out these distinctions to me, quoted a relevant proverb which roughly says, "If the roof beam is askew, then the house is awry."[11]

Face is not related to unspecified other people; it relates to very particular others, and because of this Chinese are acutely sensitive to changing conditions which affect a particular relationship. Models, as indicators of correct behavior, are very important in this regard, but the relationship to the model first stresses outward conformity of behavior rather than internalization of the model's values and motivations. This is, of course, a relative statement, but it emphasizes the fact that individuals are expected to be able to change their habits and conceptions as circumstances change, and the penalty for not doing so is loss of face, both for the individual and for the group of which he is a member.[12] Not unexpectedly, this "situational" morality tends to create a high awareness and concern over "proper" behavior and a desire to avoid extremes in interpersonal relations.[13]

10. Hsien Chin Hu, "The Chinese Concepts of Face," p. 50.

11. Shang Liang Bu Cheng Hsia Liang Wai, 上梁不正下梁歪. Generally this proverb means that inferiors are subject to bad influences from superiors so that they engage in wrong and do evil. However, as can be seen, it also carries other meanings.

12. One day a small boy came to play at my house. My housekeeper, when she found out he was in fourth grade, became quite incensed over the fact that he was no larger than my son who was in kindergarten. "You must exercise more," she sternly told him. The little fellow, crestfallen, replied that he couldn't because he had to study so hard and also watch his little sister. The point is that my housekeeper, quite ignoring the biological factors involved, assumed that he had not responded properly to circumstances and had thereby lost face for "them" to this alien child. The little boy's response indicated he felt the same.

13. One result of this concern might be the comparatively higher tolerance

It must be emphasized that the group also serves as a buffer against the personal inadequacy felt when an individual member loses face. This is an enormously important function of the group. However, one does not lightly presume on the group's indulgence, and constant efforts are maintained to prevent such an occurrence. A Chinese Air Force psychologist told me that Chinese "individualism" is really the lack of coordination that results from the inability of anyone to admit that he does not know how to do something. He felt this inability stems directly from a fear of bringing loss of face on one's family or country. In fact, Hsien Chin Hu says face is often "used by elders to stimulate the young to great effort and correct behavior. 'Don't lose *lien* for us!' not only implants in the mind of the young person the concept of *lien*, but gives him or her the consciousness of the collective responsibility which his family bears in regard to his behavior."[14]

Child Rearing and Face

What is it that makes the loss of face "come to constitute a real dread affecting the nervous system of ego more strongly than physical fear?"[15] Scholars have addressed themselves to a number of learning problems and their findings are revealing here. There is, for instance, an axiom of communications theory that states that "When two persons (or two groups, for that matter) communicate with each other about something, X, they are (by definition) transmitting information. The symbols by which they do so refer, in a direct sense, only to X. But each of them is also informing the other about himself—specifically, about himself-in-relation-to-X."[16] Theories about communication, however, have specific applications in learning situations where adults wish not only to communicate with the child about a situation X but also to develop a patterned type of response to this stimulus. Social training, in fact, consists in teaching a child to express aggression, dependency, and other social responses only in certain ways, thus developing response patterns

---

for deviant behavior in Chinese families noted by Tsung-yi Lin, "A Study of the Incidence of Mental Disorder in Chinese and Other Cultures," *Psychiatry: Journal for the Study of Interpersonal Processes*, vol. 16, no. 4 (Nov. 1953), p. 333.

14. Hu, "The Chinese Concepts of Face," p. 50.

15. *Ibid.*, p. 50.

16. T. M. Newcomb, "Communicative Behavior," in *Approaches to the Study of Politics*, Roland Young, ed. (Evanston, Ill.: Northwestern University Press, 1958), p. 246.

which form a habit complex.[17] Societies differ in their general learning procedures. John W. M. Whiting and Irvin L. Child investigated this problem, testing the hypothesis derived from Freudian theory that guilt is related to the strength of the superego, which in turn develops, at least in part, by threats of loss of love. The result—in some societies—is a sense of what Freud calls "moral anxiety."[18] Although the evidence was not clear, as the authors pointed out, two factors were found which had a slight positive effect on the development of moral anxiety. The first factor is the technique of punishment. Punishment, they found, has a dual effect, first to keep the child oriented toward a goal of parental affection, and second to arouse uncertainty about attaining this goal. All punishment contains the second of these two effects, but only three techniques of punishment have the combined double effect. They are (1) punishment by denial of love, (2) threats of denial of reward, and (3) ostracism. These three are so called "love-oriented" techniques of discipline and can be differentiated from other types of discipline such as physical punishment, threats of physical punishment, or ridicule.[19] The second major factor is the age of onset of socialization in such areas as weaning, toilet training, modesty training, training in heterosexual inhibition, and independence training. The younger a child is when training begins, the more threatening is any withdrawal of love (the child has no strong developed sense of independence to check this), and hence it is presumed that the socialization pressure is more severe. These findings are corroborated by Erik H. Erikson, who says:

From a sense of *self-control without loss of self-esteem* comes a lasting sense of autonomy and pride; from a sense of muscular and anal impotence, of loss of self-control, and of parental overcontrol comes a lasting sense of doubt and shame . . . [for] his environment must back him up in his wish to "stand on his own feet" lest he be overcome by that sense of having exposed himself prematurely and

17. Albert Bandura and Richard H. Walters, *Social Learning and Personality Development* (New York: Holt, Rinehart & Winston, Inc., 1963), pp. 20, 21.

18. John W. M. Whiting and Irvin L. Child, *Child Training and Personality: A Cross-Cultural Study* (New Haven, Conn.: Yale University Press, 1953), pp. 53, 242, 254–258. Unfortunately, the authors make no differentiation between guilt and shame.

19. The assumption is that the more severe the punishments used in imposing inhibitory control, the greater is the strength of the subsequent anxiety. Obviously what is crucial is the sensed severity. Love-oriented techniques of discipline can, with their dual nature, be most rigorous.

foolishly which we call shame, or that secondary mistrust, that looking back after a double take, which we call doubt.[20]

Robert W. Scofield and Sun Chin-wan have found that oral, sex, dependence, and aggression training are all more severe for Chinese generally than for Americans, the exception being toilet (anal) training. To me their most significant finding, however, is the age of onset of such training and the techniques used. In sexual and dependence training instruction begins at birth. Intense shaming is the technique for sexual training. In dependence training needs are always gratified, no independent activities are allowed, and there is maximum protection and close supervision. Obedience is required, while quarreling is punished and competition shamed. Oral and anal training begin around the first year, with anal training, characterized by the use of shaming techniques after the second year.[21]

Nothing here should imply that Chinese parents do not use physical punishment with their children, for they do and are sometimes quite rigorous in its application. More frequently, however, one hears the verbal injunction, "I won't like [or love] you if you do that." Parents and teachers often speak this way and sometimes place themselves in the third person when doing so, so that the phrase becomes, "Mommy [or Teacher] won't like you." If a child cries—for whatever reason, be it from having done something wrong or falling in the street or what-

---

20.   Erik H. Erikson, "Growth and Crises of the Healthy Personality," in *Personality in Nature, Society, and Culture,* 2nd edition, Clyde Kluckhohn and Henry A. Murray, eds., with the collaboration of David M. Schneider (New York: Alfred A. Knopf, 1954), pp. 199–200 (italics in original).

21.   Robert W. Scofield and Sun Chin-Wan "A Comparative Study of the Differential Effect upon Personality of Chinese and American Child Training Practices," *The Journal of Social Psychology,* vol. 52, 2nd half (Nov. 1960), p. 223. It may at first seem anomalous that in dependence training needs are always gratified yet no independent activities allowed, and some Western observers have been puzzled over the fact that Chinese children seem to be allowed everything when very little and yet become quite submissive later on. The phenomenon is less confusing, I believe, if one posits deprivation of affection and emphasis on face as the primary mechanisms for behavioral change. To the Western observer who tends to conceive of submissiveness as a result of the threat or application of force, such change in Chinese children may appear inexplicable, whereas, in fact, very powerful forces are at work. Bandura and Walters, *Social Learning,* pp. 142–143, suggest that children in whom dependency habits are strongly developed are more responsive to social reinforcers.

ever—grownups in consoling the child will use such expressions as, "Don't cry, don't cry," or "Behave, behave," or "Be good, have a good manner." Genuinely consoling words are not used. The accent is on behavior. Parental overcontrol and the suppression of individual self-expression are clearly seen in early toilet training where small children are grasped by the mother at chest level (and held slightly out) with defecation and urination responding to whistling.

David C. McClelland has isolated four types of motivational appeals which are (1) "If you do that I won't love you," (2) "If you do that, you'll be disapproved, rejected, teased," (3) "If you do that, I will punish you (or reward you)," and (4) "If you do that I will suffer (or be pleased)."[22] While all four are used in Taiwan to motivate children, major emphasis must, I believe, be placed on the first two, the first as a stimulant to correct behavior and the second as a repressant of deviant behavior. Further, they are interrelated, for if we define shame as Talcott Parsons and Robert F. Bales do as "to be displeased with oneself," we can see that the recognition of a potential number 2 situation may trigger an internalized response in terms of number 1—i.e. "If I do that, I will not love myself"—to perform the socially "correct" behavior.[23]

Schools and Shame

There is an interesting story that children read in the second term of second grade about a man who stole a buffalo from a farmer and was discovered.[24] The man begged the farmer not to tell Wang Lieh. But later Wang Lieh heard of this incident and sent the man who stole the buffalo a bolt of cloth. Everyone thought this was strange, but Wang Lieh explained that as the man was poor, he would know shame on receiving this gift and would become a good man. And this is what happened. The story is instructive for children and points out to us the subtleties of social reinforcement and punishment in behavioral change.

22. David C. McClelland, *Personality* (New York: The Dryden Press, 1951), p. 359. The first of these motivational appeals is characteristic of middle-class white Americans according to Margaret Mead, *And Keep Your Powder Dry: An Anthropologist Looks at America* (New York: William Morrow & Co., 1942).

23. Talcott Parsons and Robert F. Bales, *Family, Socialization, and Interaction Process* (Glencoe, Ill.: The Free Press, 1955), p. 89.

24. *Kuo-yu K'e-pen* 國語課本 [Mandarin Primer], new edition, book 4, lesson 26, hereafter referred to as *KYKP*.

In differentiating between these two it turns out, in fact, that social reinforcement is a slow process, used to shape customs and manners frequently of no serious social consequence. In social learning it is punishment that is usually used to inhibit responses that the child has acquired and that are deemed undesirable.[25]

Yet, obviously, reinforcement and punishment should be consistent over a considerable period of time and consistent in the various environments in which an individual finds himself if behavior is to become strongly patterned. If we find in the schools the same general types of training techniques as are used early and concomitantly in the home, then we might expect reinforcement of early learned behavior. I point this out, of course, because there are societies in which children of a subculture attend schools which are operated on the basis of the norms of another culture so that a child in school may be subjected to different types of reinforcements and punishments.[26]

In Taiwan shaming techniques are widely (and rather unself-consciously) used in the schools so that there is considerable reinforcement of early family training. In first grade in the city private school, for instance, children found to have dirty hands are told to stand at their seats for several minutes. A teacher at that school told me that, although they use a variety of methods of punishment, the most common is to require children to stand—so that the class can see them—and think about what they have done wrong. The children can also, depending on the offense, be sent to the principal's office, struck—the teachers denied they did this, but the children and many other sources indicated this happened— or even expelled. Once, at the city private school, I witnessed an examination as to whether the children had brought handkerchiefs, brushed their teeth, combed their hair, and brought cups for tea. Although checked on this every morning by their own teachers (it is a regulation, I was told, of the Ministry of Education), once a month at a time unknown to the students the teachers change classes and run a check. Children who fail in any category must go to the head of the class and write down their names on the blackboard. The names are then copied off on a sheet by the teacher and given to the assistant principal and

25. Bandura and Walters, *Social Learning*, pp. 12–13.

26. Subcultures can be differentiated on far broader grounds than simply territorial occupation or origin (Taiwanese and Mainlander, for instance). Rural/ city may be a subculture, sex may be another, and age group (as "teen" culture) another.

eventually to the parents. In a first-grade class at the country public school a child who was crying (the fall term had just started) was told by the teacher that he should not cry in school because it was not nice looking or sounding. Then the teacher, pointing out the weeping child, made the other students imitate the sound of crying and laughing.[27]

Punishments such as this contain a strong element of ridicule; at the same time, and far more important, I think, is the ostracism which accompanies it, for the individual, when so exposed, is placed outside others. The punishment serves the dual purpose of correcting the behavior of the individual at the same time that it emphasizes the group as opposed to him and reinforces the rightness of the other group members' behavior. Chinese generally refer to their actions and thoughts in the plural, emphasizing their relation to the group. "We Chinese" or "we children," they will say when expressing their own opinions. But the person who is punished is always "him," and he is outside. I witnessed the clearest example of this one day at the city public school when I was watching a morning flag-raising ceremony. Following the exercise the children marched off by classes and went to their rooms along the open verandas that surround on three sides, three stories high, the central dirt playground. Left on the playground, however, was one little girl—possibly in the fourth grade—completely alone and at attention, the object of thousands of eyes. What she had done I do not know, but she was left standing there for fifteen minutes before being allowed to rejoin her class.

In a story written about the schoolroom scene on the projective test (see Appendix 3), a sixth-grade girl at the country public school told of how a student had done something wrong. The teacher was pointing out his mistake to the whole class and telling the student to correct himself. The girl went on:

... the students were wondering if perhaps they themselves had made a mistake like this and the teacher was wondering if he ought to bring the situation up and make the student lose face or if he ought to punish this student. The teacher is wondering if in his heart the student will be aware of his shame and correct himself. Perhaps after this situation takes place and the teacher punishes the student and tells the class, this type of situation will not occur again.[28]

27. This type of shaming punishment goes on at all levels of education. A student at the Chinese Naval Academy told me that a favorite punishment is to require students to stand at attention and then goose-step in front of others.

28. One of the most interesting aspects of this story is the implicit assump-

Shame and Group Consciousness

The sense of mistrust and doubt and the sense of shame which characterize behavior on the individual level are contradicted by frequently observable group assertiveness, for the individual, by accepting and conforming to the values of the group of which he is a member, reduces the tensions he is subjected to and can boldly assert the values of his group without the fear of shame.

Compliance to group norms places upon the individual the onus for constant analysis of himself in terms of the group of which he is a member. This analysis may be formal or informal. Peter L. Berger has examined this process and has given several formal examples: "Catholic confessional discipline, Communist 'autocriticism,' and the psychoanalytic techniques of coping with 'resistance' all fulfill the same purpose of preventing alternation out of the particular meaning system, allowing the individual to interpret his own doubts in terms derived from the system itself, thus keeping him within it."[29] Self-criticism, then, of some sort, has the significant function of integrating the individual into the group. Considering how stressed group integration is in Chinese childhood training, we should not be surprised to find some aspect of self-criticism in Chinese life generally, both now (as in the small group con-

---

tion, on the part of the writer, that losing face is not a category of punishment. This is undoubtedly due to the range of feeling which face covers, and to its intimate relationship to behavior in general. It is also interesting to note how the writer conceives of the other students experiencing a sense of similar shame, a phenomenon which may help to explain the hostility of the group toward the shamed individual and why group members are motivated to participate in shaming. I do not wish to overstress (or understress) this, however, as undoubtedly many shaming situations, particularly in school, have an element of formalism in them.

29. Peter L. Berger, *Invitation to Sociology: A Humanistic Perspective* (Garden City, N.Y.: Doubleday & Company, Inc., Anchor Books, 1963), p. 52. Erik H. Erikson in *Young Man Luther* (New York: W. W. Norton & Company, Inc, 1962), p. 134, echoes these thoughts when he mentions that one (of several) elements for success of thought reform is a radical accent on brotherhood. It might appear that the desire to protect one's face would mitigate against self-criticism. There is, surely, some tendency for this to happen, but it must be remembered that, to the Chinese, the group always takes precedence over the individual. The individual may lose face but he may also gain face by a recognition of faults which, if not corrected, would cause the group as a whole to lose face. And the individual, by sacrificing himself in this way, secures his position in the group.

fessionals of the Chinese Communist party) and in the past. Helmut Wilhelm notes that a disciplinary technique of the school of Sung learning was "the conscious submission to criticism and self criticism . . . undertaken with the aim of conquering (or overcoming) one's individuality."[30] And in more modern times even Chiang Kai-shek frequently criticizes himself publicly for not fulfilling the norms of the group of which he is leader. Chiang's rhetoric includes such statements as "I have brought more stains to the revolutionary history and have failed to live up to the expectations of all my compatriots. When I think of this in the small hours of the night, I am overwhelmed by a sense of mortification and seized by a feeling of trepidation."[31]

There is a little essay in a sixth-grade workbook in which the writer discusses his good points and his shortcomings and puts them down in list form. After doing this he ends by writing: "I have spoken above of the shortcomings and good points that I myself know of. I hope that everyone will point out and tell me of still other shortcomings, and thus give me the opportunity to correct them."[32] Such self-criticism, it turns out, is a significant, if not frequent, aspect of education in the elementary schools of Taiwan. It is generally not formalized and has many different manifestations. For instance, early in 1966 a traffic safety education plan was started in the primary schools. One of the features of the plan was a "recollection list" to be posted in every classroom with the names of all the students on it. If any offenses against traffic regulations were committed, the students were expected to enter these in the space below their own names. According to a Taipei City government spokesman these entries would be regarded as a part of each child's conduct mark.[33] At the city public school I witnessed a self-government class for sixth-grade girls which was designed, the teacher told me, to train the children in democratic practices. The elected head of the class stood in the center of the room with the assistant leader at the side. The children sang the

30. Helmut Wilhelm, "Chinese Confucianism on the Eve of the Great Encounter," in *Changing Japanese Attitudes toward Modernization*, Marius B. Jansen, ed. (Princeton, N.J.: Princeton University Press, 1965), p. 293.

31. Chiang Kai-shek, "On the Birthday Centennial of Dr. Sun Yat-sen," *China Post*, vol. 14, no. 4773 (Nov. 12, 1965), p. 4.

32. *Liu Nien Tzu-hsiu*, Hsia-ts'e 六年自修下冊 [Sixth-Grade Homework, book 2] (Taiwan, 1964) 臺灣書出版社, p. 89.

33. "Traffic Safety Education Plan to Start in Primary Schools Here," *China Post*, vol. 15, no. 4873 (Feb. 21, 1966), p. 4.

national anthem, and the class leader gave a report, after which she went to the side of the room and the assistant took over. Students were then called to the front of the class by the assistant (or sometimes they raised their hands to be called on). After bowing to the class leader, the teacher, and their fellow students, the child then gave a report on her progress, or lack of it, concerning such things as staying in line on the way home, progress in carrying out some classroom task, etc.

A fifth-grade girl at the city private school wrote about the classroom scene on the projective test. She told first how one student had not obeyed the regulations and had been told to stand but that he still did not recognize his fault, thus provoking the criticism of several students. Several of her later lines are interesting:

The students were wondering if he really understood the disturbance he had caused and some of them, probably those that had seen it, took him to one side and spoke with him and made him understand about the disturbance. They told that student, "Sincerely speak out about your actions." The student who had been punished lowered his head and recognized his fault. He also expressed his sorrow to them.

In commenting on group and individual authority Hannah Arendt has said:

For the authority of a group, even a child group, is always considerably stronger and more tyrannical than the severest authority of an individual person can ever be. If one looks at it from the standpoint of the individual child, his chances to rebel or do anything on his own hook are practically nil; . . . he is in the position, hopeless by definition, of a minority of one confronted by the absolute majority of all the others. There are very few grown people who can endure such a situation, even when it is not supported by external means of compulsion; children are simply and utterly incapable of it.[34]

But many of the pressures to belong to the group are not negative, with the individual's acquiescence being forced upon him. Invoking collective responsibility as a principle of punishment is one method of developing a group sense.[35] It is not, however, the most important (or

---

34. Hannah Arendt, *Between Past and Future* (New York: Meridian Books, The World Publishing Co., 1963), p. 181.

35. Teachers seemed completely unconscious of this emphasis, however. One of the more interesting statements about the effect of an intense group environment comes from Tung Chi-ping and Humphrey Evans, *The Thought Revolution*

most common) means. The daily activities of giving choral responses, of lining up in military type formation outside the classrooms, of marching together, of competing by rows, are far more important. Teachers emphasize this. In first grade in the city public school a story was told the class about how other "small friends" lined up together when going to school, and how the children all went in step and were well behaved.[36] In the city private school groupness is emphasized by keeping the children together year after year, sometimes even moving the teacher with the students as the latter are promoted. The staff at the Mental Health Center at the city public school told me that the most effective way they have of dealing with problems of social adjustment in children is group therapy. It is interesting to note that this emphasis on group therapy is in fact a guided and directed emphasis on the main feature of that social environment, the group itself.[37]

There are many positive reinforcers for the concept of group unity and for cooperation as the ideal of group life. In the fourth grade at the city public school the teacher, in discussing characters, wrote the two characters for "selfish" on the blackboard and asked the class if the meaning was good or bad. "Not good," they all said. "Say it again," the teacher said, and the children responded, much louder this time, "Not good!" In the sixth-grade workbook, which I mentioned before, there is a review question for a lesson entitled "The Morals of Present-Day Society" which asks "How can the unity of everyone be improved and increased?" The answer (carefully provided) is cooperation.[38] In almost all the classrooms, and outside on the playground, are further injunctions. On the wall in a third-grade classroom at the city public school, in foot-and-a-half-high letters, is the exhortation "Cooperate" and in a

---

(New York: Coward-McCann, Inc., 1966), pp. 252–253, where Tung says: "There are some values on which, apparently, most Americans and people like me will never agree. The concept of privacy, I think, is one of them. In my whole life, the amount of time I have spent away from the immediate physical presence of other people is extremely small. . . . Just as [Americans] cannot understand not needing privacy, I cannot understand the need for it. I suppose one never learns to want what one has never had. In any case I suffer as much from too much privacy as most Americans do from the lack of it."

36. The word for students in the primary schools is "small friends," with the emphasis on the cooperative group sense that the word "friends" implies.

37. One American child psychiatrist told me that group therapy is not widely used in the United States.

38. *Liu Nien Tzu-hsiu*, Hsia ts'e, p. 12.

fourth-grade classroom of the same school is the statement "Happy Group." Outside a fifth-grade classroom at the city private school is a sign which proclaims: "The struggle to obtain the victory of the group is the individual's victory."

Group themes are a constant aspect of the literature which the children read. It begins in kindergarten, where in book 4, for instance, there is a section to be read which says: "I happily help my schoolmates. I do not quarrel and fight with my schoolmates."[39] In the first term of third-grade children read a story about some geese that are flying in a flock, when a small goose breaks formation and flies on his own. His companions say to him: "This kind of wild flying is wrong. When we are in a group, we should keep order [discipline] and not just leave as we wish." The small goose returns but then flies off again and is warned once more. He still fails to mind, however, and a hawk, spying this, sweeps down and catches him. When his companions think to go and help him, it is too late. Such stories are fully intended by the educational authorities to convey group values. Professor Wu Ting, chairman of the committee in charge of compiling elementary textbooks in the Ministry of Education, particularly cited the story of the small goose as an example. He went on to explain that the formation geese fly in is roughly similar to the Chinese character for man (人) and therefore the teacher can use this device to bring the point of the story into a human context.

"Who," I asked a group of first-grade children in the city public school, "is the best person in the world?" "We are!" they said, answering in the plural. Children echoed this response on the written tests which were given them. The answers to three questions concerning the individual in a group are illuminating (Table 1–1). The first question concerned a home situation, and the children were asked: "If all the family want to buy oranges but one child wants to buy bananas, what should the family do about the one child who wants to buy bananas? What do you think of that one child?" The children were roughly equal in their feelings as to whether the one child should be permitted to have his own way or not (28.4 percent Don't Know, 39.5 percent Permissive, and 32.3 percent Nonpermissive)[40] but showed a slight increase, with age, of negative feelings toward the child.

39. *Yu-chih-yüan Ch'ang-shih* 幼稚園常識 [Kindergarten Common Sense] (Taiwan, 1964) 鴻文邦刷廠.

40. There were 695 responses. References to significance in the text refer to significance at the .01 level unless otherwise noted.

Table 1–1
Attitudes toward a Nonconforming Child in the Family: Percent

Category/Grade	1	2	3	4	5	6
Don't Know	42	36.9	56.8	41.7	30.2	40.1
Positive Reaction	20	28.4	8.0	17.3	20.8	15.7
Negative Reaction	38	34.7	35.2	40.9	49.1	44.1
No. Responding	100	95	125	127	53	127

No significance: Boy/Girl or Mainlanders/Taiwanese.
Significant at the .01 level.

This somewhat expected finding was seemingly contradicted in the second question concerning a school situation in which the children were asked: "If it is your job to clean the blackboard but you forget, do you think the other children should be blamed for not cleaning the blackboard for you? Why?" Here the children emphatically state (75.9 percent No, 7.1 percent Yes, 17.1 percent Don't Know) that the other children should not be blamed. Girls are significantly higher than boys, responding No 81.9 percent of the time versus 70.0 percent for the boys. There is also a significant difference according to age, the Noes increasing with reasonable regularity from 64 percent in first grade to 88.1 percent in sixth grade, and the Yeses declining from 13 percent to 4.7 percent.[41] The responses to this question are interesting in two ways. First, a large proportion of children—41.6 percent—respond Don't Know when asked why they have answered this way. Of the remainder 56.6 percent, or virtually all the rest, answer that it is because it is the individual's job. But we should not be too surprised at this finding, for when given a task the individual is supposed to fulfill his obligations in a way that reflects to the credit of the group.[42] When the individual fails, the group may try to help him, or the group may ostracize him and hold him responsible for the failure.

41. Not significant: Mainlanders/Taiwanese. A rejection by children of the notion of collective responsibility has been noted in other societies as well. See Jean Piaget, *The Moral Judgment of the Child* (New York: Collier Books, 1962), p. 235, for a similar reaction by Swiss children. Two teachers told me, however, in answer to my question, that if it was one child's job to clean the blackboard and the child forgot, the teacher would blame the other children for not helping to do it. This would be quite expected, in spite of the children's responses, in view of the teacher's authority position and her continuous attempts to strengthen class solidarity.

42. One can question from this response whether collective responsibility,

One of the other interesting aspects of this response is that the teacher is definitely considered to be part of the class group, although in an authority position. For clearly—or so it seems to me—if the teacher were not considered a member of the class group, the children should have cleaned the blackboard in order to protect the group's face with the teacher. But because the teacher is a member of the group the child who forgot loses face, in this case, only within the group and is thus solely responsible. This notion of class solidarity including the teacher will be noted again in Chapter 3 in the section on cynicism.

Finally, in the third question, the children were asked: if they were "on a walk to a park and all the group decided to go one way but one person knows of a much shorter path should that one person say so? Why?" Here children answer overwhelmingly in the positive (85.1 percent) and show a significant increase in these positive responses as they grow older, 81 percent saying Yes in first grade and 92.1 percent saying Yes in sixth grade.[43] The second and more important part of the question was analyzed with regard to group content. Here there is a definite increase in group reasons with age as Table 1–2 shows.[44]

Table 1–2
Group Reasons as a Guide for Individual Action: Percent

Category/Grade	1	2	3	4	5	6
Don't Know	57	52.6	60.8	44.1	13.2	22.0
Group Reasons	35	43.2	35.2	48.8	73.6	73.2
Other	8	4.2	4.0	7.1	13.2	4.7
No. Responding	100	95	125	127	53	127

Significant at the .01 level.

---

which some teachers employ (see footnote 35), is, in fact, a satisfactory way of building group loyalty, or whether more positive social reinforcers are not more effective. Again we should note that learning theory stresses punishment as a means of inhibiting responses the child has already acquired rather than as a means of reinforcing existing patterns.

43. No significance: Boy/Girl or Mainlanders/Taiwanese.

44. There is no significant difference between boys and girls but there is—at the .01 level—between Mainlanders and Taiwanese. Mainlanders respond: Group Reasons, 58.7 percent, Other, 3.6 percent, Don't Know, 37.8 percent; Taiwanese respond: Group Reasons, 42.3 percent, Other, 5.9 percent, Don't Know, 51.9 percent. Possibly one reason for the greater number of group responses by Mainlanders is a minority group solidarity phenomenon related to their sense of being numerically far inferior (even if politically more powerful) to

The reasons given are interesting. For instance, some of the responses were as follows: A city private school fourth-grade mainland girl says, "Because everyone should mutually cooperate." A city private school fifth-grade Taiwanese boy replies, "Dr. Sun Yat-sen said 'We should do things for others.' Therefore we should be like that." A country public school fifth-grade mainland boy says, "Because this is everybody's job." A city public school fourth-grade mainland boy responds, "If I don't tell them, then I am really a selfish boy and not looking out for the concern of the group."

This type of response was echoed on many of the projective type test stories. A fifth-grade girl at the city private school, writing about the schoolroom scene (Appendix 3), mentioned that the student standing was being punished for playing. She concludes that "one ought not to attend class and misbehave but even more one ought not to play with things under the desk and thereby prevent fellow students nearby from peacefully attending class."

Connected with responses stressing the group itself is a marked emphasis on what constitutes ideal group membership behavior, particularly the desirability of maintaining order. Order and the "proper" way of doing things are, in fact, two of the main motifs of ingroup behavior. A fourth-grade boy at the city private school wrote that the public meeting scene (Appendix 3) was being held because there was not enough food, and the people were discussing ways of solving this problem. He went on to state that the people became happy because the situation did not arise again and concludes, somewhat off the point, that he feels this situation is good because the people know how to be orderly when holding a meeting. A girl in his class, writing about the same picture, came to the same conclusion in a negative way. She said the meeting was being held because of traffic accidents and that the people, desiring a safe and secure society, wanted the government to repair the roads and develop transportation. But she went on to say that "this situation is not good because when they are discussing this at the meeting, they ought to be orderly." At the country public school a second-grade boy discussed the vendor picture (Appendix 3), telling how a policeman was informing the vendor not to sell dirty food. Afterward the vendor felt

---

the Taiwanese. This minority group solidarity phenomenon would exist above and beyond group pressures as expressed in family and school socialization. I am indebted to Glenn D. Paige for pointing this out to me.

very bad and stopped selling the dirty food. The child concluded that the overall situation was not proper because "to quarrel is wrong."

I was at a friend's house one evening listening to a young professor of law at National Taiwan University speak on the general question of marriage and divorce in China. Emphasizing a point, he said, in passing: "To unite is a good thing, to separate is a bad thing. My father would never take a divorce case in old Shanghai."

The Group and Achievement

A senior officer in the American embassy in Taipei once told me that, despite the talk of return to the Mainland, economic development is, in fact, the primary goal of the government in Taiwan. The two objectives are not necessarily incompatible, of course, and in the minds of many are probably closely related, for economic development provides both a base for military power and proof that the Nationalist regime can provide the Chinese people with the sinews of modernization. Members of the government, and the people in general, take pride in the gains that have been made. There is also great emphasis, particularly at the higher educational levels, on the training of the engineers and scientists who will provide the intellectual basis for further growth. Yet long-range policy planning alone would not provide modernization if there were not a motivation on the part of many people to acquire the necessary training and to achieve these goals.

Psychologists generally refer to this type of motivation as *n* Achievement. There is a crucial relationship between age and the acquisition of this type of motivation. David C. McClelland has stated that "Both psychological theory and research . . . strongly suggest that the crucial period for acquiring *n* Achievement probably lies somewhere between the ages of five and ten."[45] In Taiwan, therefore, where economic development is such a basic priority, we might expect to find emphasis on achievement in the school curriculum and the development of achievement motivation among schoolchildren.

Although teachers in Taiwan sometimes use subgroup competition between classroom rows as a means to stimulate excellent performance, shaming of individual students before the whole group (the class) is far more prevalent. Beginning in first grade, the children are told, and

45. David C. McClelland, *The Achieving Society* (Princeton, N.J.: D. Van Nostrand Co., Inc., 1961), p. 415.

encouraged, to clap hands when correct responses are given. Children are almost always required to stand when answering questions. If the answer is correct, the child may sit down, but if incorrect the child must remain standing, sometimes for five minutes or more, until that section of the lesson is over or until he has correctly responded to another question. In the fifth grade of the city public school one boy who did not know an answer tried to sit down and hide behind his book. The teacher, however, made him stand while someone else correctly responded. He was then told to sit down and then to stand up again immediately, come to attention, and repeat the correct answer.

At the back of the classroom of the girls' fifth-grade class at the city public school is a chart on which marks are listed. Writing is in blue, except for failing grades, which are written in red. In the first grade of the city private school tests were handed back and those with a mark of 100—about eight children—had their names called out and were rewarded with a red slip and hand clapping. The papers were simply handed back to the others. In the city public school in fourth-grade tests for the top five children were handed back amidst loud handclapping. Immediately following this the five children with the lowest grades, starting with the worst, had their names read off and their tests handed back amidst silence.

Many of the stories which the children read in their textbooks concern achievement, some in the positive sense of how or why one achieves a high standard and others in the negative sense of the price one pays for failure. In the first grade the children learn how praiseworthy are the busy insects and birds, building homes in the spring. In the same book there is also a trilogy of stories about two water buffaloes, one of which was willing to work and the other not. At harvest time the lazy buffalo was sold and suffered afterward by having to pull his new owner's heavy cart. The good buffalo, however, was rewarded and taken out by the farmer to eat grass.[46]

Sometimes traditional themes or models are utilized. In the second grade, for instance, there are two stories, back-to-back, of this nature. The first is about Li Po, the famous poet, who was stimulated to study and persevere by the example of an old lady trying to make an embroidery needle by grinding down a stick of iron on a stone. Time, the old lady said, was all that was needed. The second story concerns an old

46. *KYKP*, book 2, lessons 14–15, 17–19.

farmer who leads his sons and grandsons out to level a hill in front of his home which is blocking direct access to the road. A neighbor, seeing this, thinks it mad for an old man to set himself such a task, but the old man explains: "The important thing is that we be willing to do something, not that we be able to finish it. My sons and grandsons can continue the work and one day the hill will be flattened."[47]

Stories involving shame are also used. In fourth grade children learn about an archer of the Sung period named Ch'en, whom people watched with marvel as he practiced. After shooting an arrow directly into the center of the target, he tells the people that he is not boasting but that really there is no one who can shoot as well as he. Then an old man comes forward who says that this talent is not a natural gift but the result of much hard and bitter practice. To illustrate his point he tells them that he is a wine seller, and taking an old copper coin with a hole in it he inserts the coin in the neck of a bottle. Standing and holding the wine high, he then pours some wine through the small coin hole directly into the bottle. The old man then states that there is no one in the world who has talent who does not owe it to studying hard. Ch'en agrees and says he has been taught a valuable lesson.[48]

These textbook lessons in achievement are reinforced in other aspects of education. In a play, for instance, some children enacted the story of the ants and the grasshopper, showing a grasshopper who would not

47. *KYKP*, book 4, new edition, lessons 28–29. Both stories are related to two proverbs: (1) Tieh Ch'u Mo Chen 鐵杵磨針 [To grind an iron pestle into a needle] (Tang Dynasty) and (2) Yü Kung I Shan 愚公移山 [Yü Kung moves the mountain] (Chou Dynasty). The second story was repeated in the *China Post*, "Old Man and Stone Stairs," vol. 14, no. 4732 (Oct. 1, 1965), p. 6, by Wu Ta-cheng who wrote of an old man, Hsu Kuo-an, eighty-seven years old, who saved for twenty years in order to build some steps in the hill leading to his hamlet near Keelung. It had been his ambition since childhood, Hsu said, to do this and thus "make it possible for my neighbors to save a lot of trouble." In the *New York Times*, Dec. 10, 1966, p. 1, in an article by Charles Mohr entitled "Chinese Are Told Key to All Problems Is in Three Mao Essays," it is mentioned how this same story is used by the Chinese Communists as an example of perseverance being the key to success.

In school the children learn that a combination of time and hard work can solve any problem. Natural ability as a factor is discounted. "He should be more studious" is the explanation given for failure. Objective circumstances mean everything; shortcomings are the result of subjective failure to recognize the needs of the objective situation—needs that can be best aided by effort over time.

48. *KYKP*, book 8, lesson 26.

work but always played and who ended by dying in the cold of winter wondering where all his friends had gone.[49] In music the themes are also repeated. In third grade, for instance, children sing "I love to play. I love to work. Play is fun, work is glorious."[50]

A sixth-grade Taiwanese boy at the city private school, describing the schoolroom scene (Appendix 3) on the projective test, wrote: "You can be sure the student will be sorry for his conduct and thank his teacher for his blaming. Afraid of being blamed, the other students will all study very hard afterwards." An analysis of the family and schoolroom projective test responses, based on whether they represent content indicating the desire or necessity to achieve, reveals certain differences in the city private and country public schools. (Table 1–3)

Table 1–3
Achievement Content: Percent

Category/School	Family Scene		Schoolroom Scene	
	City Private	Country Public	City Private	Country Public
Unknown	17.5	86.1	29.5	74
Achievement	50.0	11.6	70.5	18
Nonachievement	32.5	2.3	0	8
No. Responding	40	43	44	50

Significant at the .01 level.

Taking liberal account of the fact that country public school children have had less experience with this type of test, one still finds the lack of achievement themes for country children somewhat startling. The differences in achievement motivation between city and country children are verified by results from the open-ended questionnaire (Appendix 3). Using somewhat the same criteria of W. Mischel, who did work on Negro children in Trinidad, two questions were asked the children from all three schools.[51] They were: (1) When you grow up, what sort of

49. *KYKP*, book 8, lesson 9.

50. *Yin-yüeh K'e-pen* 音樂課本 [Music Primer], book 2, song 2.

51. W. Mischel, *Delay of Gratification, Need for Achievement, and Acquiescence in Another Culture*, unpublished paper, Harvard University, 1960, as quoted in McClelland, *The Achieving Society*, p. 328. Mischel asked the children what they would want to be if a magic man could change them into anything they wanted and found that those high in *n* Achievement frequently mentioned an occupation (policeman, pilot, etc.) or achievement-related trait (important, successful, etc.).

person do you want to be? (2) When you grow up, what kind of work do you want to do? The results were analyzed according to whether children named a high-status role (airplane pilot, scientist, businessman, etc.), a low-status role (brother, workman, etc.), an abstraction (honest, patriotic, etc.), or said they didn't know. The results are indicated in Table 1–4.

Table 1–4
Differences among Schools in Children's Achievement Orientations: Percent

	Question 1			Question 2		
Category/School	City Public	City Private	Country Public	City Public	City Private	Country Public
High Status	50.0	48.8	27.5	69.7	86.0	35.7
Low Status	3.9	2.9	3.6	3.6	0.0	3.1
Abstraction	27.3	41.3	25.9	3.3	2.9	9.8
Don't Know	18.8	7.0	43.0	23.3	11.0	51.3
No. Responding	330	172	193	330	172	193

Significant at the .01 level.

There were no significant differences between Mainlanders or Taiwanese, and only slight differences between boys and girls, the boys being somewhat more high-status oriented. The significant differences between the urban and rural children are probably attributable to the greater incidence in the surrounding environment in the city of achievement models. What this indicates is that the methods used in school to motivate achievement, while generally successful on an overall basis (for very few children were motivated to low-status roles), are inadequate in themselves. Obtaining uniformly high n Achievement seems to require the reinforcement of the urban areas where models for such achievement exist and where the banks, businesses, universities, etc., also exist and provide the formal institutional framework through which achievement goals may be obtained.

Many of the textbook stories teach children that achievement is not merely for the benefit of the individual but above all for the group, as a result of group action. In first grade there is the story of an ant finding some small pieces of rice, and while he alone cannot move the rice, all the ants together can. This is followed by an exercise where a captioned

Nonachievement-related roles or traits were such things as nice, honest, brother, baby, etc.

picture of a mother talking to her children has her saying: "If only everybody will work hard together, then anything can be done."[52] In second grade the children read how, if they all work together, they can pull up a large turnip. Another lesson tells of a child asking an old man why he plants walnuts, since he probably will not be around to enjoy them. The old man replies that everyone should work and goes on to say: "Child, I eat walnuts now, and aren't these from trees planted by people who went before? If we eat the walnuts of those who went before, we ought to plant some for those who come later to enjoy. If people thought only of themselves, we would not be able to eat walnuts now."[53]

Foreigners are sometimes held up as models for emulation. In a third-grade citizenship class the story of Abraham Lincoln was told, with emphasis on his poverty and diligence and his later contributions to society. The children were then asked to contribute similar stories of their own. In a second-grade textbook there is a story of American children saving their candy money and having a mighty ship built, called "The American Children's Ship," for even children can, and should, make contributions to their country.[54] In fifth grade, combining group and work themes, the children sing:

Good older brother and younger brother. Good older sister and younger sister. Everyone come. Exercise the body. Respect the regulations. Guard discipline. Truly active. How really beautiful. The United Spirit is good. The happiness of loving the group is beyond compare. Ha, ha, ha, ha. We like heaven and like earth. When we read we studiously read. When we play we industriously play.[55]

The supreme goal of achievement in its group context is to work for society itself. A fifth-grade girl at the city private school concluded her version of the schoolroom scene (Appendix 3) with the words: "Because the teacher is conscientious and teaches the young, when they grow up they can give even greater benefits to the country, to society, and even to mankind." A third-grade boy from the same school, writing about the same picture, said: "Reading can increase our knowledge, and after we grow up our learning will make us useful people for society." At the city public school a fourth-grade boy was interviewed, using the public

---

52. *KYKP*, book 2, lesson 26.
53. *KYKP*, book 4, lessons 6–7.
54. *KYKP*, book 4, lesson 28.
55. *Yin-yüeh Kʻe-pen* [Music Primer], book 5, song 13.

meeting scene picture (Appendix 3) as a guide. One section of the interview went like this:

Question: "What sort of person is he?"

Response: "He is a great person in the country."

Question: "How did he become a great person?"

Response: "He was very conscientious and studied hard from the time he was young."

Question: "And afterwards?"

Response: "(pause) Afterward he became a great person."

Question: "What type of person do you think is a great person?"

Response: "(pause) One who has served society."

Question: "What kind of activity is serving the society?"

Response: "To be a person of achievement."

Primary Groups and Society

Children in Taiwan, even at a very young age, have a developed sense of their membership in society as a whole. Furthermore, at least ideally, they conceive of themselves as having a primary duty and loyalty to society. In giving reasons for why a person should do this or that, why a person has succeeded, or why some person is famous, they will frequently invoke the name of society and do so with evident feelings of conviction. This is more clearly discernible among children than adults, but even with the latter there is a recognition of the growing preeminence of society. One friend, discussing face with me, gave as his opinion that face embraces much the same circle of people now as before—friends, classmates, the company one works for, the family, etc.—but at the same time, he said, it is also less strong, particularly in the family. He implicitly recognized that wider loyalties now command attention.

The emotions concerned with face and the loyalties to a group were, in traditional China, involved to a great extent with such primary groups as family or close friends. This focus, however, was always a source of societal disunity and a catalyst to political breakdown. The attempt today is to transform the particularistic relationships that characterized small groups into broader, more universal ones, yet the emotional content of the older particularistic relationship is not so readily changed.

In Taiwan there is a conscious attempt on the part of the educational authorities to maintain an emotional congruence between already established primary group relationships and the new patterns which are being formed; there is a process of identifying the primary group with the state. To some extent this is similar to traditional Confucian concepts. The difference is that the society's needs and claims are now always and unequivocably given precedence. In a book on elementary school social science teaching methods in Taiwan, the author says: "Social science ought to emphasize the development in children of moral concepts, group consciousness, patriotic thoughts, habits of cooperation, the attitude of service, and the spirit of sacrifice, etc., making children's group sense achieve adequate development."[56] Individual achievement becomes group achievement and the highest emphasis is placed on the society's achievement as a whole. This conception is widespread in education and finds expression in Chiang's statement that "All virtues are based on 'loyalty' and 'filial piety.' To fulfill the principle of complete loyalty to the state [government] and of filial piety toward the nation [people]; to be altruistic and not seek personal advantage; to place the interests of the state ahead of those of the family; such is the highest standard of loyalty and filial piety."[57]

Education may not only develop in the child a sense of awareness of society as a group to which he belongs but also make him aware of, and subject to, the values of that society. The learning process whereby actions are committed in terms of such values is a complicated one. Principles of behavior theory would suggest that a reinforcement in educational materials of certain stimulus and response patterns of primary groups may create similar patterns of behavior with regard to the society.[58]

I was visiting a class in the men's teachers' college in Taipei when the question came up of what was a proper topic of conversation for a speech class in elementary school. After discussion it was agreed that to bring up a topic such as the differences between boys and girls would be wrong. Also inappropriate would be citizenship topics, better left to the citizenship class itself. Fitting topics for discussion would be such items as "My Home" or "How We Should Respect Our Parents."

56. *Hsiao-hsüeh She-hui-k'o Chiao-hsüeh-fa* 小學社會科教學法 [Teaching Methods for Elementary School Social Studies] Wu Yüan-chieh, ed. 吳元杰 (Taipei, Taiwan, 1961), p. 16 國立教育資料館.

57. Chiang Kai-shek, *China's Destiny* (New York: Roy Publishers, 1947), p. 165.

58. Charles E. Osgood, "Behavior Theory and the Social Sciences," in *Approaches to the Study of Politics*, Roland Young, ed. (Evanston, Ill.: Northwestern University Press, 1958), pp. 223–224.

Throughout the elementary school years there is emphasis on home life, linked at the same time with development of general group spirit.[59]

Large Group Unity

The purposeful development in school of a general group spirit, which must be distinguished from nonpurposeful but equally important aspects of group training, is not without an ultimate goal. Educational authorities seek to create a powerful loyalty to Chinese society and, specifically, to the state as exemplified by the government of the Republic of China (the Kuomintang government). Political training and the rudiments of group discipline begin in kindergarten with flag-raising ceremonies quite formally carried out. There are also, during the term, simple references by the teacher to the Republic of China and the President. In elementary school the flag is introduced into the textbooks and is on the cover of the readers the children use from first through fourth grade, waving over a group of playing children. Such insertions of national symbols are by no means accidental or merely decorative; educational authorities told me that these insertions were made with the definite intention of familiarizing children with an appropriate symbol for the country. The society itself is the object of considerable glorification. In kindergarten children begin to hear "We are Chinese and we all love China. Our China's national territory is the largest, the population the greatest, and our products the most abundant."[60] In fourth grade there is a poem the children chant, each of the three stanzas starting with "China, China, lovable China, there is no other country in all the world greater than you."[61] In the fifth-grade history reader there is a series of lessons on Chinese civilization. One of them makes the statement: "The Republic of China has also the world's most exceptional race. The facts of the following historical examples can prove this. . . . Three thousand years ago, while other races of the world were still leading a primitive life, our country had already developed a writing system and simple writing implements. . . ."[62] In a sixth-grade history class the children were told about the age of exploration. The topic

59. See Appendix 2 for a breakdown to textbook topics, all of which are also used for classroom discussion.

60. *Yu-chih-yüan Ch'ang-shih*, book 4, lesson 2.

61. *KYKP*, book 8, lesson 27.

62. *Li-shih K'e-pen, Kao-chi Ti-Erh-Ts'e* 歷史課本高級第二冊 [History Primer, upper grades, book 2], lesson 11 (Taiwan, 1964) 三都紙器工廠.

under discussion was Magellan and his feat of sailing across the Pacific. No mention was made of Magellan's being the first to circumnavigate the globe; the important point was that China could now be reached from the East as well as from the West. Ethnocentrism begins early.

At the same time that children are taught to admire and respect their society, they are also introduced to a conception of priorities with regard to the groups in which they concurrently live. At first educational emphasis is on the fact that aspects of already learned behavior in primary groups are acceptable as a standard in other areas. Thus, in third grade, children will be expected to answer True to a statement in a true-false quiz which says: "In the school we are good students; in society we ought to be good citizens."[63] By fifth grade, in the citizenship reader, children are enjoined to love their relatives, and just as they love them, to love friends, the people, and the country. Start now in school, they are told.[64] There are two stories together in the fifth-grade reading primer of a mother writing to her son. Work for the country, she tells him in the first story, for sons must be brave and mothers must be brave too. Love of country must come before love of family. The moral is repeated in the next lesson when she exhorts him to kill the enemy and be brave, for the country and the people are more important than the family or an individual.

By sixth grade the priorities are expected to be well established. There is a multiple-choice question in a review section on citizenship training where the children are asked: "The responsibility of young people is to (1) read books conscientiously, (2) exercise the body, (3) build society, (4) establish the family."[65] Here all the answers are desirable goals, but, as the principal of the city public school told me, only (3) can be the right answer. The nation as a focus for one's loyalty and effort receives reinforcement outside the school as well. A sign in the T'ao Yuan local government office, for instance, requests the local people to speak Mandarin, for "To speak Mandarin expresses love for one's country."

Just as cooperation is stressed as the ideal of group life in general, so patriotism, loyalty, and bravery are the specific ideals of the good citizen. What is most to be feared, on the other hand, is national shame. Fifth

63. *San Nien Chia-ting Lien-hsi, Hsia-ts'e* 三年家庭練習下册 [Third-Grade Homework, book 2] lessons 15–16, p. 42 (Taiwan, 1965) 臺灣圖書出版印行.

64. *Kung-min Yu Tao-te, Kao-chi Ti-i-ts'e* 公民與道德高級第一册 [Citizenship and Morals, upper grades, book 1] lesson 6 (Taiwan, 1964) 臺灣省政府印刷廠.

65. *Liu Nien Tzu-hsiu, Hsia-ts'e* p. 11.

graders, for instance, learn they should act on the street as they would anywhere else because the level of a nation's education can be seen from the attitude of its people and we must not let others look down on us.[66] In third grade there is a story of a poor Italian child on a ship going from Spain to Italy who is pitied by some of the other passengers and is given some money. The child is happy at the thought that he can buy some food and take what is left over to his parents; but when he hears the passengers disparaging Italy, he hurls the money at them and cries out: "I do not want your money, you say bad things about my country."[67]

Bravery and revolutionary spirit, to work and struggle for the Republic—these are the goals that education sets for the children. For as Pu Shih, who gave money to the Han Emperor for defense of the country against the Huns, says in a fourth-grade story: "When the country is in this kind of serious difficulty, the rich ought to give money and those with strength ought to give their strength. If all in the country are of one heart, then who needs to fear that the enemy can destroy anything?"[68] Some of the responses of the children are as heroic as the stories they read. A sixth-grade mainland girl at the city private school wrote of the public meeting scene (Appendix 3) that the people were holding a meeting to discuss ways of repelling the Japanese invasion. She ended by saying:

This is a good situation because at that time Japan had committed aggression against our nation and occupied all parts of the country within three months. If our country had really been permanently occupied by the Japanese, then we would have had a life like the Jewish people with no country to defend. Moreover, we would have been scorned by other nations. Therefore, we ought to raise up every kind of resistance, defeat Japan, and restore the greatness of the people of the Republic of China. Let other countries look and see that the Republic of China is not a rotten monarchy but is one of the great nations of the world.

Above all, the goal of education is national recovery and the destruction of the Communist regime. This theme is constantly stressed. In a third-grade class at the city public school the teacher was explaining a vocabulary word, "victory." The example she used was retaking the Mainland and how the children must study hard because they will be the leaders once "victory" has been won. The armed forces are prepared

66. *KYKP*, upper grades, book 2, lesson 21.
67. *KYKP*, book 6, lesson 25.
68. *KYKP*, book 7, lesson 19.

and ready, one lesson says, for everyone believes "we must retake the Mainland and rebuild a new China."[69] We must be strong and resolute, fifth graders learn, and fight for our family home, for who wants to be old and die on this island?[70]

More will be said about anticommunism in Chapter 3, but it may be of interest to see briefly how children react to this training. One Taiwanese boy in the fifth grade at the country public school wrote of the family scene (Appendix 3). The father and the children, he said, were thinking of ways in which they could destroy communism, because this would be a great thing. Many children wrote that the public meeting scene (Appendix 3) was a gathering to discuss ways to reattack the Mainland and liberate their compatriots. A third-grade Taiwanese boy at the country school got quite mixed up about all this, however. He wrote that the meeting was one of Mainlanders, called by the President (Chiang Kai-shek) and the father of the country (Sun Yat-sen). It was a good situation, he said, because they were preparing to reattack the Mainland and overthrow the Manchu government.

69. *She-hui K'e-pen* 社會課本 [Social Studies Primer] book 4, lesson 16.
70. *KYKP*, upper grades, book 2, lesson 19.

Chapter 2

Leadership and

Political Style

The considerable pressure that children in Taiwan experience with regard to conforming to group norms is understandably accompanied by a desire for a system where group values are clearly defined.[1] Group cohesiveness demands unquestioned loyalty from group members and is maintained by leaders who articulate the goals and values by which the various members may measure their conformity.[2] The way in which leadership interacts with the group is "political style." As members of the group, leaders are themselves socialized into what are, and what are not, acceptable ways of interacting with group members. The leader, however, by the very fact that he expresses the values of the group, intervenes in the socialization process of a new generation.

In Chinese society deviance from the norms of the group involves face. Heavily reinforced in all aspects of childhood training, the degrees to which one saves face is a critical barometer to the tension which an individual may feel. Conflicting norms, or situations where norms are not clearly defined, reduce the possibility of adequate conformity, and there is a consequent strain toward elimination of conflicting values. Conformity, however, is not to some concept of abstract morality but is behavior in terms of a specific model, living or dead. The model is conceived of as embodying the proper virtues and his actions as manifesting them. It is only by imitation that one will learn correct behavior oneself.

For group members to conform best it is desirable that there be one model, or a well-defined hierarchy of models, in terms of which behavior by all members can be judged.[3] Where two or more models of equal

1. This and some of the following hypotheses I owe to the extremely interesting work of Richard H. Solomon. See his *The Chinese Political Culture and Problems of Modernization,* Center for International Studies, Massachusetts Institute of Technology, Cambridge, Mass. (C/64–38), p. 13.

2. *Ibid.,* p. 18.

3. *Ibid.,* p. 19.

authority exist, divergent actions by the models would imply more than one concept of proper virtue. Modeling by group members would produce conformity by some members to one value system and by other members to an alternate value system, with a consequent lessening of group cohesion and a threat of loss of face to some segment of the group. Persons and ideas are intimately connected; no separation is possible, for to oppose someone's actions or concept of action (his ideas) is to question his values in terms of the group's concept of proper virtue. It is also to cause him to lose face.

The leader, in a sense, epitomizes the face of the group. His actions, accepted as a model by his followers, reflect the values of the group as a whole. General orientation to one leader at any particular level of generalization would likely manifest itself in a highly unitary group structure, i.e., group members would not likely be members of other groups at the same level of generalization.

The leader is a model for group members and provides them with the cues for proper behavior; in return, followers give the leader loyalty in the form of an acceptance of his role as definer and exemplar of group values. Loyalty, in fact, becomes the modal relationship between leader and follower,[4] for if the leader, who has been accepted by the group members as a model for proper behavior, commits acts which violate the values of the members, he will have lost not merely his own face but also that of the group which he represents and by extension, that of each of its members. He will not have been loyal to the group, for he, as representative of the group, will have lost the group's face. Any member, on the other hand, who acts contrary to accepted standards set by the leader loses face with the group because the leader is its acknowledged model. If the member's actions are known outside the group, he may also lose the group's face because he will have violated the value of maintaining group cohesion.[5]

4. Loyalty may take extreme forms, by our standards. A man may follow a boss if his boss changes jobs despite his liking for his former position. Subordinates may follow a general into an extremely dangerous situation despite no legal or or moral obligation, by our standards, to do so. For Shang Hsing Hsia Hsiao 上行下效—the leader sets the example and the followers follow, as an old proverb says.

5. Conversely, initiative by any individual may seem to be lacking, or indifference manifested, not because individuals do not perceive of some situation needing action but because individual response may be viewed as disruptive of group cohesion through implied criticism of a leader's failure to act.

In commenting on the nature of the Chinese experience and tradition John K. Fairbank has written:

An equal relationship has little precedent in Chinese experience. . . . Their solution [to politics] began with the observation that the order of nature is not egalitarian but hierarchic. . . . In effect, this was a doctrine of obedience, to be manifested through the virtues of filial piety, chastity and loyalty. . . . Within the family, the patriarch was like an emperor, while ordinary family members, each in his own status, depended on the group for their livelihood, their education and social life, and even for a religious focus through reverence for their ancestors. . . . In the Chinese tradition, government is by persons who command obedience by the example they set of right conduct. When in power, an emperor or a ruling party has a monopoly of leadership which is justified by its performance, particularly by the wisdom of its policies. No abstract distinction is made between the person in power and his policies. Dissent which attacks policies is felt to be an attack on the policy maker. On this basis, no "loyal opposition" is possible. The Western concept of disputing a power holder's policies while remaining loyal to his institutional status is not intelligible to the Chinese. Critics are seen as enemies, for they discredit those in power and tear down the prestige by which their power is partially maintained.[6]

There are many examples of such conceptions of relations between leaders and followers, particularly in the ideal attitudes of the Confucian school. T'ung-tsu Ch'u, for instance, quotes this passage from the Hou-Han Shu:

During a trip of inspection to a country, a case in which two brothers accused each other over land was brought before Han Yen-shou 韓延壽, a governor. Han was deeply grieved and said, "I am lucky enough to be the example for the whole province, yet I am unable to demonstrate the moral influence, thus bringing about litigation among relatives. This is not only harmful to the customs, but it also brings shame to the virtuous magistrate, the local officials, and those who are filial and fraternally submissive in the community. The blame is on the governor of the province. . . ."[7]

Such self-abnegation is derived directly from the notion of the Confucian school that those who hold the highest positions are the ones with the greatest ability to influence. Order in society depends on the

6. John K. Fairbank, "How to Deal with the Chinese Revolution," *The New York Review of Books*, vol. 6, no. 2 (Feb. 17, 1966), pp. 12, 14.
7. T'ung-tsu Ch'u, *Law and Society in Traditional China* (Paris and The Hague: Mouton & Co., (1961), p. 253.

proper person, for the right to leadership is derived directly from one's moral influence, the two being seen as identical.[8]

Today in Taiwan the moral influence of the leader is augmented by, and identified with, the state's power and dignity. One educator has stated: "In the modern era the leaders of states not only represent the people's determination and power but at the same time symbolize the state's honor and dignity. Citizens, therefore, ought to express respect toward their leaders."[9] The same writer, talking about the desirability of encouraging children to participate in group activities of service outside the school, had this to say: "In the group, no matter what one's responsibility or work is, one ought to obey the guidance of the leader; if oneself is the leader then even more one must know how to guide others."[10]

There is a story which children read in fourth grade about how the animals have gathered together to choose the animal most capable of enduring difficulty. The spider nominated the water buffalo, who in turn named the camel, who named the ant, all being praised for the hard work they do. But the ant nominated the bee because the bee gives us things to eat, builds beautiful homes, works hard, and is not lazy. Moreover, "especially when they meet an enemy, they join hearts and effort to resist feverishly. This type of devotion and resistance manifests the group spirit. Who can do it better?" The bee is thus elected, for the

8. *Ibid.*, pp. 254, 257.

9. Kung Pao-shan, *Tao-te Chiao-yu Shih-shih Luen* [A Discussion of the Practical Application of Morals in Education] (Taipei, Taiwan, 1962), p. 31.

10. *Ibid.*, p. 88. An editorial on the first page of the *Jen-min Jih-pao* 人民日報 [People's Daily], no. 5775 (May 1, 1964), under the title "Even More Carry Out and Develop the 'Compare,' 'Study,' 'Catch Up,' and 'Help' Movement of Increasing Production and Practicing Frugality," gives an interesting comparison of this notion with mainland (or Communist) practice. The editorial said, in part: "If every place and unit wishes to take the experiences and standard of the vanguard as their own then when they start to compare and study the basis of the vanguard they must put the emphasis of their work on catching up with the vanguard and helping those behind. Moreover, when they are in the process of 'catching up' and 'helping' they must continuously compare themselves with and study the vanguard. Besides enthusiastically helping those behind, the units of the vanguard itself should constantly pay attention to overcoming the shortcomings of their own work and should humbly study the strong points of others. Only in this way can those behind become the vanguard and the vanguard itself progress even more."

bee exemplifies that characteristic which is the most important for a leader, loyalty to the group.[11]

In an interview with an eleven-year-old fourth-grade mainland boy at the city public school discussion was centered around the public meeting scene picture (Appendix 3). The chairman, the child said, had been elected because he was good to people and helped them. The conversation then went like this:

Question: "Does a group need to have a leader?"

Response: "Yes!!!"

Question: "Why?"

Response: "Because if people do something wrong, he can persuade them to do it right."

Question: "In that case what other kinds of responsibility does he have toward his subordinates?"

Response: "If his subordinates do something wrong he will urge and direct them not to do wrong. The chairman will use methods of persuasion and leadership to tell people that they cannot have attitudes which are bad for society. If they don't listen, he will tell them that the police will come and arrest them and put them in prison and that this would be very bad for the name of society and the country."

An eleven-year-old fifth-grade mainland girl at the same school also spoke on the same picture. The people who are elected chairmen, she said, "are fair and unselfish. They are people who are incorruptible and know shame." Later, in response to a question as to whether a person could do something in disregard of other people's opposition, she replied: "If everyone agrees, then it's all right, or if he takes the chairman as an example. Or it can be done if it's according to the opinion of an educational leader."

In their written stories children frequently invoked the same image of an authority figure who is a guide to good conduct and who increases the face of the group. A sixth-grade mainland girl at the city private school wrote that the family scene (Appendix 3) was one where the father was prohibiting the children from reading undesirable books. Afterward, she said, the children would not read worthless books but rather worthwhile ones and "would feel that what their father said was right, for one ought not to look at that type of book." In the same school two mainland girls, one in second grade and one in third grade, wrote

11. *KYKP,* book 7, lesson 5.

respectively about the public meeting scene and the policeman and vendor scene (Appendix 3). The first child said a policeman was speaking at the meeting and "afterward all the people felt that if they did something wrong, they would very much want to change; therefore, they were all very thankful to the policeman for speaking to them." The second little girl told how the vendor was selling dirty things and how "after this situation had developed several merchants and people who were not proper listened to the policeman's honest words and became good citizens." This is good, the child said, for "my opinion is that if people obey the policeman, then we will have a good society."

The children were asked whether, when they were playing a game with their schoolmates, they were the ones who usually decided what to play. About one third of the children responded that they were the decision makers, a half said they were not, and one sixth admitted that they didn't know.[12] When asked whether they *wanted* to be the one who decided 59.2 percent responded Yes, 27.2 percent responded No or Don't Care, and 13.7 percent said they didn't know. There were no significant differences between Mainlander and Taiwanese children, but there was a significant difference between boys and girls, the boys being slightly higher than the girls in their desire to take command.[13] There was also a significant difference between grades, with the number of Yeses (indicating a desire to be the one who decides) declining (except for a high fifth-grade figure) from 61 percent in first grade to 52.7 percent in sixth grade.

Table 2–1
Desire to Be a Decision Maker: Percent

Category/Grade	1	2	3	4	5	6
Don't Know	8	10.5	24.0	16.5	7.5	11.0
No, Don't Care	31	27.4	17.6	26.8	28.3	36.2
Yes	61	62.1	58.4	56.7	64.2	52.7
No. responding	100	95	125	127	53	127

Significant at the .01 level.

12. For 695 responses the categories were: Yes, Sometimes, 34.1 percent; No, 50.8 percent; Don't Know, 15.1 percent.

13. Total Boy responses 357: Don't Know, 16.5 percent; No, Don't Care, 22.4 percent; Yes, 61.0 percent. Total Girl responses 333: Don't Know, 10.8 percent; No, Don't Care, 32.7 percent; Yes, 56.4 percent.

It can be seen from Table 2–1 that, while many children indicate a desire to be a decision maker, the number who so desire decreases with age, presumably as realizations of female roles develop. Another important factor could well be an increasing awareness of the necessity for conformity and a hesitancy to be the one to establish a course of action which might possibly challenge an established leader or prove unacceptable to the group, for as children grow older, they show marked increases in their feelings that a leader is necessary for group action. When asked whether a basketball team (basketball is widely played in Taiwan) should have a leader or not, 82.5 percent of the children who were asked said Yes, with a slightly significant increase with age and a slightly significant difference between Mainlanders and Taiwanese, the Mainlanders being more emphatic in their desire for a leader.[14] There was no significant difference between boys and girls. When asked to explain why there should be a leader, children almost never responded with such replies as "Because the leader plays the best basketball" or "Because he is the best liked." Rather they saw the leader in group terms similar to a twelve-year-old sixth-grade mainland boy at the city private school who said that if "there is a team captain, then there will be order, and when they begin to play, no one will be reckless." Most interesting of all, there is a marked increase by grade in replies using group reasons for the necessity of a leader (see Table 2–2).

Table 2–2
Reasons Given for the Necessity of a Leader: Percent

Category/Grade	1	2	3	4	5	6
Don't Know	56	50.5	61.6	42.5	37.7	20.5
Group Reasons	44	45.3	36.8	55.9	56.6	77.1
Individual Reasons	0	4.2	1.6	1.6	5.7	2.4
No. Responding	100	95	125	127	53	127

Significant at the .01 level.

Models

How can we explain the ready willingness of children in Taiwan to conform to the authority figure? Moreover, how shall we understand children's intuitive recognition of an authority situation and their as-

14. Significant at the .05 level. Mainlanders said Yes, 84.6 percent versus 74.3 percent for the Taiwanese.

sumption that the authority figure is usually correct within that situation? Undoubtedly part of the reason lies in the dependent nature of childhood, but while such dependency may explain compliance, it is not necessarily an explanation for identification with an authority figure or for the willingness to assume the correctness of an authority figure's injunctions. A fuller explanation, I believe, lies in the type of model which an authority figure is to a child, what his status is, and the type and nature of the cues which he gives.

According to Albert Bandura and Richard H. Walters most children develop a generalized habit of imitating the responses of successful models. Approximation and imitation of a model are crucial, they say, for understanding the acquisition of social behavior patterns, while the maintenance of acquired patterns is best understood by studying the "scheduling of reinforcements."[15] There are three possible effects of exposure to a model. First, there is a modeling effect which refers to the transmission of response patterns so that the child begins to manifest new response patterns similar to those that the model would exhibit under the same circumstances. Second, there is the inhibition, or disinhibition, of already acquired response patterns. Third, there is a possible eliciting effect where a response by a model in a particular situation is a cue for releasing a similar observer response.[16] A learning situation, of course, where modeling is one aspect of the learning process, will generally involve all three of these effects.

In studying the effectiveness of modeling there are two aspects of critical importance. The first involves the extent of the individual's own motivation to achieve some desired goal. Communication theory tells us that when "A perceives X as instrumental to a desired state of affairs with respect to B, or B as similarly instrumental with respect to X, he is influenced toward co-orientation."[17] If A is an observer and X and B are models, A will be influenced to co-orientation providing he perceives the model as instrumental to a desired state of affairs. Generally stated if B talks to A about X, and X is desirable and A trusts B, the chances are that A and B's cognitive and cathectic orientation toward X will be more

15. Albert Bandura and Richard H. Walters, *Social Learning and Personality Development* (New York: Holt, Rinehart & Winston, Inc., 1963), pp. 4–5.

16. *Ibid.*, p. 106.

17. T. M. Newcomb, "Communicative Behavior," in *Approaches to the Study of Politics,* Roland Young, ed. (Evanston, Ill.: Northwestern University Press, 1958), p. 247.

similar than it was before.[18] The shift of A and B do not need to be equal, however, and if A is a child and B an adult, the chances are that A's shift will be considerably larger.

The second important aspect of modeling is that reinforcement procedures are more effective when the model is a high-prestige versus a low-prestige person.[19] As Llewellyn Queener points out, the sheer number of attitude cues does not mean that an attitude will be formed, nor does it even guarantee that the opposite attitude will be attenuated. What is critical is the prestige, in the observer's eyes, of the cue giver.[20]

Briefly, what these points mean is that if children do not conceive of some end as desirable, or have not been taught so, then a model who upholds such an end is not likely to be very effective. In addition, if a model is perceived as having low status, he will again not be very effective. Where the goal is desirable and the model of high prestige, however, there will be a powerful impulse to conform to the model's behavior and attitudes. In childhood socialization particularly the model not only establishes the correct hierarchy of preferences with regard to goals but also exhibits the socially approved ways of orienting to these goals.

The Family

Children look upon their parents as the settlers of disputes and the solvers of problems. Typical is the response of a fifth-grade Taiwanese girl at the city private school who was writing about the family scene (Appendix 3). The children, she wrote, had taken something to eat, but the older brother had grabbed first and had not shared with his little sister. This was bad, the father said. The little girl concluded this minor tragedy by writing: "I definitely do not think this type of situation will develop again because Father understands and will explain it to them. Later this kind of quarreling between the children will not occur." Whether such sentiments of the parent as the knowing solver of problems generalize to other individuals or not is still largely unknown. F. N. Cox, trying to assess whether children's attitudes toward parents generalize to other individuals, found some significant correlations but

18. *Ibid.*, pp. 249–250.

19. Bandura and Walters, *Social Learning*, p. 10.

20. Llewellyn Queener, "The Development of Internationalist Attitudes" (II, "Attitude Cues and Prestige"), *Journal of Social Psychology*, vol. 29 (1949), as mentioned in Herbert H. Hyman, *Political Socialization: A Study in Political Behavior* (Glencoe, Ill.: The Free Press, 1959), p. 162.

was very cautious with his results and was reluctant to generalize beyond the samples he studied.[21] Fred I. Greenstein, discussing the complexity of the process, points out that no definitive proofs have yet been adduced for this theory.[22] The assumption in the literature of psychological testing is that some linking exists, but whether it is a simple or complex association is unknown. Robert D. Hess and David Easton, for instance, have posited a relationship between a child's affective view of his father and his view of the President.[23] Very possibly the attempt to link directly fathers and political figures is erroneous. What is more important at this stage, I think, is to determine whether generalized responses to authority figures develop to the extent that we can observe a congruence of behavior patterns and emotional responses between primary and secondary group authority figures generally.

With regard to specific political learning, it is conceivable that affect and behavioral responses toward a father and a political leader may develop separately, as a result of a "step" socialization process. That is, a parent (invested with affect and high prestige by a child) may encourage school learning in general. One aspect of school training may be political in nature, and the child will respond to this training in terms of the family model's favorable attitude toward learning and not to the model's attitude toward a political figure or to the political situation in general. This assumption would have to be modified, of course, depending on the nature of political discussion in the home: where there is a great deal of discussion, what is learned about politics in school may be submerged; where there is little political discussion, what is learned at school may be of prime significance.

In assessing the role of the family in the political socialization process, it seems to me, based on the reasoning in this chapter so far, that there are four critical variables to be considered: (1) affect of the child for his or her parents, and whether the parents are of high or low prestige in the eyes of the child; (2) the importance of school learning as a goal; (3) the nature of response to authority in the home; and (4) the extent of direct training in politics in the home.

21. F. N. Cox, "An Assessment of Children's Attitudes towards Parent Figures," *Child Development*, vol. 33, no. 4 (Dec. 1962).

22. Fred I. Greenstein, *Children and Politics* (New Haven, Conn.: Yale University Press, 1965), p. 50.

23. Robert D. Hess and David Easton, "The Child's Changing Image of the President," *Public Opinion Quarterly*, vol. 24, no. 4 (Winter 1960).

According to the Chinese parents I talked with, discussion of topics directly related to politics is not brought up in front of elementary-school-age children. Undoubtedly fear or apathy may enter in as explanation of this phenomenon. Chinese parents tell me, however, that this reticence is mostly due to the fact that, generally speaking, topics concerning matters outside the family are not discussed before children. Politics is a man's business, commented upon like all men's real business, outside the home with other men. Inside, women rule and family matters are supreme.

Very likely what Chinese parents say is largely true, that extensive conversations on political matters are not introduced into the home with children; however, comments and remarks touching on politics may, in fact, be just as important, and I must confess that I do not have data on this type of communication. A remark by a father that "that damned mayor is lining his pockets" may be far more important in forming attitudes than a lengthy discourse ever could be.

If the extent and nature of actual political training in the home is difficult to assess, the emphasis by parents on education as a goal is not. No other topic in Taiwan is of such consuming interest, and children early learn that education is a goal of paramount importance. The emphasis is undoubtedly greater in some homes than in others, the rich versus the poor and the urban versus the rural, for instance, but despite such differences it is a topic generally emphasized throughout the society.

The nature of discussions between parents and children does not encourage the child to criticize or question. One friend told me that, although one loved one's child, raising children was somewhat analogous to raising an animal. The child is not a little adult; he knows nothing and must be taught everything. Most Chinese parents feel that it is not necessary to explain to children why they have to do something. Children are supposed to do something because the father or mother (and later, in school, the teacher) said so. Furthermore, certain subjects are not discussed by either the parent or the child. If a child brings up the subject of sex, for instance, he may be rather angrily told that it is not a fit topic for discussion or thought. In later years good friends may discuss sex, but the introduction of such a subject to new friends is always sensitive because of the possibility of rejection by others for not knowing shame. In short, children begin to develop quite early a response to authority figures that is outwardly unquestioning and uncritical, a response in which the actions of the authority figure are deemed to be correct by definition.

This type of outward dependence on the correctness of the parent is reinforced by the development of strong inner dependency. Many Chinese children sleep with their mothers well into grade school. As a car washer once complained to me, "Children like their mothers better because they get to sleep with them." When children misbehave and criticism of the parent would be construed as misbehavior, children are threatened with withdrawal of affection. "I'll tell the teacher" is also sometimes used as a threat, a threat which reinforces the teacher's role by investing it with parental support.

There is much mutual reinforcement between the school and the family. Support by the family for education and for the teacher is echoed by the support given the home in school. In education, much of this support revolves around the concept of filial piety as the root of all proper relations to authority. A story that children read tells of a little boy who is given some fruit to eat by his aunt but who saves it for his mother and father and is praised for doing so. In a home study review book a question is asked related to this story: "The most important way that one can be filial to one's parents is (1) to give good things to parents to eat; (2) to make good clothes for parents to wear; (3) to help parents do things; (4) to obey one's parents."[24] All are desirable responses, but (4) is obviously correct, for it is not the giving of food itself which is important but the fact that the giving is only a way of manifesting a more basic obedience and filiality. At the country public school a third-grade class devoted a session to discussing the topic of filial piety. Pictures were put on the blackboard along with some slogans, which were as follows:

"How Should We Be Filial to Our Parents?"

1. "Mind what they say."
2. "Help our parents to do things."
3. "Love and protect our younger brothers and sisters."
4. "Be careful and guard our health."
5. "Follow the regulations," etc.

Overt training in filiality begins in kindergarten and is most marked in the early years of school. As in the slogans just mentioned there is an

---

24. *Tzu-hsiu Liang-yu, Erh Nien Hsia-ch'i* 自修良友二年下期 [The Self-study Companion, second grade, second term] (Taipei, Taiwan, 1966) 良友書局.

attempt to link filiality with other desirable goals. In both terms of first grade, for instance, love of parents and love of flag are put back to back in the lessons.[25] In the exercises following these lessons—in the book used in the second semester—emphasis is put upon filial piety and love of country.

Obedience to parents is reflected generally in the responses of children writing about the family scene (Appendix 3). Very typical is the second-grade mainland girl at the city private school who told of a father scolding his children because they had not memorized their lessons. The father's heart is sad, she says, to raise children who do not know to be industrious and study hard. But "they want their father to forgive them and their father, knowing that they know how to change, is happy and does forgive them." Afterward the children do not play but study hard. Another child, a third-grade mainland boy at the same school, wrote about the policeman and the vendor scene. He sketched a story of a vendor whose mother became sick and who was weeping as he sold fruit. A policeman gave the vendor some money because he knew it was a good thing to buy medicine for one's mother and wanted the vendor to do this for his parent. It is a good situation, the child said, "because the vendor is filial and the policeman is willing to help the poor."

I asked some fifth-grade girls at the city public school who the best people in the world are. One child answered, "Americans," but the others quickly said, "No, Chinese." I said I did not mean a nationality but a person, and then they all answered, without exception, "Mother" or "Father," with "Mother" predominating. These somewhat spontaneous affirmations of the affect children grant their parents is borne out in other ways. Children were asked who the most likable person they knew was. Of the 695 children who answered, 59.5 percent named their parents or grandparents.[26] On other aspects of prestige, however, parents did not come off quite so well. To the question of who the smartest person is, the same children gave parents or grandparents only 7.8 percent of their choices. On this same question 37.7 percent of the children responded Don't Know, while a little over 30 percent of the children named a nonauthority figure such as a school friend.[27]

Although the affective relationship may be the strongest between

25. *KYKP*, book 1, lessons 15–16; book 2, lessons 2–3.
26. 4.6 percent named Chiang Kai-shek or Sun Yat-sen.
27. 6.5 percent named Chiang Kai-shek or Sun Yat-sen.

child and parent, the child also recognizes the parent's decision-making role. This role, however, is recognized by present-day children as differing from the generally held stereotype of the traditional Chinese father who was conceived to be the ultimate arbiter on matters of overall importance to the family. Many adults told me that as children they remember their father as a supreme but distant individual. Mothers were quite close to their children, but the separation between a father and his children was quite great. As one woman said in a revealing remark, "Not even my brothers talked freely with our father."

Observations in parks, on playgrounds, and on the streets of the way children now react to parents show some divergence from the more traditional and probably idealized model. One has a sense that many fathers are very close to their children, openly exhibiting warm and intimate feelings, and, further, that by no means are men unchallenged masters of the home. As one man said, women are emancipated from the home now and are companions, not just wives.

These observations of modern family patterns lead one to wonder whether traditional concepts of Chinese family patterns can be accepted in their entirety. F. W. Mote, in private conversation, has mentioned seeing lower-class fathers in poor, rural villages on the Mainland turn out with their small children at the end of the day to play with them while talking to other men. Indeed, according to him, it was the mothers who were the greater disciplinarians until the age of about five or six, when the fathers began to take over this task. In contrast to this open affection for small children, Mote noticed that middle-school and college-age children, especially boys, seldom had good talking relations with fathers unless some unusual situation, like a family crisis, brought them together. There is no reason to believe that these patterns he cites are markedly different from those of more traditional times, and one senses therefore that remembrances of fathers by adults in Taiwan are remembrances of their youth rather than early childhood. It is more than this, however. Formal respect for and a sense of avoidance of the father were idealized responses (approximated most closely in practice by the "gentry") which indicate not only what the relations with the father were during one period of childhood and adolescence but what they ought to have been at all times. To the extent that this is so, the responses of adults, although they submerge an earlier and happier recollection of fathers, reflect the socially accepted father-child relationship typical of their generation. For while an affective relationship was not ideally discouraged in traditional China—indeed, far from it, it was encouraged and undoubtedly realized in many instances—this affect was to be expressed by very prescribed forms of filiality which in practice were always more important than any warm affective relationship itself and which tended to dampen any spontaneous expressions of intimacy. Undoubtedly there was considerable pressure to conform to this ideal from even the fathers themselves, who were good models of the correct role relationship despite whatever their personal feelings may have been.

Modern children's values concerning male dominance and generational deference also are at variance with the ideal traditional model. When asked to pick between boys and girls as to who gets new clothes first or who gets to eat an apple first, only a little over 18 percent of the 695 children gave boys for both answers (not unexpectedly, however, there was a significantly higher percentage of boys, 25.8 percent, who answered this way than girls, 10.2 percent). The lack of generational deference is roughly comparable. When asked to pick between younger and older people as to who gets the best things to eat or who sits in the most comfortable seat, only 15.3 percent of these children answered elders for both (there was a slightly significant difference between boys and girls, 17.6 percent versus 12.3 percent).

A general form of question was used to determine who makes decisions in the family. Two questions were asked: (1) If you wanted to change schools, who in your family would you ask? (2) In a family discussion about whether to buy a new radio, who would decide? The first question relates to the child's own plans in an important area of his life and the second to economic decisions in the home. The results are shown in Table 2–3.

Quite obviously, while the mother is not often accorded the sole

Table 2–3
Locus of Decision Making in the Family: Percent

Category	Question 1	Question 2
Father	38.0	43.1
Mother	13.1	10.9
Father & Mother	36.7	28.8
Other	2.7	5.6
Don't Know	9.5	11.7
No. Responding	695	695

decision-making role, the father is by no means omnipotent either.[28] Roughly one third of the children see parents as codeciders. When children are asked who the head of the house is, however, fully 63.2 percent answer Father, with 5.2 percent answering Mother, 21.5 percent answering both parents, 4.5 percent answering Other, and 5.8 percent responding Don't Know. Whether the father ever had the actual decision-making powers accorded him by the traditional model is again, I think, open to question. In any case he does not now, although he is generally looked upon as the family head.

According to the responses given, most children, 81.4 percent, had warm, favorable feelings toward the family head, who, as we have seen, was generally recognized to be the father.[29] This favorable response contrasts sharply with the avoidance that some older Chinese have mentioned as characterizing their relations with their fathers. If this approbation on the part of modern children is not due simply to their young age or to a fear (undoubtedly important) of expressing unfavorable feelings, then there has been a change in the ideal types of affective patterns within the Chinese family. Actual observable patterns of formal modern family interaction may have shifted only slightly from the actual patterns of traditional times. This, however, would not lessen the implications for present-day political socialization that would result from continuing changes within the family in the attitude behind the formal style of interaction, i.e., in generally held ideals regarding the primacy of correct behavior versus freely expressed intimacy. It must be stressed, however, that such intimacy involves the expression of positive affect only. Expressions of negative affect by the child are still strongly proscribed.

We know that in traditional times there was a fear of government manifested in a desire to stay out of the magistrate's yamen. These generally avoidant feelings seem also to have been felt by most people with regard to their fathers as well. Such avoidant feelings were as-

---

28.   There is a division, of course, in the Chinese home with regard to decisions, the mother generally deciding about matters of family concern and the father dealing with outside matters. I chose these two particular questions after consulting my Chinese friends because they are relatively ambiguous between the two roles and hopefully therefore would reveal, when there is ambiguity, who has the crucial say in the home.

29.   Negative feelings were expressed by 3.5 percent of the children while 15.2 percent were indefinite or didn't know.

sociated with the customary role of the father and the sanctioned ways he had for dealing with other family members. It was also undoubtedly due, as Marion J. Levy points out, to the father's responsibility as the head of an economic unit outside of which there was no sanctioned way of making a living.[30] It was the father's responsibility to ensure that the unit and its members survived.

The primacy of the family with regard to economic survival has declined, however, in the last few decades with a corresponding growth of larger group identification. Paradoxically, however, as the family's importance as an economic and political unit has declined, its cohesiveness from an affect standpoint may have increased. The father's ideal position as an absolute authority figure at or near the top of a well-defined family hierarchy has lessened, the avoidance involved in maintaining that position has declined as well, and the father is able to fraternize more freely with his children and other family members.[31]

These changed father-child relationships have two very important results. First, the development of an intimate relationship between a child and his father is not subordinated to an overriding need for manifesting proper relations, and to the extent that there is a connection between positive affect for a father and affect for a political leader there is likely to be an increase in affective feelings for the latter, or, more importantly, a decrease in avoidant feelings. Second, as the father begins to take over some of the personal, expressive, and emotional attributes that the mother traditionally had, he may very likely begin using some of the means mothers traditionally used to obtain their objectives. The father may technically still be the instrumental leader (as indicated in the children's choice of him as family head) yet use expressive versus instrumental means to obtain his ends. For instance, the father may seek an instrumental end for his child, such as success in school, and use expressive means, such as withholding love, to obtain this end.[32] It has

30. Marion J. Levy, Jr., and Shih Kuo-heng, *The Rise of the Modern Chinese Business Class* (New York: Institute of Pacific Relations, 1949), pp. 1–5.

31. This may even result in ineffectual noninvolvement with the affairs of one's children as they grow older, something Robert J. Lifton has pointed out about Japanese fathers. Robert J. Lifton, "Youth and History: Individual Change in Postwar Japan," *Daedalus*, vol. 91 (Winter 1962), mentioned in James C. Davies, "The Family's Role in Political Socialization," *Annals of the American Academy of Political and Social Science*, vol. 361 (Sept. 1965), p. 13.

32. For an extremely interesting article about some of these factors see Wil-

been pointed out earlier how powerful withholding love is as a technique of discipline with Chinese children.

In Taiwan fathers represent the family and have high prestige. They may not be the sole decision makers in the family, but their opinions and directives are not openly questioned. They provide early models for children of an authority figure whose injunctions must be uncritically accepted. At the same time there seems to be a growing acceptance of an open intimacy between the child and the authority figure, and the disciplinary techniques associated with this involvement are additional and powerful mechanisms for orienting the child toward goals espoused by the authority figure. To the extent that positive affect is transferable, fathers also provide an early model of a benevolent relationship between leader and led.[33]

Part of an interview with a second-grade Taiwanese girl at the city public school went like this:

Question: "How ought parents to be toward their children?"

Response: "They should pay attention to how they feel and to their health."

Question: "Is what parents say always correct?"

Response: "Yes." (very positive)

Question: "Is there any time when they are wrong?"

Response: "No."

Question: "But if they are wrong, what then?"

Response: "They won't be wrong." (laughs)

Question: "Must we do what parents tell us to do?"

Response: "Yes."

Question: "But what should we do if they are wrong?"

Response: "Don't listen to them."

Question: "Can we criticize them?"

Response: "No . . . (pause) Sometimes."

---

liam R. Larson and Barbara G. Myerhoff, "Primary and Formal Family Organization and Adolescent Socialization," *Sociology and Social Research*, vol. 50, no. 1 (Oct. 1965).

33. The government, knowingly or unknowingly, attempts to utilize this. There is an interesting sign on a barracks in Taipei which proclaims: "Our leaders are our family heads. Our barracks are our homes." This type of usage has its parallel from traditional times when the name for a hsien magistrate, both officially and popularly, was Fu-Mu-Kuan 父母官 [Parent Official]. While the usage is similar, the affective content may be quite different.

Question: "When can we and when can't we?"
Response: "When they do something that's wrong."
Question: "What is something that's wrong?"
Response: "Playing mah-jongg."

The Schools

In the schools there is a hierarchy of strictly defined roles. At the apex is the principal. Under him, depending on the size of the school, there may be one or more assistant principals. Next in rank come the department heads, teachers who spend part, or all, of their time giving overall direction to maintenance, health, curriculum, teacher affairs (absences, changing schools, poor teaching, etc.), and discipline (lining up, regulations, safety outside the school, etc.). Last are the teachers themselves.

Among the students each class has its own class leader and assistant class leader. In addition, each row has a row leader, and there may also be a column leader for every two rows. (There are generally eight rows in each class and four columns, which are made up of two rows with their desks side by side.) Each student rank is clearly delineated. The class leader has three stripes on his uniform, the assistant class leader two, and the column leaders one. In addition to these ranks, but much rarer and at the teacher's discretion, students may be appointed specifically to be in charge of keeping order, of keeping up the bulletin board and other items related to studies, of recreational activities, of sanitation, and of class money matters. The positions of class leader and assistant class leader are elective, although in first and second grade the incumbents are usually appointed by the teacher. Row or column leaders may be elected or appointed, the latter method being used particularly when the teacher desires that the holder of the position be able to help the other students with their studies. At most schools there are also police boys and girls whose special function is to keep order on the playground and help the children get home safely. Student government with a student council does not generally exist, although an experimental council was tried at the city public school some years ago.

Boys seem to be picked more frequently than girls for such jobs as starting games, and this tendency seems to carry over into the selection of class leaders. In the city private school I analyzed the sex of the class leader and assistant class leader for all grades for the spring term of 1965. In all, girls held these posts 19 times versus 17 times for boys. When examined in detail, however, it can be seen that by the upper

Table 2–4
Sex of Class Leader

Grade	Boy		Girl	
	Class Leader	Asst. Class Leader	Class Leader	Asst. Class Leader
1–3	4	4	5	5
4–6	7	2	2	7
Total	11	6	7	12

grades girls are not frequently elected to the top position (see Table 2–4).

Such results are not very conclusive, but they buttress observations that with age boys are increasingly chosen for leadership positions. It is difficult to assess whether the choice of boys is due to their greater aggressiveness or to a growing association in the minds of the children of the male sex with leadership. Certainly there is a marked emphasis on boys as heroes and leaders in childhood stories.

In class the plethora of leadership positions, particularly among the students, seems astounding at first. It becomes perhaps less so when one realizes that the tasks of the various leaders are to maintain group order and the hierarchy is utilized for this goal (there are, after all, on the average of 65 to 70 students in each class).[34] This need for order was stressed by many children in answer to a question as to why a basketball team ought to have a captain: "It is just like a country. If no one comes to lead it, then it will collapse." "He can keep the group in order." "The group will then have a leader." "If there is a leader, then there is order, and the team is not confused."

I witnessed two sixth-grade class meetings, one at the city public school and one at the city private school. In the former, the teacher was out of the room, and there was some fooling around which the class leader suppressed by cuffing a few heads, throwing some chalk, and ordering one boy to stand up and come to attention, which the boy did. In the city private school the class leader was conducting a discussion concerning regulations while a subordinate was keeping discipline by shouting out commands for quiet and cuffing heads. Such commands of peer group leaders are, like the commands of the father, met with un-questioning acquiescence. The same acquiescence occurs when the class

34. For comments on leadership selection and types of group structure see Philip M. Marcus, "Expressive and Instrumental Groups: Toward a Theory of Group Structure," *The American Journal of Sociology*, vol. 66, no. 1 (July 1960).

breaks into groups for independent work. In a third-grade class I witnessed several children appointed to lead small work groups. He (or she) asked questions from the reading, and the children in the group raised their hands to answer in a very orderly way. Each group was composed of from 16 to 18 students.

The status of student leaders is quite high, possibly because, according to one teacher, leaders are selected not simply on the basis of intellect but also on the basis of leadership factors. Elections are carried out in class meetings, the procedures for which are precisely set forth.[35] Nominations are made from the floor, and the names are written on the blackboard. In some classes the children then stand up and, with remarkable candor, praise and criticize the candidates for their strong and weak points. The children then write their choice on a piece of paper, fold it, and give it to the row leader, who takes the collected slips to the class leader. After another student has been delegated to observe that the class leader reads the results fairly, the ballots are opened and checks put against the name of each candidate as he receives a vote. There is often much cheering as the result of each ballot is read off. In one case a teacher made comments after the election, saying that the opinion of the class was shared by her as this child was very diligent, not naughty, and constantly improving. In this case, at least, the elected child's status as a model for emulation was heavily reinforced by the teacher's praise.

Children see selection to leadership as based on universalistic criteria such as intelligence and ability to work hard. I asked them three questions in this regard: (1) A child grew up to become a famous person in the government. What do you think the reason for this was? (2) A soldier could not become an officer. What do you think the reason for this was? (3) A child was not elected class leader. What do you think the reason for this was? In all cases particularistic criteria were mentioned by only .5 percent, or less, of the children. On the first two questions approximately 40 percent of the children did not know the reason, whereas roughly 60 percent mentioned universalistic criteria. On the question concerning the class leader, 23.2 percent of the students answered Don't Know while 76.8 percent gave responses such as intelligence or diligence. On all questions there was a significant increase of universalistic re-

---

35. *Kung-min Yü Tao-te*, upper grade, book 1, lesson 8, which states that because the modern age is democratic and free, we must learn to be citizens and to run a meeting.

sponses with age. Unquestionably, it would seem, Chinese children see leaders as ideally possessing qualities which merit the respect of all group members.

Such respect and concomitant high status are also afforded the teachers and principals themselves. One fourth-grade mainland girl at the city private school described her principal in these glowing terms, "Very nice. When we do something wrong, she tenderly talks to us." This recognition of a principal as compassionate and good was shared by a second-grade mainland boy at the same school. He wrote of the meeting scene as one between the parents and the principal after a traffic accident when some children were taken to the hospital. (A tragic bus accident in which many children were killed had taken place shortly before, just outside Taipei.) He makes the principal say: "I feel that your children are my children, so that what has happened to you is just as if it has happened to me. I feel so sorry for you."

It must be remembered that the status a child accords a teacher may be quite different from the status accorded the same teacher by an adult. Traditionally in China the calling was honorable enough, yet teachers were also occasionally held in contempt. Arthur H. Smith quotes a revealing proverb which says, "If one has a few bags of grain on hand, he is not obliged to be king over children."[36] The status of an elementary school teacher in Taiwan is not the highest nor is the pay very good, yet it is generally a respected position, particularly for working mothers.[37]

Regardless of adult attitudes, there is certainly strong reinforcement for children to accord quite high prestige and status to the teacher, and even more so to the principal. There is, for instance, a prominent sign at the front of a third-grade classroom in the city public school which reads, "Respect teachers; be filial to parents." The Chinese language itself emphasizes status in the terms employed as titles. A particular principal is always addressed as Principal so-and-so and a teacher as Teacher so-and-so, emphasizing the position which is held. In the first grade in the city private school the children were studying characters, among which was (長) [Chang], meaning, when used in titles, head or leader. The teacher asked the children to make up words on the basis of this character. The children mentioned several, and then the teacher said

36. Arthur H. Smith, *Village Life in China* (New York: Fleming H. Revell Co., 1899), p. 73.

37. Although, as one principal told me, the status of teachers and principals is not nearly so high now as it was under the Japanese.

"principal" and "mayor," two words which use this character. The teacher then brought up a word which does not use this character, "president," and gave a short talk to the children about President Chiang Kai-shek. Following this, examples using the character were again brought up, this time at the children's own level. They were "class leader" and "row leader." Discussion centered on the nature of authority at all levels and the appropriate titles that should be used. Association of the principal's title with that of mayor and president clearly lent prestige to the head of the school. The prestige already associated with the principal flowed in turn to these other status roles.

There is a conscious attempt in education to utilize the feelings children have toward the teacher and principal. In the second term of fourth grade, for instance, there are three lessons together that clearly reveal this attempt. The primer begins with a story about how studious Sun Yat-sen was. This is followed by a lesson on Lincoln and his love of reading. In the third lesson a teacher praises an industrious student to the class.[38] Political figures are used as models, yet it is the teacher who serves as the one who praises this activity and who sanctions it for the class by his approval.

In the fifth grade there is a story in the primer that categorizes the teacher as loving and nurturing. The children are precious, the teacher says, because they are like a family. Then we get a repetition of the loyalty theme, for the teacher makes his affection conditional upon the absolute acceptance of his authority position. The children are like a family; more than this, the teacher wants the class to be just like a family—responsible and obedient.

Although in first and second grades the children see the principal and the teacher as approximately equal in authority, by third grade an appreciation of the principal's higher status has been clearly recognized.[39] When asked who was in charge in the school, 75 percent of the 695 child-

38. *KTKP*, book 8, lessons 1-3. See Appendix 2 for remarks concerning how educational authorities organize textbook lessons in order to obtain a sequence of training content.

39. The children were asked who in school decided when an assembly was going to be held. In first grade children responded 38 percent Teacher, 22 percent Principal, and 40 percent Don't Know or Other. By third grade the responses are 16 percent Teacher, 64 percent Principal, and 20 percent Don't Know or Other. The number responding was 100 and 125, respectively. "Principal" is the correct response since it is actually this person who decides. There was a significant difference between grades on this question in the direction indicated.

ren who responded named the principal, while 10.8 percent did not know and 14.2 percent named someone else, such as the teacher or mayor. An overwhelming majority, 78.0 percent, indicated very positive feelings toward this leader, whoever he might be; 18.7 percent didn't know how they felt while 3.3 percent expressed negative to neutral sentiments.

There is considerable effort expended in the teachers' colleges to train new teachers to develop affective ties with the students. Teachers, it is felt, are examples of leaders and a powerful moral force. They should not be strict as teachers were in the past but should love the children and show them sympathy. In the men's teachers' college in a speech class there was a discussion of the teacher's "face." This problem of maintaining face would best be solved, they concluded, by rejecting a rigid and distant attitude and fostering a friendly relationship with the children. At the same time the teacher must be a helper.

In practice teachers often reveal themselves as friendly and helpful. However (and this may be partly due to the large class size), these expressions of affect are never allowed to interfere with the two primary goals of obedience and acquiring knowledge. The withdrawal of affection, in fact, is one of the more powerful techniques used by teachers to motivate children toward these two goals. Children's acceptance of these two objectives, at least as ideals, is readily observed. In a sixth-grade class at the country school, for instance, boys and girls were acting out a skit of calling at a home and practicing the expression for "Thank you. I am flattered." Invariably a boy was the caller and in the course of the conversation said, "I hear from your older brother that at home you are always very filial and at school very studious," to which the girl would reply, "Thank you. I am flattered." Obedience responses to appropriate cues also occur spontaneously quite early. In the second grade of the city private school a hand puppet show was given by two teachers. Two pieces of fruit, an orange and a banana, were talking about the advantages of vaccination. At one point the banana said, "Because I am old, I hope all the children are behaving," at which point there was a spontaneous reaction, and the children all sat up and put their hands behind their backs.

Training in respect for authority is a part of school life at all levels. Criticism and questioning of the teacher, even of the most simple problems, is not encouraged and is hardly ever observed. At the start and finish of all sessions students come to attention at the command of the class leader, face the teacher, and at a second command, bow. The teacher then bows in return. Elementary school students bow when they meet a teacher or the principal in the hallway.[40] Uncritical acceptance of commands is made a game. In the fifth grade of the country public school the children played, with great enthusiasm, a game to see who could follow orders best. Attention, right face, dress right, at ease, etc., were called out by the teacher. Gym classes also frequently stress the same theme. At the city private school each class has physical education four times a week. When the sun is too hot for games, training is given in marching. The class leader lines the children up, and they march to the field, where they line up again. When the teacher comes, the class leader bows to him, the teacher bows back, and the class is then turned over to him. The teacher marches the children around the field five or six times, blowing a whistle to keep them in step. After stopping, the children come to attention and then do right and left faces, shouting out "One, two!" as they execute the commands.[41]

If it is true, as the theory of cognitive dissonance posits, that participation breeds a shift in feeling and cognition toward acceptance of that which is done or said, then we should expect that day-by-day training in making certain response patterns would produce acceptance of these patterns, particularly when such behavior is reinforced in other areas and where there is no initial reluctance on the part of the individual to conform. Further, it may be possible by such incremental learning to associate certain models and symbols so that a response to the model will generalize to the symbol, and vice versa. Reinforcement of certain responses, and association of models and symbols, would clearly seem to be the intent

40. Teachers frequently claim that the practice of bowing is a holdover from the Japanese period (although, in fact, it was standard in mainland schools), yet no great effort seems to be made to break the habit. On the contrary it seems institutionalized as one aspect of schooling. The first book of the arithmetic primer, for instance, opens with a picture of children going to school and bowing at the gate to a male adult. *Suan-shu K'e-pen, Ti-i-Ts'e* 算術課本第一冊 [Arithmetic Primer, book 1] (Taiwan, 1964) 三都紙器工廠.

41. A less obvious indicator of the strength of the value of uncritical acceptance of a leader is in the memorization training in school. A friend told me that he noted that with the children of the family he lived with it was not the multiplication method that was memorized but each individual problem. A Chinese friend once mentioned to me that success on exams depended purely on whether one was asked a problem that had been memorized. There is no training in initiative because the leader provides this; all that is necessary is that one memorize the appropriate response.

of the morning exercises held each morning at all schools. It is worth describing these exercises, I believe, for their cumulative effect upon the children is significant, and they provide one of the clearest examples of leader-led relations within a Chinese school group context.

At about 8 :00 A.M., although sometimes earlier, the children arrive at their classes to finish homework. At 8 :20, with the exception of children who might be sick or who are being punished, sweaters and coats are taken off, uniform caps are put on, and the children, in uniform, form in military fashion outside the class room and mark off. When the loud-speaker music starts, they march to the playground and form by classes, marking time until told to stop, a command which they obey with a resounding shouts "One, two!" Then the children close order, dress right, and come to attention. Directly in front of the children is the flagpole, and there may be a bust of Sun Yat-sen near by. In many schools (it was so at the two public schools I visited) there is a raised platform in front near the base of the flagpole. The teachers line up on both sides of this platform facing the students, the department heads standing in the middle.

After the children have come to attention, a teacher mounts the plat-form and conducts the singing of the national anthem. Then the flag is raised, and the principal mounts the platform, the flag at his back. The students bow, and the principal, from his prestigious vantage point, bows back. A talk about citizenship follows, although occasionally other topics are discussed. One morning, at the city public school, the students were brought to attention and told to take out handkerchiefs and hold them up. Those who held them up were then told to kneel down, and those without handkerchiefs were displayed for the others to see. At other times there are presentations of awards. At the city private school an award is periodically given to the best-behaved class. Awards for good academic performance are also made. During these ceremonies certain students are called forward and line up in front of the platform. A student then mounts the platform, salutes the principal, and is given the prizes to distribute to the others. As the morning exercises come to an end, a student leader, standing slightly in front, again calls the child-ren to attention. They are then ordered to bow once again to the principal who bows in return. The principal then comes down from the platform, and the student leader mounts in his place. More commands are shouted out, and the children wheel in the proper direction for heading back to class, shouting "One, two!" as they turn. The music starts, and off they march to class. Outside the classrooms the children halt and march in place. At an order they shout "One, two!" and come to attention. At a further order they shout "One, two!" again and face in the direction for entering the class. Then the final command rings out, and the children file by columns into the classroom, stand by their seats, and wait for the order to bow to the teacher and for class to begin.

Political Training

A second-grade mainland girl at the city private school wrote about the meeting scene (Appendix 3): "The position of the man giving the speech is relatively high, and the position of those listening is relatively low. The man on the platform directs the people down below. He is speaking to the people down below." She goes on to explain that this leader, whoever he might be, is exhorting the people to observe safety on the streets. This is good, she says, and ends with these words: "The clothes the people down below are wearing are all different, but they are not necessarily bad people. The man on the platform is wearing clothes like Sun Yat-sen's. Behind him is the national flag, and there is also a picture of Sun Yat-sen and some characters written by some one who has just recently died. Therefore, he definitely is a good man." A fourth-grade mainland girl at the same school had a similar response: "I think what's going on in the picture is good," she said, "because at the back of the platform where they are talking is a picture of Sun Yat-sen and also the national flag."

At a very early age children develop an awareness of certain national symbols. The generally favorable identification with such symbols is probably due to their association, quite early in the child's experience, with models, such as the principal, who are accepted as leaders in the child's own immediate environment. It seems that a response developed during something like morning exercises, where political symbols and school authority figures are often paired, may generalize to individuals other than someone known to the child who is also associated with such symbols. I would posit that the association with the principal and teacher is far more important with respect to learning about specific political symbols than are parents, for school authorities are most closely associated with these symbols. Both parents and teachers provide general-ized training in authority situations, but it is in school, under the influence of the school authorities, that organized political learning really begins.[42]

42. In connection with this point it is interesting to note the assumption that

A recent work on American children states that "Evaluations and affective knowledge about political leaders seem to precede the factual information on which they might be based."[43] Because the feelings one may have toward parents and teachers may generalize to individuals in the secondary environment, these secondary relationships "become invested with deep personal feelings, sometimes in the form of direct reflections of primary group relationships, sometimes in the form of compensating reactions to them."[44] Easton and Dennis feel that it is the early personification of the government in terms of national leadership that accounts for the strong affective attachment American children show quite early toward the institution of government and to the social system generally in which they are raised.[45] There is, in fact, at this stage a very idealized image of the President. American children at lower grade levels say he works harder, is more honest, likes people more, and has more knowledge than most men.[46] Hess and Easton propose "that the first step of political socialization is initially completed with essentially no information about the political figure himself except that he is an authority figure whose status exceeds that of the authorities with whom the child has been familiar."[47] He is "a central orientation point to an increasing awareness of other elements of the political system."[48] Only later in the second major step in political socialization is there role differentiation. In later years, however, when critical knowledge of the President as a person is learned, the respect which was the earliest acquired orientation remains. To the extent that such respect is based on early strong parent-child or teacher-child ties, it may be one of the largest contributors to the stability of a political system.[49]

---

children with strong dependence habits (such as are developed in the home) are more influenced by social reinforcers (such as specific political training in school might be) than children with weak dependency habits. Bandura and Walters, *Social Learning*, p. 10.

43. Fred I. Greenstein, "The Benevolent Leader: Children's Images of Political Authority," *American Political Science Review*, vol. 54 (Dec. 1960), p. 936.

44. *Ibid.*, p. 941.

45. David Easton and Jack Dennis, "The Child's Image of Government," *Annals of the American Academy of Political and Social Science*, vol. 361 (Sept. 1965), p. 57.

46. Hess and Easton, "The Child's Changing Image of the President," pp. 636–637.

47. *Ibid.*, p. 643.

48. *Ibid.*

49. *Ibid.*, p. 644.

James C. Davies has found that children, by seven years of age, have a warm and positive attachment to their schools, to the beauty of the country, and to the goodness of the people. Attachment to the flag becomes almost religious, with this attitude reaching a plateau by the time children are nine or ten years old.[50] This is certainly true in Taiwan. In the first grade of the city public school, when told to draw pictures of the out-of-doors, 23 of 69 students included the national flag as some part of the picture. In Taiwan, however, the most intense feelings surround not the flag but the political leaders, and there is a conscious effort throughout all the school years to foster and encourage this feeling. This is not to posit, however, that the two symbols are not frequently used to reinforce each other, because they are. Thus, for instance, in the first part of second grade, there is an exercise sentence about every house hanging out the flag and every classroom having a picture of Sun Yat-sen.

The leader represents the people and personifies the nation as a whole. In fourth grade the children learn that on a date commemorated as National Recovery Day Chiang Kai-shek was captured at Sian by two generals, Chang Hsueh-liang and Ch'ang Hu-ch'eng, who had been incited by the Communists. These generals tried to force Chiang to sign some unacceptable conditions, but he replied that they could kill him but that he is the representative of all the people, the personality of 400 million people, and that if the personality is wounded, the people cannot survive. Therefore the generals released Chiang, and when he returned to Nanking, the soldiers went wild, considering this the best holiday of all. The children, the story concludes, thought Chiang was really magnificent.[51] In sixth grade, in the history primer, the children learn about "The People's Savior: President Chiang." Sun Yat-sen, they are told, "praised and admired [Chiang], considering him to be the most excellent and the most loyal revolutionary cadre." All his life he worked for the country, but then the Communists, aided by the Russians, deceived the people; everything collapsed, and the government fled to Taiwan. Chiang, who had retired, came back. The lesson ends with these unequivocal sentences: "All his life the President has been loyal to the party and patriotic to the country. Struggling for the revolution, he has continued to carry out the teachings of the Father of our Country [Sun

50. Davies, "The Family's Role in Political Socialization," p. 15.
51. *KYKP*, book 7, lesson 21.

Yat-sen] and has industriously labored to build a new China. He is the savior of the Chinese people and the greatest man in the whole world."[52]

It may be true that in all societies it is through identification with the political leader that children learn to relate themselves to the nation and the government. Jeremy R. Azrael has made the statement that in the Soviet Union the cult of Lenin and Stalin was considered the best way for children to develop an undifferentiated commitment to the nation, the government, and the party as well. Love of country progresses most easily through a feeling of love for the leaders. Biographies of leaders are therefore structured so that children will associate character traits such as love of labor, devotion to revolutionary and scientific ideas, and personal sacrifice, with building and defending the state.[53] There is a great similarity between this educational philosophy and that which prevails in Taiwan.[54] But there are, I think, in addition, deep-rooted values in Chinese group life, consciously reinforced by educational policy, which assign to the leader a heightened responsibility for exemplifying group values.

There is an interesting story which children read at the end of second grade about a village where everyone lined up indiscriminately at the well to get water and where no one was orderly. A scholar saw this, and for several mornings he went early and lined up the buckets so that those who came first could be served first and water could be taken in an orderly fashion. He made the people listen to instruction on getting water. Afterward the people learned to be orderly and did not struggle to be first or fear to be last in taking water.[55] Here is the leader par excellence. He sets the norms of the group, leads the members, and is a model of desirable behavior. In such a way children in sixth grade learn to be good to others, to reform the wayward by kindness and by being a good example. They learn that the good official helps the people and protects them from invasion, famine, and flood.[56] In fourth grade they

52. *Li-shih K'e-pen* [History Primer], book 4, lesson 16.

53. Jeremy R. Azrael, "Soviet Union," in *Education and Political Development*, James S. Coleman, ed. (Princeton, N.J.: Princeton University Press, 1965), pp. 238–240, 243.

54. The Kuomintang, it should be remembered, is modeled on Leninist concepts of party organization. That other Communist concepts should also be held should therefore not be too surprising.

55. *KYKP*, book 4 (new edition), lesson 25.

56. *KYKP*, upper grades, book 3, lessons 12–13.

learn about Koxinga, his flight to Taiwan, and his bravery; they learn that "We must each one of us have Koxinga's spirit so as to be able to restore China."[57] But above all they learn that Sun Yat-sen and Chiang Kai-shek are the best models for emulation. From them also is acquired an identification of desirable behavior with the good of the state. In an exercise section of the second-grade primer, for instance, are two true-false questions (of six): "Sun Yat-sen was brave from the time he was little" and "Sun Yat-sen established the Republic of China."[58] In Chiang's writings, speaking on filial piety, he says about his mother: "She impressed upon my mind that to be merely a dutiful son does not fulfill all the exacting conditions of the principle of filial piety; the principle demands also an unflinching devotion to the cause of the nation."[59] In the second term of second grade the primer starts with a story of Chiang and how as a young boy he was very industrious and studious and helped his mother around the house. "President Chiang," it says, "developed the habit of industry from childhood and therefore did not shirk hard and bitter work when he grew older—doing the work of saving the country and the people."[60] When I asked a second-grade boy at the city public school what the meaning of this story was, he promptly replied that it was to work hard like Chiang did as a small boy. He went on to say that Chiang has a medal (a picture with the story shows Chiang with a medal) because he is a great man.

The impact of Chiang Kai-shek and Sun Yat-sen as high-status models is constantly reinforced. At the front of many classrooms, for instance, is the sign, "I Respect the President; I Respect Mr. Sun Yat-sen." In all newspapers, whenever the names of these two men appear, a blank space is left directly before the name. In traditional times this was only done for one's parents or for other respected persons.[61]

A third-grade mainland girl at the country public school, writing

57. *KYKP*, book 8, lesson 18.

58. *KYKP*, book 3, exercises following lesson 11.

59. Chiang Kai-shek, "Some Reflections on My Fiftieth Birthday," quoted in Pichon P. Y. Loh, "The Politics of Chiang Kai-shek: A Reappraisal," *The Journal of Asian Studies*, vol. 25, no. 3 (May 1966).

60. *KYKP*, book 4, lesson 1.

61. One does not find Chiang portrayed as kind and humble, descriptions which, according to Richard H. Solomon, are found about Mao Tse-tung in Communist literature. Sacrifice, industry, bravery, and loyalty are the themes usually stressed with regard to Chiang.

about the meeting scene (Appendix 3), said the people were going to reattack the Mainland and strike the Communists. When asked what feelings the people would have afterward she replied, "They will be grateful to the President." On a bulletin board at the front of a first-grade class at the city public school were posted some pictures done by the children themselves showing children bowing to a portrait of Sun Yat-sen. When I asked in a third grade at the same school who the best person in the world was, they predominantly answered, "Sun Yat-sen."

In answer to the question of who their greatest hero was, 66.8 percent of 695 children responded by naming some authority figure, 4.0 percent gave some nonauthority figure, and 29.2 percent did not know.[62] There was no significant difference in these responses by either sex or age criteria, or between Mainlanders and Taiwanese. Nor was there any significant difference between Mainlanders and Taiwanese or boys and girls when the authority responses (464 in all) were analyzed for distribution between family and government. Family figures were named in 23.9 percent of the responses, 73.9 percent named some person or occupation associated with government, and 2.2 percent gave some other category (such as athlete). There was some slight significance (.05 level) between grades with a decline in family responses from 37.3 percent in first grade to 17.3 percent by sixth grade, and an increase in government responses from 61.0 percent in first grade to 76.6 percent by sixth grade. However, of the original 695 children who responded to this question, only one half of them (49.3 percent) named some government figure, past or present, as a hero. Within this one half who named government figures, 162 children, or 23.3 percent of the original 695, answered either Chiang Kai-shek or Sun Yat-sen. The number who name these two men is significantly higher in first and second grade and declines, more or less regularly, with age.

The same group of children was asked if they knew who the head of the city government of Taipei was. Some government figure or occupation was named by 54.3 percent of the children, 42.5 percent of the children responded that they did not know, and 3.3 percent named some other person or occupation. Not surprisingly there was a significantly higher percentage of children who did not know from the country public

---

62. An authority figure, besides including specific figures such as teachers, principals, parents, government leaders, historical heroes, policemen, also included the military. Thus, if a child responded "our Air Force," this was included.

school than from the Taipei city schools. There was a slightly significant difference between boys and girls, the girls responding 47.7 percent Don't Know, 48.3 percent Government, and 3.9 percent Other, while the boys answered 37.8 percent Don't Know, 59.4 percent Government, and 2.8 percent Other. Mainlanders and Taiwanese showed no significant difference in response patterns. Among grades there was a significant increase in government responses with age, from 42 percent in first grade to 62.2 percent in sixth grade.

More interesting than these gross results is an analysis of the 377 children (54.3 percent of the total) who named a government figure or occupation. Overall, the city children again were able to pinpoint far more accurately the actual incumbent or occupation of mayor. It was interesting to note, however, that when the children did not name the mayor they generally named the President, revealing either a lack of knowledge of other government organs or an assumption that it is the President alone who is of real importance. Between schools the responses were those shown in Table 2–5.

Table 2–5
Responses Naming Some Government Figure for the Head of the Taipei City Government: Percent

Category/Schools	City Public	City Private	Country Public
Mayor	72.6	75.6	20.0
Chiang Kai-shek	24.2	19.5	56.7
Other	3.1	4.9	23.3
No. Responding	194	123	60

Significant at the .01 level.

There was no significant difference between boys and girls and only a slightly significant difference between Mainlanders and Taiwanese, Mainlanders being more able to identify the mayor than the Taiwanese, naming Mayor 68.6 percent, Chiang Kai-shek 23.1 percent, and Other 8.3 percent, while Taiwanese responses were 52.4 percent Mayor, 40.5 percent Chiang Kai-shek, and 7.1 percent Other. With age children become progressively more able to name the mayor. For methodological reasons the second-grade responses were anomalous (see Appendix 3), but the general pattern is quite clear, as shown in Table 2–6.

Unfortunately, the political climate in Taiwan is such that I felt a reluctance to ask any questions which directly related to the President.

Table 2–6
Responses Naming Some Government Figure for the Head of the Taipei City
Government: Percent

Category/Grade	1	2	3	4	5	6
Mayor	40.5	69.0	35.0	57.1	59.4	81.0
Chiang Kai-shek	40.5	27.6	60.0	28.6	31.2	15.2
Other	19.0	3.4	5.0	14.3	9.4	3.8
No. Responding*	42	58	60	49	32	79
Percent of Total Responses Naming Some Government Figure	42	61	48	39	60	62

Significant at the .01 level.
*Some children failed to answer what grade they
were in and were thus excluded from this analysis.

There is reason to believe, however, that first- and second-grade children
are already very familiar with the President and Sun Yat-sen. Certainly,
as has been shown, there is a conscious effort from kindergarten on to
familiarize children with these two leaders, an effort which is apparently
successful, since children, especially in the early years, have a tendency
to name Chiang and Sun as heroes. The same level of awareness is not at
all in evidence with regard to the mayor. Not only is the overall percentage of responses naming some government figure or occupation as the
head of the city government lower in the early grades, but there is also
a tendency at that age, when mentioning the government, to name the
President as the responsible political figure. This is quite in accordance
with Greenstein's findings for American children in New Haven who
often incorrectly attributed to one aspect of the political environment
features of another aspect. Thus Greenstein found that the children he
studied sometimes saw the President or governor in terms of the mayor.
By fourth grade (age nine), however, he found that New Haven children
were almost universally aware of the President and mayor, both being
known by name by more than 90 percent of the children at that grade
level.[63] New Haven's mayor, Greenstein felt, was probably atypical,
being extremely dynamic and popular. However, Taipei's mayor was
also extensively in the news. One must ask, therefore, what other factors
could account for the fact that by fourth grade Chinese children are still

63. Fred I. Greenstein, "More on Children's Images of the President," *Public
Opinion Quarterly,* vol. 25 (Winter 1961), p. 649.

not responding with any great percentage of accuracy (only 28 of 127 fourth-grade children who responded, or 22 percent, answered Mayor to the question of who is the head of the city government). By fifth and sixth grades the responses begin to be more accurate, yet by sixth grade only 50 percent, or 64 of 127 responses, correctly named the mayor. It is impossible to state, as Greenstein does about American children, that the modal sixth-grade child is familiar with the state level of government and clearly aware of federal and local government.[64] This is the more surprising when one realizes that by sixth grade Chinese children have received fairly extensive political training in class and in their citizenship primers (versus American children, who often get no formal civics training in the elementary school years) and have certainly been familiarized with the role of the mayor. The difference may be partly explained by the greater degree of political training in the home in America, a training which both reinforces factual knowledge and makes politics important.

In the minds of children in Taiwan politics is uniquely associated with the President and with Sun Yat-sen. The large number of Don't Know's on the city government question at all age levels may reflect both a knowledge by many children that running city government is not the President's job as well as ignorance as to just whose function it is. It may also indicate the low level of salience (but not necessarily a lack of interest) which the political process has for these children. In Taiwan, as in many other developing nations, the heart of local politics is more often intraparty rather than interparty. As such, the crucial aspects of local politics are frequently masked and not apparent. The excitement and importance of interparty conflict which American children sense is not part of the environment of Chinese children.

A lack of salience for local politics in the lives of children, and an only

64. Greenstein, *Children and Politics*, p. 63. It will be noted, however, that the political knowledge of sixth graders in Taiwan shows a truly remarkable increase over fifth grade. David Easton and Jack Dennis, "The Child's Image of Government," *Annals of the American Academy of Political and Social Science*, vol. 361 (Sept. 1965), p. 44, note that in the United States only 27.29 percent of second graders express uncertainty as to what government is, declining to 12.41 percent in sixth grade and 9.79 percent by eighth grade. However, although American children are more knowledgeable concerning politics than Chinese children in Taiwan, it must be remembered that politics is still relatively unimportant in the lives of American children.

partially sensed awareness of what is crucial in politics, may also explain why differences between boys and girls in Taiwan are not marked. Boys did show a slightly higher likelihood than girls to name a government figure when asked who runs the city, but there were no other real differences between the sexes, and, in fact, on almost all the questions I asked, the response patterns of boys and girls tended to be virtually the same. Certainly from these data one could not say, as Herbert H. Hyman does about American boys, that Chinese boys show an early direction toward politics and by sixth grade have a better knowledge than girls of political phenomena.[65] In the general learning process girls may be associated more with the immediate home environment than boys, but such differences do not seem to translate into any appreciably greater political awareness for boys. Differences in nonpolitical orientations, which Greenstein feels may be reflected in different political responses, may perhaps not be as great between boys and girls in Taiwan as between boys and girls in the United States.[66]

The Taiwanese are largely excluded from participation in the national government in Taiwan. This inability to participate may explain the differences between the Taiwanese and mainland children, with the Taiwanese somewhat less able than the Mainlanders to identify the mayor as the head of the city government. On the other hand, Taiwanese children were more likely than Mainlanders to see the mayor's role in terms of the President. The surprising aspect of this is that the mayor of Taipei is, in fact, Taiwanese. Moreover, much of local political power is in the hands of Taiwanese. If nothing else, these facts make more poignant the assumption that the political process for children in Taiwan, and Taiwanese children in particular, has no real salience in their daily lives.

These conceptions of political behavior are borne out on a question that was designed to test perceptions of what is, and what is not, a proper government function. The children were asked who in Taipei City ought to decide whether a new park should be built (a piece of legislation which I thought might have some personal appeal to children). I was interested mainly to see whether children could identify this as a government function. Of 695 respondents, 57.6 percent were able to identify some governmental body or figure as responsible, 7.9 percent pointed

65. Hyman, *Political Socialization*, pp. 30–35.
66. Greenstein, *Children and Politics*, pp. 123–125.

to some nongovernmental agency, and 34.6 percent didn't know. Not surprisingly there was a significantly higher percentage of Don't Know's from the country public school. There was no significant difference between boys and girls. Mainlanders were more able to name the government than Taiwanese, as Table 2–7 shows. Between grades the results were also significant, showing an increase in government responses with age and a decline of Don't Know's. In Table 2–8 we note again the sudden increase in political learning that seems to take place in sixth grade.

Table 2–7
Who in Taipei City Ought to Decide whether a New Park Should Be Built: Percent

	Mainlanders	Taiwanese
Government	61.9	46.1
Nongovernment	6.8	11.1
Don't Know	31.2	42.8
No. Responding	221	271

Significant at the .01 level.

Table 2–8
Who in Taipei City Ought to Decide whether a New Park Should Be Built: Percent

Category/Grade	1	2	3	4	5	6
Government	33	51.5	50.4	55.9	54.2	74.0
Nongovernment	14	8.4	8.8	5.5	12.3	7.1
Don't Know	53	39.9	40.8	38.6	33.7	18.9
No. Responding	100	95	125	127	53	127

Significant at the .01 level.

Political Style: Leader and Follower

The leader represents the group and sets the style for group action. Ideally, followers should be passive and accept the goals of the group as they are defined by the leader. They must not break the group's unity. A first-grade mainland girl at the city private school, writing of the policeman and vendor scene (Appendix 3), noted that "the unclean fruit being sold by the man selling fruit gave the people who ate it a tummyache. Everybody told the government and the government sent a policeman to investigate." The people themselves do not interfere or accuse the vendor; they tell the leader or the government. A sixth-grade mainland boy at the same school wrote about the meeting scene. The man on the platform is the village leader, and the people in front are listening to him talk about health measures that should be taken in the summer. "They think that what the village leader says is correct. They remember that before they were wrong and afterward they will certainly pay attention to health. This is good because this type of thing can make the whole village clean and really reduce sickness."

The people receive instructions. They may sometimes criticize, but the most sanctioned expressions and actions are loyalty to the leader and the group. An interview with a thirteen-year-old sixth-grade mainland boy at the city public school went like this (discussing the meeting scene, Appendix 3):

Question: "What's going on here?"

Response: "A lecture has started. There's a speech."

Question: "Who's giving the speech?"

Response: "The Father of our Country."

Question: "What kind of person is the Father of our Country?"

Response: "Very learned. A statesman. A person who has especially studied medicine."

Question: "What do you think the Father of our Country is speaking to them about?"

Response: "Scheme for the Establishment of the Nation. Outline of Principles for the Establishment of the Nation, or The Three Principles of the People." (three works by Sun Yat-sen)

Question: "Is everything the Father of our Country says correct?"

Response: "Not necessarily."

Question: "If there was a time when he was wrong, what would happen?"

Response: "The people or the representatives of the National Assembly would correct the place that was wrong."

Question: "Can we criticize the Father of our Country?"

Response: "No."

Question: "Why?"

Response: "Because he has made great sacrifices for the Chinese race."

Question: "In that case, can we criticize ordinary leaders?"

Response: "We can't do it just as we please. But if there's a time when they say something very wrong, then we can."

Question: "What responsibility does the leader have for his followers?"

Response: "He should do his utmost to protect them and make their lives peaceful. He should also accept ideas which are raised by the people."

Question: "How ought subordinates to be toward him?"

Response: "(Pause) They should carry out his orders and respect him."

Question: "Must we obey everything the leader says?"

Response: (smile) "If what he says is very wrong we can request representatives of the National Assembly to make him take back his order."

Question: "Can the leader do something that everyone doesn't want done?"

Response: "It has to be seen if there is or isn't any benefit to the country. If there is benefit, then it should be done."

Question: "Can a person disregard other people's opposition and do something?"

Response: "You have to see his whole stand. If his father was killed and others wouldn't let him get revenge, then it would be wrong."

Question: "Is a leader necessary in a group?"

Response: "Very much needed."

Question: "Why?"

Response: "If there's no chairman, then the group cannot agree."

Question: "What sort of person can be chairman?"

Response: "A person who can accept the ideas of the members, who perseveres, and who can accept being corrected."

Question: "Can we criticize the chairman?"

Response: "We can talk with him privately."

Question: "When is this?"

Response: "When he has done something wrong."

Question: "Should everybody obey what the chairman says?"

Response: "I think they should because the majority of people have already agreed."

Question: "Is there anyone who can disagree with the chairman's opinion?"

Response: "No."

Question: "But if there were some who disagreed, how would you feel about those people who didn't agree?"

Response: "I would devise a way to advise and correct them."

Question: "What would you do if the chairman did something bad?"

Response: "I would advise and direct him. I would not obey and would try to have him recalled."

It is interesting to note how this child sees the leader in group terms. He does not disagree with criticism, but his reluctance to do so openly is quite obvious, I think, and reflects a desire to be outwardly loyal to the leader. In like manner he does not want others to criticize and, far from allowing them this right, would try to correct them. This attitude exists despite the rather explicitly stated notion that the right to authority is conditional upon performance.

Great emphasis is placed on loyalty to the leader. Over a school on the outskirts of Taipei is a huge sign on a hillside which proclaims "Serve and Be Loyal to the Leader." But loyalty and service work both ways, for in the stories the children read Chiang and Sun are themselves the paragons and exemplars of loyalty to the nation. In third grade the children read two consecutive lessons; the first is about Sun Yat-sen's revolutionary spirit, how he was kidnapped and imprisoned in the Chinese legation in London but, persevering, "went through many dangers, yet he was not disappointed but finally overthrew the Ch'ing government and established the Chinese Republic." Then, in a lesson entitled "Patriotic President Chiang," the children learn how Chiang, "brave since he was a child and loving his country, entered the army school to prepare to protect his country in the future." Studying in Japan, Chiang, alone of his Chinese classmates, stands up to a Japanese professor after the latter has made disparaging remarks about China. "The Japanese professor had not thought that among the Chinese students there was this type of brave and patriotic young man."[67] The leader protects the group's interests; he is loyal and fights for them. He never forgets them and exposes himself to danger for their sake. In like manner they return this loyalty. In third grade the children also read how in the city of Kaifeng, on the Mainland, in the busiest part of town, it is discovered one morning that Mao Tse-tung's picture, hanging on the wall of a tall building, has been ripped down and Chiang's picture put in its place subscribed with the words "Long Live President Chiang." The people all crowded around to see, and the Communists dispersed them and had Chiang's picture obliterated. But the next day the same thing happened. Then the Communists feared guerrillas, but a search of the city revealed nothing.[68]

The children learn that affirmations of loyalty are both good and expected. In the newspapers one frequently reads statements which proclaim that the leader sets the group norms. In one editorial, for in-

67. *KYKP*, book 5, lessons 27–28.
68. *KYKP*, book 5, lesson 12.

stance, there is a sentence saying "The instructions of the Father of the Country and the President are especially relevant for establishing an index of human relations."[69] During the election period the *Chung-yang Jih-pao*, the government paper, ran an increased number of interviews in a section entitled "Daily Biographical Visits." The topic, boldly lettered, was "We Need the Leadership of the President." First is a 'middle school boy who talks about the great achievements of President Chiang, building the nation and opposing the Communists, surmounting crises and overcoming difficulties, leading us to victory. He ends with the words "All youth are of one heart! All youth and all the military are loyally and sincerely united around the President. We will always follow the President in the great work of restoring and rebuilding the nation." A Taiwanese middle school girl follows with thanks to the President for giving her a chance to go to school and for improving the whole life of the Taiwanese people. She concludes "So I loudly proclaim 'We Need the Leadership of the President.' "[70] It should come as a surprise to no one that Chiang ran unopposed for office.[71]

David Easton and Jack Dennis gave a test to several thousand American children, grades two to eight, in which they endeavored to analyze the development of cognitive images of government with regard to symbolic associations.[72] Out of a set of ten pictures children were asked to pick two in response to a question of which two first came to mind when they thought of government. The pictures the children were given were of a policeman, George Washington, Uncle Sam, voting, the Supreme

69. Editorial, *Chung-yang Jih-pao* 中央日報 [Central Daily News], no. 13718 (May, 1, 1966), p. 2.

70. *Chung-yang Jih-pao* 中央日報 [Central Daily News], no. 13664 (March 8, 1966), p. 4. I have refrained here from making comments on the emotional content of such statements. What is important is to note the form of such statements and the fact that they were made. See Chapter 3, "Hostility."

71. Many people may assume that an unopposed election is rigged for reasons of personal ambition for power. One frequently hears this with regard to Chiang since he has now been reelected twice beyond original constitutional limits. I do not intend to minimize Chiang's ambition (the record here is rather clear, I think) or to minimize rigging, except to state that in this case, as usual, it is done quasi-legally. I would like to point out, however, that our moral judgments of this should include cognizance that in a Chinese group context Chiang may feel a powerful obligation to the group to be their leader, and the group may feel similarly in return.

72. Easton and Dennis, "The Child's Image of Government."

Court, the Capitol, Congress, the American flag, the Statue of Liberty, President John F. Kennedy, and a final space for "I Don't Know." Assuming that any pictures which received 20 percent or more responses were significant, they found that only four pictures achieved this status, those of George Washington, President Kennedy, Congress, and voting. The results were quite interesting for they showed that while in the early years Washington and President Kennedy were very important, by eighth grade these figures had been supplanted in importance by Congress and voting. The results are indicated in Table 2–9.[73]

Table 2–9
Development of a Cognitive Image of Government—Symbolic Association: Percent

Grade	George Washington	President Kennedy	Congress	Voting
2	39.47	46.26	5.93	4.32
3	26.77	46.81	12.94	8.36
4	14.19	37.25	28.97	10.83
5	6.93	38.51	49.08	19.23
6	4.94	30.52	49.66	27.99
7	3.44	27.89	44.22	39.44
8	1.72	22.91	49.14	46.77

I attempted to replicate this test with a much smaller number of Chinese children in grades one to six. There was, naturally, some difference in the pictures used, but the type of symbols Easton and Dennis utilized were approximated as closely as possible. The pictures used were of a policeman, Sun Yat-sen, Double Ten (the national holiday), voting, a law court, the presidential palace, the legislative Yuan, the Chinese Nationalist flag, Three Principles of the People (the official political ideology in Taiwan), President Chiang, and a final space for "I Don't Know." Using the same criterian of assuming that 20 percent or more responses were significant, I discovered that for Chinese children the important pictures were Sun Yat-sen, the flag, the Three Principles of the People, and President Chiang. The results for all pictures are shown in Table 2–10.

When I discussed this test with the assistant principal for education at the city public school, he remarked that the children all "ought to

73. *Ibid.*, p. 45, extracted from Table 2.

Table 2–10
Development of a Cognitive Image of Goverment—Symbolic Associations:
Percent

Category/Grade	1	2	3	4	5	6
Policeman	3.33	2.22	5.55	8.88	5.55	1.11
Sun Yat-sen	78.81	69.93	45.51	46.62	43.29	49.95
Double Ten	4.44	8.88	1.11	2.22	3.33	1.11
Voting	3.33	7.77	5.55	11.10	22.20	12.21
Law Courts	2.22	3.33	12.21	12.21	8.88	7.77
Presidential Palace	9.99	4.44	18.87	12.21	13.32	16.65
Legislative Yuan	5.55	4.44	16.65	6.66	4.44	13.32
Flag	37.74	27.75	27.75	27.75	23.31	13.32
Three Principles of the People	11.10	12.21	26.64	18.87	36.63	28.86
President Chiang	36.63	56.61	34.41	47.73	36.63	55.50
Don't Know	6.66	2.22	5.55	5.55	2.22	0
No. Responding	90	90	90	90	90	90

Because of the double response, percentages will equal 200.

select Sun Yat-sen and President Chiang." It turns out, in fact, that these
two responses were the most popular at all age levels. Voting and Congress (for the Chinese children the Legislative Yuan), the two responses
which for American children show a marked increase with age, remain
quite low for children in Taiwan. Instead it is a political ideology, the
Three Principles of the People, that shows a comparable increase.[74]

It is interesting to plot these different results on figures side by side
(see Figure 2–1). For purposes of strict comparison only the five years
from second to sixth grade, the years which both tests mutually covered,
are shown. The Chinese "plot" is not a smooth line and undoubtedly
reflects the smaller sample size. The overall configuration, however, is
illuminating.

74. It is of interest to note that of 270 boy responses 55.87 percent selected
Sun Yat-sen, 22.94 percent selected Flag, 21.83 percent picked the Three Principles, and 49.95 percent selected President Chiang. For 270 girls the responses
were 54.76 percent Sun, 29.60 percent Flag, 22.94 the Three Principles, and 39.22
percent Chiang Kai-shek. Only in the category of the President are the girls obviously lower. This says nothing about political knowledge but does seem to indicate that girls relate less to a male political figure. For 156 Mainlanders the
responses were 55.77 percent Sun, 27.56 percent Flag, 21.15 percent Three Principles, and 46.15 percent Chiang, while for 200 Taiwanese the responses were
52.0 percent Sun, 20.5 percent Flag, 27.5 percent Three Principles, and 38.0
percent Chiang.

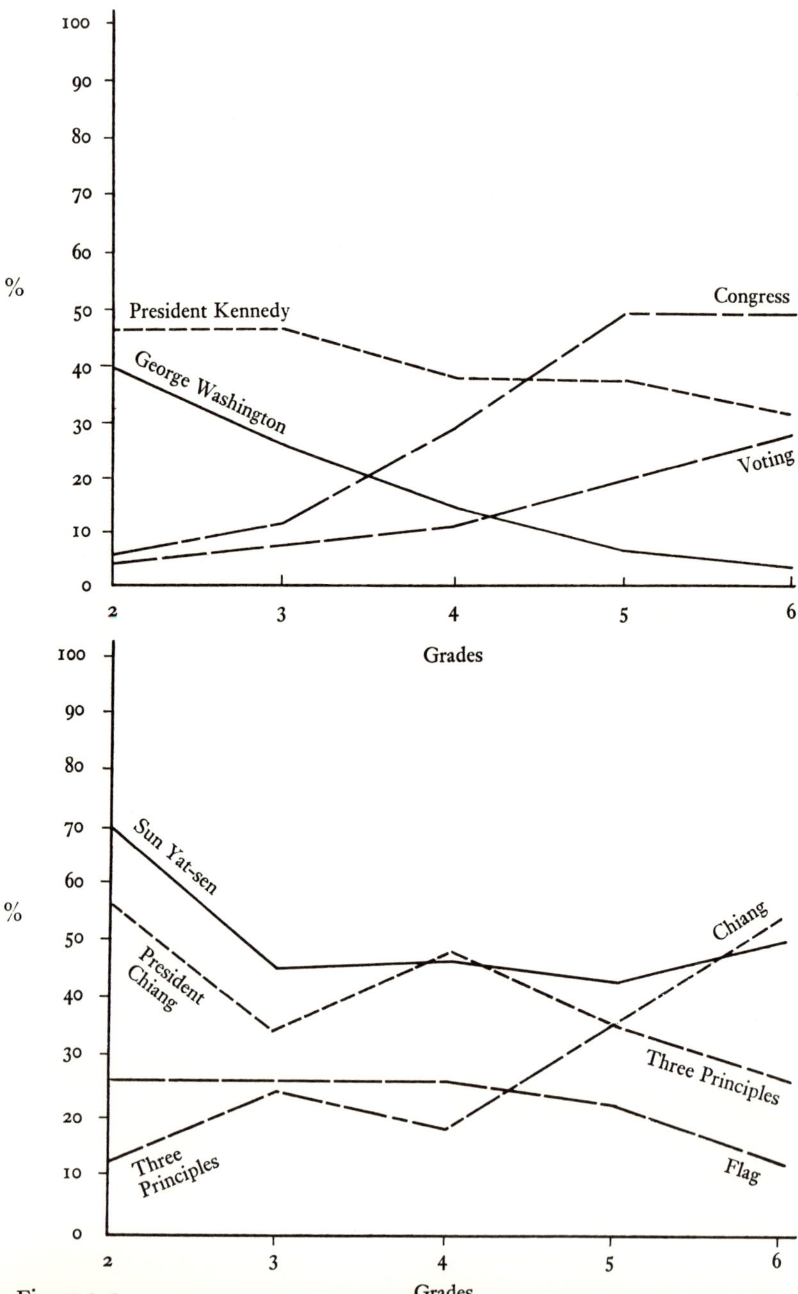

Figure 2–1

Cognitive Images of Government: Most Important Symbolic Associations for Chinese and American Children

Using the same group of pictures, I asked the Chinese children a second question: Who makes the laws?[75] The children were again asked to select those two pictures which in their opinion best answered the question. The results of this test, by grades, are shown in Table 2–11.[76]

Table 2–11
Development of an Awareness of Who Makes the Laws: Percent

Category/Grade	1	2	3	4	5	6
Policeman	14.43	2.22	11.10	6.66	3.33	1.11
Sun Yat-sen	27.75	18.87	34.41	32.19	46.62	46.62
Double Ten	0	1.11	2.22	2.22	0	0
Voting	9.99	26.64	7.77	6.66	5.55	1.11
Law Courts	25.53	28.86	46.62	39.96	34.41	37.74
Presidential Palace	9.99	0	3.33	1.11	0	0
Legislative Yuan	22.20	37.74	45.51	53.28	48.84	66.60
Flag	9.99	16.65	5.55	6.66	5.55	0
Three Principles of the People	2.22	13.32	5.55	25.53	23.31	36.63
President Chiang	45.51	26.64	33.30	23.31	31.08	8.88
Don't Know	32.19	21.09	4.44	2.22	1.11	1.11
No. Responding	90	90	90	90	90	90

Because of the double response, percentages will equal 200.

Again, if a criteria of 20 percent or more is used as an indication of significance, it will be noted that five pictures, Sun Yat-sen, Law Courts, the Legislative Yuan, the Three Principles of the People, and President Chiang, are predominantly chosen (the Don't Know category was also important in the first and second grades but drops off to virtually nothing). If these results are plotted by grades from one to six, we get the pattern indicated by Figure 2–2.

Hess and Easton gave their sample children four choices, the President, Congress, the Supreme Court, and I Don't Know, and tested them for

75. Because there is no tense in Chinese this question could be read: Who made the laws?

76. On this question there were no startling differences between boys and girls or Mainlanders and Taiwanese. Girls were, however, slightly more inclined, 32.94 percent versus 25.16 percent, to choose the President and less inclined, 42.55 percent versus 48.84 percent, to name the Legislative Yuan. Country children answered Legislative Yuan and Sun Yat-sen less frequently than city children but spread the difference over the other answers so that there was no great difference elsewhere.

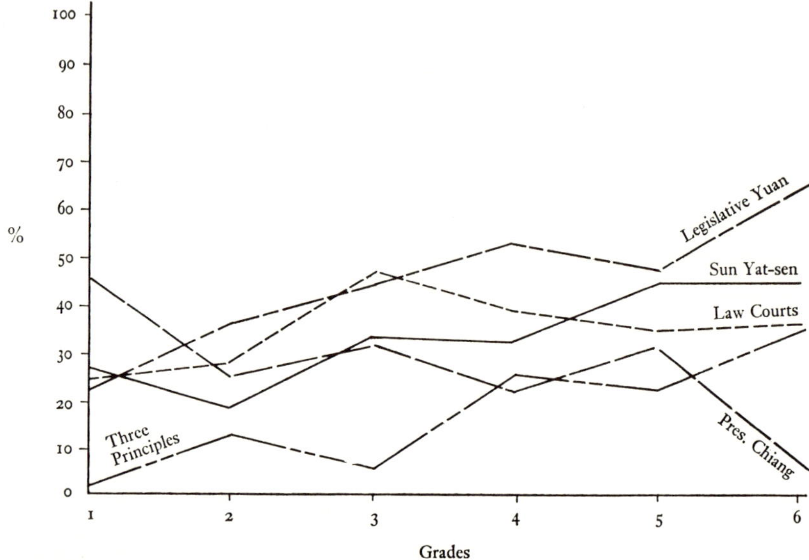

Figure 2–2

Most Important Associations Concerning Development of an Awareness of
Who Makes the Laws

the development of an awareness of the chief lawmaker. They found that
for American children the percent who answered Congress rose from
4.79 percent in second grade to 85.33 percent in eighth grade; for President a reverse trend was noted of 75.55 percent in second grade, decreasing to 5.44 percent in eighth grade; the Supreme Court showed a
slight decline over the same years from 11.49 percent to 7.87 percent,
and I Don't Know's decreased from 8.17 percent to 1.36 percent.[77] Viewing Hess and Easton's total data for both questions, American children
show the gradual development of symbolic associations of government
relating to Congress and voting and an increasing awareness by age
of Congress as the chief lawmaker. They conclude that while younger
American children may think of government in terms of the President,
older children and adults conceive of it in terms of legislative functions.

Chinese children, like their American counterparts, show an increasing
awareness of the legislative body as the chief lawmaker and a recognition
that it is not the President who performs this function. But there is also

77. Hess and Easton, "The Child's Changing Image of the President," Table
3, p. 641.

an increasing tendency for Chinese children to name Sun Yat-sen as the person who made (makes) the laws; by sixth grade Sun, in fact, is second only to the Legislative Yuan as a choice for lawmaker.

Like Americans, Chinese children are inducted into the political system through an early knowledge of, and identification with, supreme political leaders. Such leaders are models in the child's socialization in general and in political socialization in particular. In America, however, children reveal a growing personal identification with the political process. The growth of associations surrounding Congress and voting are indicative of this, for voting is an important means of personal identification with the political process and Congress is an extension of this identification through a representative.

Chinese children do not develop this same sense of identification, for, individually, it is only through their group membership and in coordination with others that Chinese children enter the political process. When they identify with the political process, they identify predominantly in terms of their group leader, who is the symbol and representative of the group and the initiator and arbiter of group politics. These feelings are formed and reinforced by training in the home and school.[78]

As a feeling of national identity develops, there is a concomitant development of a relationship to the national leader. The symbolic associations of government which are attached to political leaders develop as early in Taiwan as in America, but they are also felt with greater intensity. They weaken only slightly with age. As children learn of the Three Principles of the People, an ideology intimately linked with its author, Sun Yat-sen, and his disciple, Chiang Kai-shek, it also becomes an important symbolic association. It is true that in the test responses this association may be due largely to the fact that the Three Principles of the People can be regarded as the national basic law. Still significant, however, is the fact that, in the minds of the children, the Three Principles are closely linked to Sun and Chiang.

Children are increasingly aware that the Legislative Yuan is the chief lawmaker (they are specifically taught this in school),[79] yet they also

78. The fact that most Chinese have been trained in habits of uncritical obedience, and participate in the political process only as directed, should not obscure the fact that there are individuals, especially among the better educated, who are very politically conscious and sometimes willing, indeed, to engage in politics in a way not sanctioned by the prevailing political system.

79. Chinese adults are not so aware. They hesitate when one asks this question

view lawmaking in terms of Sun Yat-sen and the Three Principles, revealing a deeply ingrained habit of seeing politics in terms of a leader and his principles. They give the functional answer of the Legislative Yuan but intuitively link this response with the leader, in terms of whom they feel legislation should, and does, take place.

---

and say that it is confusing, that perhaps the really crucial decisions are made in military councils or by the President. The children do not reveal this sophistication but view lawmaking in terms of the formal legal patterns they are taught in school. There the distinction is clear between the President as executive administrator and the Legislative Yuan as lawmaker. Significantly, neither adults nor children mention voting, the one response which would indicate a sense of personal involvement with the lawmaking process.

Chapter 3
Hostility

Since one of the most important aspects of political interaction is the mediation of conflict, and since conflict is usually invested with hostility, some analysis of this emotion—the means by which it is generated and the ways in which it is expressed—is an essential part of any political culture study.

I am not a psychologist, and thus it will not be my attempt to analyze the myriad ways in which hostility among individual children manifests itself. Rather, I will focus upon certain broad generalizations about hostility in the social system of Taiwan as a whole, and in the elementary school system in particular. Within this framework I shall discuss how the behavioral characteristics of groups and group leaders, set forth in the preceding two chapters, are modified or reinforced under the impact of conflict and hostility.

A realization of the importance of the shaming techniques of punishment so widely used on Chinese children (see Chapter 1, "Group Orientation") is critical to an understanding of the generation of hostility. To be shamed is to be exposed and looked at; it is expressed by a desire to bury the face. But this "turning away," Erikson feels, is "essentially rage turned against the self. He who is ashamed would like to force the world not to look at him, not to notice his exposure. He would like to destroy the eyes of the world, instead he must wish for his own invisibility."[1]

In addition to shame there is also doubt, which is related to shame. Doubt is linked with toilet training, something which begins relatively early for Chinese children and is associated with a consciousness of "having a front and back—and especially a 'behind.' "[2] Doubts and fears arise about this area and about the power of others to attack one's

1. Erik H. Erikson, *Childhood and Society* (New York: W. W. Norton & Company, Inc., 1950), p. 223. This feeling exists despite the fact that the destructiveness of shaming is balanced in many cultures by devices for saving face.

2. *Ibid.*, p. 224.

autonomy in this area and to designate the products of bowel movements as evil. "This basic sense of doubt in whatever one has left behind forms a substratum for later and more verbal forms of compulsive doubting; this finds its adult expression in paranoiac fears concerning hidden persecutors and secret persecutions threatening from behind and from within the behind."[3]

There is a strong motivation for Chinese children to suppress doubt and minimize shame by conforming to group values. Such conformity, however, while it may tend to mitigate the most extreme tension associated with doubt and shame, serves only as a palliative and not as a cure. Indeed, recent work in learning theory suggests that while non-reward emphasizes the removal of disapproved behavior, active punishment only suppresses the behavior rather than eliminating it.[4] Punishment by use of shaming is an active part of family and school life for the Chinese child. Corporal punishment is used as well, reasonably frequently in the home, and sometimes even in the schools. The conformity of behavior which is readily observable among Chinese children in certain well-defined group situations—family, school, etc.—may reflect both the extent of the punishment and the desire to mitigate the shame and doubt arising from that punishment. Socially undesirable side effects may result from the suppression of certain behavior, however, when there is no legitimate intrasocietal way for it to be expressed. Inner rage or hostility, associated with shaming, would be types of such suppressed behavior. Some authorities, notably Richard H. Solomon, have suggested that "traditional Chinese attitudes toward authority were based upon *great anxiety about the hostile emotional energy that would be released [or generated] should the 'proper' set of social authority relationships [roles] break down.*"[5]

Conformity to group norms is one by-product of Chinese child-rearing practices. A contributing factor to this conformity may be the nature of leader-led relations themselves (the " 'proper' set of social authority relationships"). Children, as has been pointed out, see the leader in group terms. That they may often see the leader in positive

<hr>

3. *Ibid.*

4. Albert Bandura and Richard H. Walters, *Social Learning and Personality Development* (New York: Holt, Rinehart & Winston, Inc., 1963), p. 14.

5. Richard H. Solomon, *The Chinese Political Culture and Problems of Modernization*, Center for International Studies, Massachusetts Institute of Technology, Cambridge, Mass. (C/64–38), p. 13 (italics in original).

group terms, as helpful and loving, and as one who leads the people to a better group spirit, should not obscure the fact that the leader's capacity to penetrate directly into the group and act on any individual, sometimes in a predatory or punitive way, is not checked by intervening or countervailing authority and may give rise to hostility feelings. (It will be remembered that class leaders, in maintaining order, could cuff heads and throw chalk at schoolmates with impunity.) This ability to penetrate, in fact, is one of the characteristics of authoritarian leadership. Some psychologists have posited that there are distinct differences between democratic and authoritarian leaders in the way they solve group psychological needs. Cecil A. Gibb, quoting R. B. Cattell from a personal communication, has written:

we may notice two important differences in the psychological accounts: (1) the autocratic leader creates needs, e.g., by bringing to the group fear, insecurity, and frustration by which they were not originally stimulated, and (2) he exploits regressive, primitive, unconscious needs instead of helping the group to outgrow them, e.g., father dependence, vicarious satisfaction through identification, superego projection in place of individual conscience.[6]

I would suggest that fear, insecurity, and frustration are created at the level of national group life in Taiwan and are also prevalent in the school and home. These emotions derive from the capacity of the leader of whatever group to initiate shaming against a member, and they are a manifestation of the suppressed hostility which is generated by this type of punishment.

The sense of conformity which children express manifests itself in a desire to make adaptions of behavior which will fit with the authority figure's conception of what is right. I asked three groups of third-grade children at the city public school what they would do if they saw one child badly hitting another on the playground but where neither child was a friend. All unanimously said they would tell him to stop. Intervention with peers is perfectly acceptable, but when I changed the subject and asked whether a policeman should hit me if I did wrong, one child said he ought, others said he should not, but many said I should just change my ways.

Children grant to authority figures the right to punish. They frequent-

<hr>

6. Cecil A. Gibb, "Leadership," in *Handbook of Social Psychology*, Gardner Lindzey, ed. (Cambridge, Mass.: Addison-Wesley Publishing Co., Inc., 1954), p. 909.

ly see this as done for their own good, as when I asked why parents punish children. Of the 695 children who responded, 79.9 percent gave answers that indicated they felt punishment was done for their own benefit such as "to help me grow up to be a nice person"; 18.9 percent answered Don't Know; 1.3 percent said Other. The children also concede that under certain circumstances the authority figure has the right to be punitive. One question asked why they supposed a person who was driving a car had gone through a red light and how they thought a policeman ought to treat this situation. Children show a significant increase by age in supposing that the policeman will make some punitive response to this situation (take the man to prison, scold him, etc.). See Table 3–1.

Table 3–1
Response of Police to a Lawbreaking Situation: Percent

Category/Grade	1	2	3	4	5	6
Don't Know	55	46.3	59.2	47.2	39.6	31.5
Punitive	38	46.3	30.4	46.4	52.8	59.8
Nonpunitive	7	7.4	10.4	6.3	7.5	8.7
No. Responding	100	95	125	127	53	127

Significant at the .01 level.

The realization that an authority figure may make a punitive response to a situation socially defined as wrong is accompanied in many children with fear of the authority figure. A sixth-grade Taiwanese boy at the country school writing of the schoolroom scene (Appendix 3) describes how a child is not able to answer a question posed by the teacher because he wasn't listening and how the other students think this student ought to be punished. The child will change and thank the teacher, the boy writes, and "afterward they will be even more diligent because they will fear punishment by the teacher." A fifth-grade mainland girl at the same school writing of the meeting scene tells a story of how the people were watching a performance and the police came. The people didn't know who the police were looking for, but they (the child writes "we") were frightened and ran away.

In an interview with a first-grade Taiwanese boy at the city public school the discussion was centered around the policeman/vendor scene. One portion of the conversation was as follows:

Question: "Do you think the policeman is always right?"

Response: "Yes."
Question: "Is there any time when he does something wrong?"
Response: "No."
Question: "Is there any time when your Daddy, Mommy, or teacher make mistakes?"
Response: "No."
Question: "What happens if a policeman makes a mistake?"
Response: "We ask someone higher up to arrest him and kill him."
Question: "Can we criticize a policeman?"
Response: (frightened) "No. We must say he is good. If we say he's bad, we'll be arrested."
Later the talk shifted to the public meeting scene:
Question: "Who is the person up here?"
Response: "He's a great person."
Question: "Why can he be a great person?"
Response: "He is a person who shoots a gun; he's a person who fights together with the Father of our Country."
(It appeared from later evidence that the child was referring to Chiang Kai-shek.)
Question: "When he speaks, will everyone down below obey him?"
Response: "Yes, they'll all obey him. Not to obey wouldn't be right."
Question: "What happens if they don't obey?"
Response: (pause) "They'll be arrested by the great man."

The authority figure is granted the right to punish group members, but the children do not concede to members the right to question or object to such treatment. The projective tests show little inclination on the part of children to write of situations where the nonauthority figure even desires or thinks about questioning or rebelling against the authority figure, a finding anticipated in the results of Chapter 2 where it was pointed out how learning to accept uncritically the injunctions of authority figures is an important aspect of childhood training. In the city private school such attitudes were expressed in only five out of 171 responses, all on the policeman/vendor scene. In the country public school only one such response is recorded from 186 responses, this one being in the public meeting scene. There the child wrote of the people questioning why they should accept birth control measures advocated by the speaker when they do not want them. Interestingly, no questioning of authority occurs in the school or family scenes, areas with which children have the most familiarity. The children in these pictures are seen as obeying without question. Resentment, ill-feeling, or doubting do not seem to be elicited whether the overall situation is viewed as one of punishment or nonpunishment. In the responses of the city private school children to the schoolroom scene, for instance, there is a sudden and significant increase in fifth and sixth grade in viewing the scene as one of punishment but still no tendency to write of the nonauthority figure in any but passive terms.[7]

Shaming techniques of punishment and emphasis on ideals of group loyalty may provide for great intrasocietal stability. At the same time, however, the stability derived from such techniques must be balanced against equally inherent destructive characteristics. The majority of behavioral norms are couched in group terms or define relationships within a group. Disobedience, because it places one outside the group, is feared and is potentially explosive, for outside the group these norms no longer apply. Much energy is therefore expended, primarily through the use of shaming techniques, on preventing disobedience and bolstering group cohesiveness. When normal intergroup relationships break down, anarchy may result. People accept the norms of the group because they have been socialized to believe in the predominance and primacy of the group itself. Deviance from the norms is, virtually by definition, action against the group as a whole.

The individual does not clearly differentiate himself from the group of which he is a member (at any level of generalization), either with regard to his individual identity or his ideals. But in order for the individual to identify clearly with all groups of which he is a member (family, school, nation, etc.), there is both a rank order of groups and a clearly defined hierarchy of models so that the leader of the society as a whole is the supreme model by whom models in groups lower in the hierarchy and all members can measure their conformity. There is a strain toward a single ideal of behavior within the hierarchy of models. Within this system there are generally no institutionalized avenues for withdrawal for the individual which would diminish the controls of the group. There is, as Tsung-yi Lin has noted, a comparatively higher tolerance for deviant behavior within Chinese families, a factor which undoubtedly acts as a defense mechanism against undue group pressure and which allows individuals to become more than mere group robots.[8]

7. Possibly because of increasing examination pressures, among other things.
8. Tsung-yi Lin, "A Study in the Incidence of Mental Disorder in Chinese and

Nevertheless deviance in Chinese group life, when it is so defined, must remain within the system with a concomitant greater hostility, mistrust, and fear of disillusion.[9]

Group members do not differentiate between the leader and his policies. To attack or criticize the leader is therefore to attack the ideals of the system for which he stands and the ideals of the leader's friends and subordinates as well.[10] When the leader loses face, group members also lose face because their judgment in supporting him is called into question. The leader, in a sense, represents the face of the group; he is at the apex of a face pyramid because followers, by accepting a leader, involve their own face in his actions. Here again we note how absolutely essential it is to be aware of the reciprocity between the individual and the group with regard to the concept of face, for to attack the leader, to criticize him or to go against him, is, in fact, to attack the self and is thus to be avoided at all costs.

Criticism of the leader places one not simply in opposition to him but also in opposition to the group he leads. Since societal organization is unitary in nature, this has the effect of destroying the basis for one's normal social existence. In opposition, compromise and face-saving techniques will tend to be employed within the group rather than direct confrontation (a leader will retire or become sick, etc., but never be deposed). When open conflict with the leader does occur, no alternative exists but to organize a new and distinct group. Conflict will not be resolved until one of the two groups has been destroyed and orthodoxy restored.

Inhibitions against criticizing the leader undoubtedly strengthen the position of the leader and increase the unitary nature of social life. However, one should not mistake feelings of group solidarity for "authoritarian submission," despite the verbalized emphasis on such values as obedience, deference, etc.,[11] and the undisputed evidence in Chinese

---

Other Cultures," *Psychiatry: Journal for the Study of Interpersonal Processes*, vol. 16, no. 4 (Nov. 1953), p. 333.

9. Harry C. Bredemeier and Richard M. Stephenson, *The Analysis of Social Systems* (New York: Holt, Rinehart & Winston, Inc., 1962), p. 163, and Orville G. Brim, Jr., and Stanton Wheeler, *Socialization after Childhood: Two Essays* (New York: John Wiley & Sons, Inc., 1966), p. 45.

10. Solomon, *The Chinese Political Culture*, p. 19.

11. Godwin Chien Chu, *Culture, Personality and Persuasibility*, unpublished doctoral dissertation (Mass Communications Research), Stanford University,

group life of maintaining a definite (albeit sometimes idealized) distinction between superiors and inferiors. The Chinese are submissive to authority, but it would be missing the point to say that this is the sole basic cultural norm. Submission to, and defense of, group norms, I would suggest, is another equally basic value. Otherwise, how can one explain deviance and repeated rebellions? Submission to authority may partially account for a reluctance to rebel, but one can do so if the authority figure is seen as violating group norms.

In all political systems decision makers and their opponents tend to try to legitimize the goals they seek by using symbols (such as the flag, freedom, etc.).[12] But what if the major symbols are the leaders themselves? Then to disagree would be to repudiate the leader; it would be impossible to disagree since one could not invoke the symbol of the leader to obtain a goal which the leader himself personally opposed. To disagree openly one would need to discredit the whole system and invoke new symbols. One would have to rebel.

Gibb has posited an interactional theory of leadership in which leader and follower are "united by common goals and aspirations and by a will to lead, on one side, and by a will to follow on the other, i.e., by a common acceptance of each other."[13] He has stated that "The function of the leader is to embody and to give expression to the needs and wishes of the group and to contribute positively to the satisfaction of those needs. To the extent that he does this he may remain the leader; when he fails to perform this function he will be superseded; and he fails as soon as the followers perceive his needs and his goal to be divergent from their own."[14] But how does a leader become displaced in the Chinese milieu? Rebellion, as has been mentioned, is one method. Factional disputes carried out behind the scenes, or the organization of secret societies which undermine political stability and often support the politically disaffected, are other, and far more frequent, ways. In either case the

---

1963, postulated this (p. 10) but did not, in his tests, find any significant relationship between persuasibility and this supposed norm of authoritarian submission, although it was in the predicted direction for males (p. 130). Personally I am not surprised at this, for I would hypothesize that the link is more between norms of group solidarity and persuasibility.

12. Richard M. Merelman, "Learning and Legitimacy," *The American Political Science Review*, vol. 60 no. 3 (Sept. 1966), pp. 548–561.

13. Gibb, "Leadership," p. 915.

14. *Ibid.*

expressed purposes for deposing the leader, whatever the actual underlying power motives might be, while often based on arguments of incompetence also usually contain appeals to some objective set of standards that the leader has no virtue—that he has violated basic group values and has thereby lost his mandate.

The claim to moral leadership is an essential aspect of authority. In many leader-follower groups, but particularly among the Chinese, to question a leader openly in terms of his right to moral leadership causes the leader to lose face. Such questioning is an indication that the leader no longer represents the whole group but only a faction. But in Chinese terms a leader must represent the whole group because he is the ultimate model for behavior and personifies the face of that group. Open criticism, therefore, reveals that the leader no longer fills this role for some members. If group unity is to be maintained, a new leader must be sought or the critics eliminated.

Children in school learn what correct behavior is and how ideal leaders should personify this behavior. They also learn that their particular leaders personify these ideals. More particularly, they become aware of how serious criticism of leaders, in terms of loss of face for themselves and their group, can be. They learn as individuals not to question lightly the leadership of authority figures. Only when the leader violates group norms, as defined by the majority (and herein, of course, is the difficult question), can the leader's mandate be openly questioned.

In their responses older children frequently state that a leader should be able to accept criticism and some go further and state that he can be "recalled" if he performs badly in office. Such statements undoubtedly reflect the training in citizenship and government that begins in earnest in fifth grade. Criticism, however, is almost always phrased in terms of the leader's moral behavior and a violation of group norms. In the first grade the authority figure is still seen largely in terms of his whole person. At the city public school an interview with a first-grade Taiwanese boy went, in part, as follows:

Question: "Can we criticize the policeman as being this way or that?"
Response: "No, we can't."
Question: "Why?"
Response: "If the policeman is good, then he's completely good. We can't say this is good, that part's no good."

But later, when discussing the principal, the following responses emerged:

Question: "Do we need to obey the principal completely?"
Response: "Yes."
Question: "But if he is wrong?"
Response: "We need to."
Question: "Do we need to obey him if he wants us to do something bad?"
Response: "No, we don't."
Question: "But in that case what ought we to do?"
Response: "We don't need to do it! Let him go do it himself!"

In fourth grade these feelings are somewhat better articulated. A fourth-grade mainland boy answered this way:

Question: "What method can we use to get rid of the chairman?"
Response: "Because the chairman is elected, then if he isn't good, he can be recalled."
Question: "When will the chairman accept criticism?"
Response: "When his behavior is not right, then he should be persuaded."
Question: "For instance, what kind of bad behavior?"
Response: "For instance, if he goes and does something bad with several people and people see him do it and try to persuade him not to, then sometimes he'll listen and sometimes he won't listen."
Question: "If the chairman does something wrong, does everybody still have to obey him?"
Response: "No, they shouldn't. The people will oppose him. Otherwise everybody will do something wrong."

Criticism of authority figures is never casually tendered, and much of a child's socialization reinforces this value. Nevertheless, the group as a whole is always ideally more important than any one individual regardless of that person's position. The responses of this sixth-grade Taiwanese girl are typical in this regard:

Question: "Can we criticize the chairman?"
Response: "Yes."
Question: "When?"
Response: "Whenever he does something wrong."
Question: "Can the chairman do something that everyone else doesn't want done?"
Response: "Yes, he can."
Question: "In that case everybody will do as the chairman tells them?"
Response: "Not necessarily."

Question: "What is your feeling toward those people who don't do as
he says?"

Response: "They probably feel they ought not to."

Question: "In that case what do you feel ought to be done?"

Response: "They probably feel that what the chairman has said is
wrong."

Question: "But what do you feel should be done if the chairman has one
idea and another group of people have a different idea?"

Response: "The minority should obey the majority."

Sanctioned Expressions of Hostility

Hostility against the group, and against the group's legitimate leaders,
is strictly prohibited. Opposition, when it exists, finds expression in
covert cynicism, in clandestine organizations, in factions operating
"behind the scenes," or, as a last resort, in rebellion. The politics of
opposition seems polarized between periods of outwardly passive
acceptance and moments of violent outburst, between group conformity
and total overthrow.

There are, however, sanctioned targets in the political system for
hostility. These are the so-called outgroups composed of those who do
not support the group, people who have done something wrong or
improper, or, most of all, those who are conceived to be outside the
group itself. Often these heterogeneous entities are seen as somehow
interconnected. The "evil identity" which Erikson believes is an amalgam
of "the images of the violated (castrated) body, the ethnic outgroup, and
the exploited minority" is synthesized by people into whole good or bad
imageries "in order to make one battle and one strategy out of a bewilder-
ing number of skirmishes."[15] The hostility which one may feel (but not
be able to express) against one's parents, teachers, or political leaders is
displaced onto this composite evil image and often justified by some
belief. John Dollard discusses the development of such stereotyping:

Either rivalry or traditional patterning creates a stereotyped image in the minds
of current members of society of a class of individuals who may be more or less
painlessly detested. These images usually denote men who are to some degree
released from the moral order which binds us and who are feared because "anything" may be expected of them; because they do not accept our mores, they are
also regarded as inhuman beings to whom "anything" may be done. It is an effect

15. Erikson, *Childhood and Society,* p. 215.

of this stereotyping to produce the categorical treatment which is given those against whom prejudice is felt; individual discriminations tend to drop out and the differential treatment accorded to ingroupers is omitted. Within our own group we judge people according to their deserts and not according to standard classifications, but not so with the group against whom prejudiced stereotypes exist.[16]

The intensity of feelings against outgroups is undoubtedly some function of the intensity of those hostility feelings which derive, in part, from the nature and severity of socialization practices themselves. In America, for instance, it has been found that highly aggressive boys are generally those with parents who prohibit aggression in the home but reward it outside.[17] It seems conceivable that intensity of expressed hostility in a society like China, where ingroup aggression is strongly prohibited, may in addition also depend on the number of permissible outside targets. Where the evil identity composite is narrow one would expect the hostility per outgroup to be higher due to selectively higher reinforcement.

When the outgroup is viewed as quite powerful, hostility may be accompanied by fear. The power of the outgroup alone, however, is not the major factor influencing this emotion. Rather, fear tends to vary with the strength of anxiety about aggression and with the strength of the tendency to be aggressive.[18] In Taiwan, where there are few socially ingrained prohibitions against verbalized suspicion,[19] such fear and anxiety about aggressiveness may be accompanied by what appears to be social paranoia concerning the aggressiveness of others.

Over seventy years ago Arthur H. Smith hinted that tension and disequilibrium in Chinese society occur because there is no prescribed and sanctioned way in the family for the expression of certain feelings—notably, but not solely, hostility feelings.[20] Relations between members,

16. John Dollard, "Hostility and Fear in Social Life," *Social Forces*, vol. 17, no. 1 (Oct. 1938), p. 21, quoted in John W. M. Whitting and Irvin L. Child, *Child Training and Personality: A Cross-Cultural Study* (New Haven, Conn.: Yale University Press, 1953), p. 278.

17. Bandura and Walters, *Social Learning*, pp. 18–19.

18. Whiting and Child, *Child Training and Personality*, p. 318.

19. From a conversation with Mr. Yang Kuo-shu, a psychologist at National Taiwan University.

20. Arthur H. Smith, *Village Life in China* (New York: Fleming H. Revell Co., 1899), particularly the two chapters "Unstable Equilibrium of the Chinese Family" and "Instability from Family Disunity."

icularly marked. High walls surround the houses, and barred windows are a common sight. There is some justification for this in Taiwan as thievery is widespread, yet combined with this is the sense, implicit rather than explicit, that thieves are to be feared less because of the act itself than because they have voluntarily defied the norms. Theirs is an occupation where actions are purposely concealed and unpredictable. The foreigner may be unpredictable from ignorance; for the thief it is calculated premeditation which is an especially fearful thing.[23]

Most of all, however, hatred and fear are directed toward those members of society who are purposely disloyal to the group. This type of target is not an especially Chinese one, yet, as with thieves and foreigners, it is the intensity of feeling which is notable rather than the object itself. These objects of hostility are a class of internal traitors, those who repudiate the leader and his followers and organize a competitive loyalty structure. Such people have not merely violated group norms but have sought to change or destroy the group itself. They are thus especially detestable. This is never more true than when their actions are secret and covert.

"How would you feel about people who didn't obey [Chiang Kai-shek]?" a first-grade Taiwanese boy was asked in an interview structured around the public meeting scene picture:

Response: "I'd have them arrested and locked up."

Question: "Why, what would happen without him?"

Response: "Without him we would lose to the Communists."

A sixth-grade mainland boy in a later interview was asked:

Question: "Do you think everybody will agree with the village head?"

Response: "That's not possible."

Question: "What sort of feelings do we have toward those people who don't agree with the village head?"

Response: "(pause) We'll dislike them."

Question: "Is there anything else?"

Response: "If it goes too far, then there will be fighting or quarreling."

Question: "How ought it to be?"

Response: "If ought to be that the minority obeys the majority."

At the same school (the city public school) a fifth-grade Taiwanese boy was questioned. During the interview the same meeting scene picture was used. Part of the conversation was as follows:

23. I am indebted to Richard H. Solomon for pointing this out to me.

but most crucially between those with authority and those without, are prescribed by certain rules and norms. Despite continuing changes within the family concerning authority relationships (as noted in Chapter 2), much effort is expended to make members outwardly comply with societal norms, for violation would put one in a shameful position. Outgroups in Chinese society are not, however, composed simply of these luckless family members. At the highest level of generalization they are all those who do not know shame. These people, who care nothing for their face, "can no longer count on the network of social relationships to help them out, for they have isolated themselves by flaunting moral standards. . . . For example, people who turned traitors against their country in its hour of greatest need are said to 'have no [face]' at all, meaning that they have laid aside all pretensions of being decent human beings."[21]

Among this outgroup of shameless people is one large segment composed of those who have simply never been part of the ingroup. These are foreigners or "outside country people," to give literal translation to the Chinese word which graphically expresses the relationship. The problem with foreigners is that they do not know the norms to begin with, nor do they fit into any prescribed social relationship. One does not live in Taiwan long before one is keenly aware of one's foreignness —people stare, and children shout "American," or, just as frequently, "Big nose, big nose," to name two of the less subtle types of indicators. In the schools I was a mere object of curiosity until I was identified and my role specified. After that I was bowed to and accepted, rather without question, much as most foreigners who accept things Chinese are accepted. Nevertheless, the bulk of foreigners are, as one Chinese Air Force psychologist explained to me, an identifiable target against whom pent-up feelings of hostility are channeled with particular emphasis.[22]

Within Chinese society itself the fear and hatred of thieves is part-

21. Hsien Chin Hu, "The Chinese Concepts of Face," *American Anthropologist*, vol. 46, no. 1, pt. 1 (Jan.-March 1944), pp. 51–52.

22. One might view the traditional Chinese tribute system as a hostility-reducing mechanism peculiarly adapted to reducing Chinese senses of hostility by giving foreigners an identifiable niche in the Chinese social order. The notion that foreigners who accept the Chinese way of life are no longer targets of hostility leads one to believe that hostility against foreigners is not based purely on ethnic grounds. Rather, it seems to be primarily a function of frequency of contact of foreigners with Chinese, plus an unwillingness, or incapacity on the part of the foreigner, to make concessions to Chinese custom—as in Shanghai thirty years ago or in some areas of Taiwan today.

Question: "How ought subordinates to be toward the leader?"
Response: "(pause) Obedient."
Question: "Do you think everybody should obey the leader?"
Response: "No."
Question: "What sort of feelings do those who obey have toward those who do not obey?"
Response: "They despise them."

Purposeful Channeling of Hostility

A well-defined focus of hostility serves the very important function of draining off energies that might be directed elsewhere. It is more than this, however. It may well be a necessary factor for the development and maintenance of group cohesion. Focused hostility may serve as a group integrator in that it becomes a channel of communication where shared values are delineated.[24] Hostility may influence learning by emphasizing a frame of reference into which segments of reality can be selectively incorporated. In the sense that a focus for hostility establishes a readily observable we-they matrix, not only does it identify the object of hostility but also it is another means for identifying one's own group.

Adults often perceive political developments in terms of early childhood preferences, selectively evaluating new data according to this already established political position. Despite the fact that early preferences are based initially on only the haziest of discriminatory criteria,[25] the hostility image may be well defined and, as one aspect of early preferences, be an extremely important, perhaps necessary, part of the political environment.

When the children (695) were asked the question, "Who is the worst person?" 28.9 percent answered "the Communists." Boys responded this way more frequently than girls (34.4 percent versus 23.3 percent) and Mainlanders more than Taiwanese (33.2 percent versus 24.2 percent), but overall, and for any group, this was the single most defined response. The Communists as an answer constituted 20 percent of the

24. For an interesting exposition of this argument about small groups see George A. Theodorson, "The Function of Hostility in Small Groups," *The Journal of Social Psychology*, vol. 56, 1st half (Feb. 1962). For a more general exposition see Lewis A. Coser, *The Functions of Social Conflict* (Glencoe, Ill.: The Free Press, 1956).

25. Fred I. Greenstein, *Children and Politics* (New Haven, Conn.: Yale University Press, 1965), pp. 81–82, 154.

responses in first grade, rising to 30.6 percent in second grade and remaining at approximately that level thereafter.

Whether such a response is a true indication of how children feel or is only what they feel adults want them to think is unknown to me and is, in any case, somewhat beside the question. The point is that nearly one third of the children spontaneously perceive the Communists as an object of hostility in their society, an identifiable "they" in the we-they matrix. This is not altogether surprising, however, for quite early children begin to receive indoctrination concerning outgroups generally and the Communists specifically.

With regard to outgroups generally, such training is effected through stories such as that of the lion and the buffaloes which the children read in third grade. There the buffaloes, chased by a lion, form a ring and drive the predator away.[26] This story, an important one for children to learn, was acted out in a school assembly under the title "Unity Is Strength." At the end of the skit, as the lion lies defeated, the children who play the part of buffaloes each hold up a large sign with a character on it. Taken together, the characters all read, "Unity Can Destroy the Enemy." Many lessons repeat this theme—ants unite to defeat grasshoppers, oldsters show that many chopsticks bound together cannot be broken although one by one they can be snapped easily—and each story reveals a primary concern with the unity of the ingroup. Other stories (such as one where Confucius is made to say, "When the state is invaded by the enemy, the people ought to resist strongly; they ought not to rejoice when the state perishes and also ought not to work for the enemy.... Why do such people deserve respect?"[27] reveal how one should feel toward members of the outgroup. A favorite of the children, in fact the hit of one assembly, was the story of Koxinga, an early hero in Taiwan, who came to the island and thwarted the mainland Ch'ing soldiery. After this skit everyone in the audience stood up and clapped. Stories like these are intermixed with stories of the Communists and serve as reinforcers for the development of ingroup consciousness and outgroup identification.

On the backs of the history books is the slogan: "The thought of opposing the Communists and resisting the Russians is everywhere.

---

26. *KYKP*, book 6, lesson 1.

27. *KYKP*, book 6, lesson 27. This story is immediately followed by a story of Sun Yat-sen and Chiang Kai-shek, stressing the bravery and loyalty of Chiang.

Everything should reflect our dedicated effort to love the country and help the people." In addition to such slogans, which are encountered frequently in school and out, the children read stories such as the third-grade one about a man in a village who did many good things. When the Communists came, they put the squeeze on this man until he wondered, out loud, how long this could go on. But the Communists heard this and decided to kill him cruelly. They called a "people's meeting" and forced the village people and some vagrants to agree with them. Because the trial was rigged, some people, planted in the audience, spoke out for killing the old man, and this pronouncement was declared to be the will of the people. The villagers, however, said, "If even this kind of good man can be cruelly killed, what is the world coming to?"[28] Accompanying this story is a picture of an old man, arms tied, kneeling on the ground, surrounded by ruffians, one of whom is piercing the old man with a bayonet. The blood is spurting out.

The Communists, the children are told, are wickedly destroying the family. They also oppress any workers who speak out against increasing exploitation. Above all, however, the Communists are cruel and in-human. There is a story in third grade of a man who drowns himself because a tax placed on his family is too high. The Communists, however, fish his body from the water, weigh it, and subtract his weight from the amount of tax due. The children see an accompanying picture of a corpse on the scales, attended by a villainous creature. They also read the final ringing words of the wife of the drowned man who angrily shouts: "Despicable Communist bendits! When the National Army comes that will be the time of your death."[29]

The return of the National Army is, in fact, an integral part of anti-Communist indoctrination, for the ingroup will not be passive; they will strike back and root out the inhuman and aggressive evil. From their geography book the children learn that they will first visit Taiwan, "which is the base for attacking the Communists and resisting the Russians and will then visit each province on the Mainland. After we have clearly understood the real condition of our wonderful country, we then can know the importance of reattacking the Mainland and recovering our lost territory."[30] In fourth grade there is a poem about flying from

28. *KYKP*, book 6, lesson 13.
29. *KYKP*, book 5, lesson 9.
30. *Ti-li K'e-pen, Kao-chi Ti-i-ts'e* 地理課本, 高級第一冊 [GeographyPrimer, upper grades, book 1] (Taiwan, 1964), lesson 1 老共同美術印刷廠.

east to west toward the sun and how pretty everything is, for flying is like a floating cloud or a flying bird. The poem, after this start, ends with these words, "We will bestride the narrow seas, and see our blood-besmirched old homeland. We will break down the iron curtain, and take the news of our counterattack."[31]

The counterattack, however, is constantly threatened by two great evils—spies and the Russians. These dual villains are the major actors in a plot which borders on the paranoidal. In citizenship the children are taught that the world is divided into two camps, one headed by the United States and the other by Russia. The nature of the Russian camp is not left in doubt. In geography the lesson concerning the Soviet Union is entitled, "Our Enemy Country—Soviet Russia." The Kremlin is described as the place where "Soviet Russia controls all Communist countries and is the center for aggression against the world."[32] In fourth grade the children read how after the Red Mao bandits came to Nanking, the rats who lived south of the Yangtse River were threatened with starvation. The rats, therefore, called a meeting and deputized representatives to go north and see where the provisions were hidden. They found nothing and finally felt they would have to go outside the country "beyond the pass." Finally they came to a large granary and saw that all the rice from China was being prepared for the Russians to eat in World War III.[33] The worst thing about the Russians, however, is not that they have long been aggressors against China (although the children are frequently told this) but that without them the Chinese Communists would never have come to power. This aid, the children are told, is the real reason the Mainland was lost. There is no equivocation. As the *China Post* puts it in an editorial "the Chinese Communists were able to seize the Mainland entirely because of the support they obtained from the Soviet Union."[34] The sense of having been victimized is high indeed.

Aiding the foreign schemers and plotters is an insidious internal enemy whose machinations are no less to be feared. Signs warning of

31. *KYKP*, book 7, lesson 14.

32. *Ti-li K'e-pen*, upper grades, book 4, lesson 8 全勝彩色印刷廠. During class this sentence was written boldly on the blackboard as the key to the lesson.

33. *KYKP*, book 8, lesson 21.

34. "Treacherous Russia", *China Post*, vol. 14, no. 4758 (Oct. 28, 1965), p. 2. It is interesting to note how the use of the Russians as the exaggerated enemy parallels the use of the United States (and now, interestingly, the Russians also) on the Chinese Mainland.

this enemy are everywhere, on street corners, in the public buses, at theaters, etc. One large poster in an elementary school at T'ao Yuan, outside Taipei, showed children keeping quiet after seeing a file of government troops march by. The slogan underneath says, "Don't Talk about Government Secrets." At the back of a fifth-grade class in the city public school were hung samples of the children's brushwork. One such proclaimed, "In Public Places Don't Talk of the Country's Secrets." In fourth grade, in a story entitled "Guard Secrets and Protect against Spies," the little child in the story learns from his parents how suspicious it is when an old friend, whom one hasn't seen in years, meets you and the conversation turns to military affairs, for, the father admonishes, Red spies often use dear friends to get information.[35] It was possibly this story which prompted a fourth-grade mainland girl at the country public school to write in the conclusion to her story of the policeman-vendor scene (Appendix 3): "Because he is a policeman, he must keep watch at the main entrance. If spies falsely take advantage of certain people and ask about recent news in the country, nobody will know [of their false intentions] and will directly speak out. The country's affairs will then be divulged."

Identification of the Communist enemy in all his myriad forms is not consigned solely to the literature but is also an active part of class discussion even in noncitizenship classes. In a fourth-grade class on composition at the city public school, for instance, the children were instructed to make up sentences using certain vocabulary words. The sentences were read, and afterward there was a discussion. The children were not guided as to what sentences were preferable, but certain sentences were lightly commented on while others drew praise and were used as the basis for further instruction. Three such model sentences using the word "really" were: "The patriotic man was really fine"; "They had a really strong country"; and "The Communist bandits' insults were really horrible." Another word was "to improve." The teacher strongly approved of the sentence of one child, which was "We must improve the society's strength in order to attack the Mainland." In the fourth grade at the city private school a similar class was held and the vocabulary word was "military." A child made a phrase saying, "The military of the Communist party." "That is correct," the teacher said, "but the sentence would have been better had it been phrased, 'The

35. *KYKP*, book 7, lesson 25.

military of the Communist bandits!' " At the country public school, in connection with a lesson on the meaning of the Mid-Autumn Festival, sentences were written on the board. They proceeded in tone from the meaning of the festival itself to why we should be thankful and to the enemy who may destroy this happy occasion. These two question-answer sentences are samples: "Whom should we most revere—Our soldiers." "Who are the worst in the world—Not just the Communist bandits but the Russians."

This class on the meaning of the Mid-Autumn Festival was part of a course on common sense in the second grade. The teacher first told the story of the original moon cakes and how the Chinese used them to overthrow the oppression of the Mongols some six hundred years ago. Then, turning to the blackboard over which hung a portrait of Sun Yat-sen and the motto "Bravery," the teacher took a display poster and hung it for the class to see. The picture, as pointed out by the teacher, showed a happy family in Taiwan eating moon cakes. The figures in the picture all appeared well clothed and well fed. Another poster, with the caption, "The Pitiful Plight of the People on the Mainland," was then put on the blackboard alongside the first. On this poster were several pictures, all of which were described by the teacher. One was of a farmer being whipped. The last was a scene showing a person being shot, and when the teacher arrived at this point, she asked the class who this person was. "A dead person," the class responded. "Who did it?" the teacher asked. "The Communist bandits," came the answer. "Are the Communist bandits bad or not bad?" was the next question. "Bad," the children all said. Finally the teacher asked the class what they were going to do about it. Two boys immediately sprang up, one exclaiming, "Retake the Mainland," and the other saying, with equal feeling, "Destroy the Communist bandits."[36]

The development of a cognizance of a defined focus of hostility, and the intensity of the hostility feelings engendered, are difficult to measure. However, a second-grade mainland boy at the country public school,

36. The release of hostile feeling against a defined target, as described here, has its corollary elsewhere. Charles Mohr, in an article entitled "Now Mao Declares Class War," *The New York Times*, Dec. 4, 1966, sec. 4, p. 4, wrote: "Evidence reaching Hong Kong indicates that this official sponsoring of class consciousness has been greatly exacerbated by the release of pent up animosities and passions that took place when the Red Guard youth movement was allowed to run loose, both physically and ideologically."

writing about the classroom scene, when asked what the people in the picture were thinking about, answered, "Of their compatriots on the Mainland." In an interview with a third-grade Taiwanese girl at the city public school the child described the public meeting scene as one led by an honest, patriotic, and brave President Chiang who became President because "a long time ago the Communists persecuted the people, and the President led the people in a revolution." The interviewer then asked:

Question: "What do you think the President ought to do for the people?"

Response: "He ought to make the people happy and peaceful."

Question: "What do you mean by happy and peaceful?"

Response: "We must retake the Mainland."

The President, the child went on, is someone who is always correct, like Mommy and Daddy and Teacher. Then the interviewer asked:

Question: "What kind of person can become President?"

Response: "Someone who doesn't do bad things."

Question: "What do you mean by bad things?"

Response: "To tell the Communist bandits the country's secrets."

She used this theme again later to explain why the President did not need to tell the people everything and why he can sometimes do things the people don't want. A fourth-grade Taiwanese boy at the same school described the meeting scene as one led by a chairman "talking about something related to the government."

Question: "What government?"

Response: "The country's."

Question: "Who is the chairman talking to?"

Response: "To the people."

Question: "What people? Who are they?"

Response: "Those people involved with reattacking the Mainland."

He is a chairman, the boy went on, because he is brave and is "a person who desires to reattack the Mainland." He is a person, like the teacher, whom we obey whenever he speaks and whom we can't criticize. Moreover, in his ideal relations with the people, he is a person who "should recommend to everyone to go and save our compatriots on the Mainland."

Nonsanctioned Expressions of Hostility

Deviant or nonsanctioned behavior takes place when people behave in a way which violates the group norms publicly declared to be the proper forms of behavior. In this study the sanctioned patterns of behavior were set out first because it is on the basis of these that we define deviance. Expressions of deviance, present in every social system, must be contained and managed if the system is to continue to exist. An analysis of the socialization process is critical for an understanding of this, for not only can one glean information concerning ideal behavior values and the intensity with which adult members of the society conceive that such values should be held, but one also can gain an understanding of the mechanisms of social control used to repress deviant behavior and the anxiety and hostility that may result from this repression. Moreover, clues are revealed as to how the anxiety associated with socialization may be expressed. There may be overcompensation toward performance of ideal patterns; there may be displacement of hostility onto legitimate targets; there may be an attribution to others of one's own tabooed thoughts; and there may be a rationalization of deviance in terms of some specified criteria.[37] In any society we observe distinctive utilization of these patterns as unique social phenomena. In Taiwan, for instance, we see overcompensation in terms of real concern about proper behavior, hostility is displaced onto the Communists, who are also attributed with possessing one's own tabooed thoughts, and one also hears rationalizations for deviant behavior in society, particularly with regard to unscrupulous financial gain.

Nonsanctioned behavior is not necessarily associated with hostility feelings, or vice versa. One must be clear on this. Placing family loyalty above loyalty to the nation, for instance, may be deviant in terms of the ideal norms of the society, but hostility feelings are engendered only when there is a situation of confrontation between these values and when compliance in terms of national loyalty is enforced at the expense of a stronger family loyalty. Otherwise, there is no conflict between these values as both are sanctioned.

Conflict may also arise between proper behavior and behavior that is clearly nonsanctioned in terms of any ideal standard. Various forms of corruption might fall into this category. Again, hostility may be engendered where compliance in terms of the ideal behavior is enforced. Here, as in the example in the preceding paragraph, an expression of hostility is illegitimate, for its manifestation reveals an open violation or contempt of ideal group norms.

37. Bredemeier and Stephenson, *The Analysis of Social Systems*, pp. 138–139.

If deviance is widespread within a group, conforming members may feel hostile toward those who deviate. This is a perfectly legitimate expression of hostility since those who deviate are clearly violating sanctioned group norms and have, to some extent, placed themselves outside the group. Where the deviants are the leaders of the group, however, such expressions of hostility may themselves be deviant in terms of values of loyalty to the leader. The manifestation of this hostility may therefore be a quietly expressed cynicism, an aspect of hostility that allows release of pent-up feelings at the same time that the individual is permitted to maintain his standing in the group by not overtly violating proper norms of behavior. Obviously, however, cynicism may involve withdrawal of support from the leaders, and where cynicism is an inadequate mechanism for the release of hostility, its appearance may be the prelude to openly expressed hostility to the leaders.

In the next two sections it is my intention to analyze expressions of nonsanctioned hostility as manifested in two widespread phenomena—subgroup conflict and political cynicism.

Subgroup Conflict

About twenty years ago Kenneth Scott Latourette wrote some lines which express vividly some of the dilemmas of Chinese group life. They are worth quoting:

> Chinese society has been and is an interplay of groups, some of them united by blood, some by economic ties, and some by political, professional, or religious interests. . . . All these many kinds of associations make Chinese society extraordinarily complex. They are one reason why the uninitiated finds particular problems and situations in politics and business so difficult to understand. Even an intelligent Chinese frequently fails to know all the elements involved.
>
> It is also apparent that such a society develops marked skill in effecting compromises and adjustments among its many groups and that secret parlays and intrigues flourish. Not only must the individual, if he is to succeed and often if he is even to survive, associate himself with as strong a group or groups as possible, but he must frequently be an adept at playing off one against another and at diplomacy, perhaps underhanded and tortuous. . . . Still another side of the picture must not be forgotten. Many, both foreigners and Chinese, regard the Chinese as rather unsuccessful at cooperation. They point out that much of existing concerted action is under the pressure of strong necessity. . . . [and] that most Chinese find it impossible to believe that the organizer is acting from sincere public spirit. . . .[38]

38. Kenneth Scott Latourette, *The Chinese: Their History and Culture* (New York:

Within the restrictions of a common national focus of loyalty, conflict may arise between subgroups, for the problems of intensity of loyalties are very complex indeed, and it is around this point that much subgroup conflict arises. Under most situations loyalty to one's own family, friends, and colleagues is only minimally challenged by the demand to give paramount loyalty to the nation and its leaders and to give precedence to group cooperation at the national level. The demand for loyalty in China is nowhere more pressing than in the subgroups themselves. In traditional times the intensity of these loyalties was frequently greater than that of other loyalties and often manifested itself in moments of critical confrontation such as dynastic crisis, in a decision to adhere solely to one's subgroups.[39] As was pointed out in the first part of this study, great effort is now being expended to change the foci of loyalty decisively to the national level.

Intersubgroup hostility may be reduced by a shared adherence to a larger group. Such adherence may not, however, completely restrict the desire to maximize gain for one's own subgroup, and if maximization is done at the expense of other subgroups, the hostility engendered may be very real indeed. As long as the common group membership at the next higher level of generalization is recognized and values of cooperation and loyalty at that level are sanctioned, open expressions of hostility may be muted. Fear of outright suppression and of being stigmatized as outsiders may also limit expressions of hostility. These emotions of fear, however, may have the consequence of intensifying primary loyalties in order both to minimize the gains of other subgroups and to reduce the tension of being termed an outsider in terms of the larger group con-

---

The Macmillan Company, 1950), pp. 684–685 (3rd ed., rev.). The manifestations of group spirit in Taiwan seem always to be indifference to and lack of consideration for outsiders, and loyalty, consideration, and cooperation within the group. The existence of group spirit is often situationally defined. For instance, students in the same school can be very cooperative in a school-defined context and yet shove and push while waiting at a bus stop. Citizens may loyally do military service together, and yet families living next to each other may be totally inconsiderate, playing loud music, keeping livestock, throwing garbage out, etc. (Lest such actions be considered acceptable social custom which only foreigners take umbrage at, it should be noted that Chinese frequently voice upset over such conditions as well.)

39. Before assuming that this is a peculiarly Chinese phenomenon, it is well to remember Robert E. Lee's famous choice to join the Confederacy rather than remain with the Union.

text. Thus we can have a closed circle where subgroup loyalty leads to attempts to maximize one's own subgroup's position, thus arousing the fear and hostility of members of other subgroups, which leads to an intensification of subgroup loyalties.

It has been noted by Hyman that in the United States large differences in attitudes can be correlated with differences in parental income by ninth grade.[40] What this suggests is that in America subgroup awareness, on the basis of income, is reasonably well articulated by mid-puberty and probably has its beginnings in childhood. Within the schools in Taiwan, however, one does not observe, at least superficially, subgroup cleavages based solely on economic criteria. School group loyalty apparently suppresses such cleavages within each school itself. There is a noticeable difference between rural and urban children (all the tests reflected this difference, which is, of course, partly economic in nature), with the urban children always significantly more able to respond on the questionnaires. There was not, however, any noticeable hostility between these two groups. Within the schools there is one subgroup differentiation, however, that is frequently tabulated and openly exhibited in the principal's office and on charts outside each room. This is a statistic showing from which province in China each child's family came. The Chinese use this statistic as a means of identifying a loyalty larger than the primary family group and as a way of expressing a further sense of individual identity. The province of a family's origin has always been a basic fact about each individual for which there is no parallel in American society. Such statistics seem to gain merit for the cosmopolitanism of a school. More than this, and while no concrete evidence is available to substantiate this assertion, such data are perhaps also exploited by the educational authorities for the purpose of submerging the simpler issue of Taiwanese-Mainlander hostility. For although there is no apparent hostility in the school based on provincial criteria, hostility between adult Taiwanese and Mainlanders is one of the largest unresolved political problems in Taiwan.

Observed incidents of open conflict in the society between Mainlanders and Taiwanese are quite rare, although one does occasionally see them. More frequently one hears about such incidents, particularly in the countryside, but usually not from an actual observer or participant.

40. Herbert H. Hyman, *Political Socialization: A Study in Political Behavior* (Glencoe, Ill.: The Free Press, 1959), p. 65.

Conflict in the past was on such a large scale, however, that many people over thirty witnessed scenes of strife or enforced humiliation. It is also in this age group that one encounters the greatest intensity of hostility. Among younger people, who demographically are now a very large proportion of the population, less hostility among peers is noticed. Many Mainlanders, particularly, express no hostility at all, although they are aware they may be the target of Taiwanese hostility.

Stories of discrimination against Taiwanese are frequently heard, and it is known, for instance, that there are virtually no senior Taiwanese military officers in any of the services. Taiwanese participation in government at the highest level is also highly circumscribed. On the other hand, local gossip claims that the Taiwanese control the wealth of the island, being active and successful in business and finance. Most of the agricultural wealth is also reportedly in their hands.

It is certainly conceivable that different social classes may develop different attitudes because of different conditions of existence. As has been noted several times in the data presented so far, there are differences in the responses of Mainlander and Taiwanese children. Taiwanese children, for instance, do not seem to be as aware of the government as their mainlander counterparts. In their cognitive associations of government they name Chiang Kai-shek less frequently, and in their identification of hostility figures they are less likely to choose the Communists. Nevertheless, while a difference between the two groups themselves may be noted, it should be mentioned that the percentage of Taiwanese children who name Chiang Kai-shek (38.0 percent) or who choose communism (24.2 percent) is not inconsiderable.

On the projective tests four children at the country public school (none elsewhere), all Taiwanese, identified the characters in their stories as Mainlanders. In two stories, both about the public meeting scene, Sun Yat-sen and Chiang Kai-shek were mentioned as being Mainlanders. In one family scene the group was identified as Mainlanders, possibly because the adult male figure is wearing Western-style clothes. One schoolroom scene story notes that the children were Mainlanders. In none of these stories, however, was there any sense of hostility. Rather, Chiang and Sun were praised for their ideals, and in the other two stories the Mainlanders were held up as models for emulation—for obedience and studying hard.

Why is there not greater evidence in the schools of conflict between the two groups? It could be, of course, that there is no real tension in the society of an overt nature which the children might reveal in their responses, but this is not a tenable argument since it violates very readily obtainable evidence to the contrary. It could also be that the children simply told me what they thought I wanted to hear. This is also not a very adequate explanation, for beyond the fact that children are poor dissemblers, there was no other evidence in the schools to contradict the test responses. The sample, obtained in the Taipei area, may not have reflected the higher feelings of hostility which I am informed exist in the southern and central parts of the island. Whatever the reason for the lack of evidence, the question is still of great importance, for many competent observers have noted that the Taiwanese have not accepted Nationalist rule as final and that there are strong feelings among them about establishing an independent Formosan republic.[41] There are also observers who see political circumstances on the island in terms of the most tyrannical oppression.[42]

However, while hostility exists between the two adult groups, a hostility reflected at least partially, perhaps, in the Taiwanese children's less enthusiastic adoption of mainland political symbols and goals, there has also been a shift in Taiwanese attitudes toward support for the Nationalist government. Certainly there are a growing number of Taiwanese who have entered the elite, and who feel that stability is more important for their future than political turmoil. These adult Taiwanese may have feelings of hostility; they may also feel that the independence of their island is an ideal goal; but most of all they feel that time, rather than revolution, is their best ally. Indeed, their political leaders, most notably Thomas Liao, who led their independence movement from abroad, have now returned to Taiwan and have publicly disavowed the rebel cause.

41. See O. Edmund Clubb, "Sino-American Relations and the Future of Formosa," *Political Science Quarterly*, vol. 80, no. 1 (March 1965), pp. 10–11, and Maurice Meisner, "The Development of Formosan Nationalism," *The China Quarterly*, no. 15 (July–Sept. 1963), p. 102.

42. As a sample of such a point of view, Albert Axelbank, "Chiang Kai-shek's Silent Enemies," *Harper's Magazine*, Sept. 1963, opening paragraph, has this to say: "Behind the mask of a benevolent, freedom-loving Chinese Nationalist Government on Formosa, there exists today an unpopular, elite party dictatorship that rules the island with an iron hand. In the guise of 'mobilization for counter-attack against Communist China,' the regime of Generalissimo Chiang Kai-shek has trampled upon basic human rights and stifled free political expression. Under the cloak of 'national emergency' it has waged a campaign of police terror."

It is not my intention to minimize the fact that fear of repression is one of the major reasons, if not the major reason, why open hostility is not expressed by the Taiwanese. Yet it is also true that if longest-held attitudes are important in molding the behavior patterns of individuals, a thesis supported in this work, then early training in showing respect for the leader and the political system should prevail over the desire to criticize openly; if the educational system has been successful in inculcating a loyalty to the society as a whole, much effort would be required of an individual who has experienced such training to reject this focus in favor of any subgroup's aims. Last, there seems some justification for feeling that professions of loyalty to the society as a whole, and of working for their country which children openly make in school, will produce attitude changes in the direction expressed in the statements.

An example of children's desire to conform to educational goals comes from a teacher at the country public school. He mentioned that, although there was conflict between the Taiwanese and Mainlanders which children were well aware of, the children had learned to respect their teachers to such a degree that they would never express such feelings openly if they knew the teacher would disapprove. One European scholar in southern Taiwan, a man very close to the local people, stated that the Taiwanese were more concerned about the ethics and morality of a leader than about which particular subgroup the leader belonged to. If a leader is moral, he stated, the Taiwanese, both children and adults, will follow him loyally whether he is Taiwanese or not.

It is comforting for some, perhaps, to believe that repression alone impels compliance to Nationalist rule and that without such repression many individuals would behave quite differently. It is a well-known method of dissonance reduction to rationalize compliance by magnifying the amount of reward or punishment involved. Such sentiments apply not only to the Taiwanese but also to those disaffected Mainlanders who covertly express their opposition to the Nationalist government.

Beyond inducements to conform because of fear of physical repression, however, are other fears, latent or manifest, which may serve as explanations for loyal behavior. Taiwanese children have learned to revere the leader and condemn the disloyal. They also dread to be stigmatized as outsiders and to become part of the evil stereotype they themselves abhor.

Expressions of open hostility, then, are largely muted and are only covertly expressed. They form one part of what, in Chinese society, is the outstanding characteristic of nonsanctioned political hostility—cynicism.

Political Cynicism

It has been said that friendship in China is "a mutual web of exploitation." Loyalty to other members of one's group is the society's most outstanding value and this loyalty requires that friends and relatives go to extreme lengths to honor their obligations to each other. The disloyal person is a person without face. Much of childhood training involves acquiring an understanding of this concept and its implications with regard to interpersonal relations, and learning to differentiate between when one must become involved and when it is better to avoid commitment. The strictures of face apply to all groups of which one is a member, but the most stringent implications are always in primary groups with those individuals one knows personally and where affective ties are generally strongest.

Within any society there are conflicting values, and it is not my intention to enumerate these in any exhaustive sense for the Chinese case. Let me mention only that goals such as personal prestige, wealth, and political power have historically been noticeable objectives in Chinese society and are certainly not unknown in Taiwan today. The attempt to maximize such objectives in favor of one's own group may violate standards of loyalty and cooperation at a higher level of generalization. A trivial example would be when a man arrives at a bus stop and steps ahead into line with a friend (one witnesses this frequently). This action may be understood by others as the obligation one friend owes another, while at the same time such behavior is deviant in terms of the larger group, the line, of which all are members. Or again, one may go into a store and find that, if one does not know the store owner, a higher price will be charged for the goods. Clearly the store owner is attempting to maximize his own gain (and his family's) at the expense of a more attenuated loyalty he owes his fellow citizen. When I asked children about the store owner's actions, however, they said he was not really dishonest since both sides know the rules of the game. The fact that children say people know the rules of the game reveals how accepted and ingrained in habit are the many small actions and customs whereby one is expected to maximize the advantage of one's own and one's subgroup at the expense of others.

Although preferential loyalty toward one's own subgroup may be understood by members of the society, specific aspects of such preference by others may be resented if they operate to one's own disadvantage. When political leaders favor their own family or associates, or do not prevent certain members of society from maximizing gain for themselves, a critical attitude toward the leader may develop. Open criticism may be suppressed, however, because of fear and a need to be loyal. The result is cynicism, a pattern of behavior characterized by an inner personal alienation from aspects of the political system, coupled with covert criticism expressed to those whom one can trust. Such alienation is likely to be particularly acute where actions by the leaders themselves, or actions by others which the leaders allow or cannot prevent, are clearly in violation of all commonly held values and the minimum obligations owed other members of the society. Corruption, in its many forms, is the term usually used to describe such actions. I would hypothesize that political cynicism occurs when ideal behavioral patterns are blatantly and consistently violated and where political leaders cannot, or will not, prevent such behavior.

Loyalty is the greatest strength, and the greatest weakness, of the Chinese political system. When the leader's actions conform to the moral attributes that people are trained (and rigorously so in Taiwan) to believe justify their loyalty, then group cohesiveness is very strong indeed. At the national level it manifests itself as a unified dedicated citizenry. But because one's loyalty to a national group especially is intimately connected with one's "face," any loss of face of the leader may imperil one's own face. Affective ties with other members at the national level are often weak and of much less importance than identification with the group's goals through the leadership, so that loss of face of the leader may lead to an attenuation of one's sense of loyalty to the group or system the leader heads. There will also be a concomitant cynicism regarding the inability of the national leader to prevent members of subgroups, particularly those whose loyalty has become extremely attenuated, from increasingly maximizing the gains of the subgroups to which they belong. When such cynicism is accompanied by a fear that the maximization of others, if unchecked by the leadership, will take place at one's own expense, there will be a tendency for a further attenuation of loyalty to the large group (plus an increase of concern for one's subgroup) and a further loss of confidence in the larger group's leadership.[43]

43. Friends in Taiwan have told me that one reason citizen groups do not form

Political cynicism exists in Taiwan just as does subgroup conflict, but in no sense, I think, can one call either an increasing phenomenon. In any case, cynicism is not an attitude that is prevalent among primary school children. Rather, it tends to begin in some individuals after, or during, adolescence as part of a general questioning of authority. Nevertheless, points of fracture in the spectrum of ideal behavioral patterns are known and are early observed by children. One can begin to note indicators in children of the attitude changes which may later lead to cynicism.

Cheating and helping others in class are frequently observed and only sporadically corrected, as if the teacher expected such peer group cooperation. However, other types of help are often not forthcoming, whatever the ideal attitudes might be. I asked a fifth-grade girls' class at the city public school what they would do if they saw a child hit another on the playground. "Help," they unanimously responded. Later I watched playground activity for about fifteen or twenty minutes during which period there was continual fighting between boys which no one attempted to stop. There was no adult supervision. Quite obviously help is conditional upon other criteria than its pure necessity.

Despite such lapses, the school environment is relatively disciplined and cooperation the mode rather than the exception. Not so outside the school, for not only is cooperation between children less observable after class but also the ideals of public service learned in school are sometimes forgotten. At the post office, for instance, a jeep drove up with two naval officers in it. Thinking they were police, a little child, the lookout, ran down the street shouting "The police are coming! The police are coming!" At this the sidewalk vendors began to push their carts away. No onlooker appeared surprised by this behavior, nor did anyone become concerned at the park when another lookout warned the vendors that a policeman was coming. The vendors hid or fled, but a little boy,

---

for, say, purposes of local improvement is that they fear the government would immediately arrest the leaders. Any group, I am told, which could possibly be a present or future threat is dealt with in this way. What this seems to suggest is that independent intermediate leadership is prevented from forming by political engineering. The result of this tactic could well be an identification, in the minds of the people, of whatever intermediate leadership now exists with national leadership. A loss of confidence in either level, therefore, would tend to leave only primary groups as alternate foci of loyalty, i.e., there would be no way to minimize the effect on the national level of any loss of support.

standing next to me, asked his father, "Are they going away?" "It's all right," the father replied, "they'll be right back," as indeed they were once the policeman had passed. The actions of all three parties—the vendors, the policeman, and the onlookers—seemed to imply a knowledge that this was the way the system worked.

Such examples would be relatively unimportant in themselves if they were not reinforced by far more serious types of deviance, for in the schools themselves the children soon become aware of (in fact, are partners in) probably the most talked-about example of corruption in society. Indeed, the discontinuities between sanctioned and nonsanctioned behavior are nowhere more obvious than in the schools themselves. One of the curious anomalies in Taiwan, in fact, is that the very institution which attempts so strenuously to mold "correct" attitudes is also the one which gives children their first systematic introduction in the evasion and undermining of the ideals that are taught.

Children who wish to take the middle school examinations find it almost a necessity to have extra tutoring, and this has led to an institution of cramming sessions known as supplementary education.[44] Such cramming sessions are illegal, yet so important is additional education that parents and children find themselves forced to resort to the sessions in order that a child not be at a competitive disadvantage. For the teachers the sessions are a source of badly needed income because the tutoring is not free of charge (and this is the part that is specifically contrary to law). The teachers and the students, sometimes with the knowledge and participation of the principals, must deceive higher educational officials. The children must be taught and enjoined not to reveal the secret, and even to lie to cover up the illegal sessions. In addition, it is occasionally reported that teachers, in order to force children into the cramming sessions, will sometimes withhold, during regular class hours, certain information necessary for the examinations. Parents and children are afraid to complain, however, because of the difficulty of proving such a charge, and because the result may be a retaliatory lowering of the child's grades.

The evidence of improper behavior, even if not absorbed into a coherent logical framework, is available to the children for their scrutiny. It becomes at their age, I think, not a source of cynicism but simply

44. Compulsory education has now been extended in Taiwan through ninth grade, partly to end this abuse.

a part of their environment. They see such things as the cramming sessions, police corruption, and vice as contrary to the moral codes they are taught, but not as something sanctioned covertly by the adult world and their national leaders in particular. Because they are children, they do not yet understand their own relationship to such deviances and the ambivalent attitudes which may be held toward them. This is not to imply, however, that children are not influenced by improper behavior of adults.

In citizenship classes at school, for instance, children learn about school and government organization. They learn of the rights and duties of citizens and about the constitution. Included in this indoctrination is training concerning the correct behavior of officials and how these officials are supposed to treat the people. At the same time, children become aware of deviant aspects of the adult political process. The following four headlines from a Taipei paper are indicative: "Hualien Mayor Indicted for Embezzlement"; "Wartime Austerity? Why Is It Necessary for a Commissioner to Use Two Cars, Three Houses at Government Expense?"; "TPG [Taiwan provincial government] Offices Vacant on Saturday Afternoon despite Government Order"; and "Tainan City Council Vice-Speaker Arrested in Taipei." Then, in October 1965, an editorial appeared mentioning that many primary schools in Taipei were electing "little mayors" in their schools in an effort to teach the children more about democratic practices. The election process was one the children had learned in school, being patterned after those of mayors and district magistrates in Taiwan. The editorial continued;

Everything about the elections of "little mayors" is good and deserves commendation except for one thing, which, if no timely action is taken against it, will seriously affect the practice of democracy in our country. We mean bribery. As in the elections of adults, candidates for the "mayorality" in schools are in many cases bribing "voters" in their "electioneering campaigns." No cash, of course, is being used to bribe "voters." However, candies, toys, pencils, ballpens and things popular among children are being "freely" and "abundantly" distributed among the "voters."[45]

While there are indications of cynicism and disaffection among adults, the evidence in children is far less abundant and more open to question.[46]

45. "Little Mayors," *China Post*, vol. 14, no. 4736 (Oct. 5, 1965), p. 2.
46. Perhaps the best example is that, of 7,357 students who came to the United States from Taiwan to study between 1957 and 1963, only 481, or 6.5

Nevertheless, some evidence does exist. When the children were asked, for instance, what they thought the head of the Taipei City government was like, they showed a small but increasing tendency to express negative sentiments and, after second grade, a decreasing tendency to express positive sentiments[47] (Table 3–2). It should be mentioned that while the mayor of Taipei himself has never been proved to be corrupt, stories, later retracted, have appeared in the press linking his name with financial fraud. In a well-publicized case, the brother of the mayor was actually indicted on such charges.

Table 3–2
Sentiments toward the Head of the Taipei City Government: Percent

Sentiment/Grade	I	2	3	4	5	6
Don't Know	58	39.0	48.8	55.1	45.3	51.9
Negative	2	1.1	4.0	7.9	7.5	10.2
Neutral	2	3.2	0.0	0.0	7.5	1.6
Positive	38	56.9	47.2	37.0	39.6	36.2
No. Responding	100	95	125	127	53	127

Significant at the .01 level.

It is interesting to observe the responses of the city private school children on the projective tests when an analysis of their written stories was made for affect. The attempt, admittedly very subjective, was to analyze the general tenure of feelings the nonauthority and the authority figures held toward one another. In the public meeting scene picture the children generally attributed positive feelings to both the listeners

---

percent, returned (International Association of Universities, *Bulletin,* vol 14, no. 1 (Feb. 1966), pp. 33–34). Naturally, only a percentage of those who did not return did so for purely political reasons. I would still hypothesize, however, that some sense of alienation was present in a majority of these students.

Old "China Hands" remember clearly the extremely pervasive cynicism present on the Mainland prior to the Communist victory in 1949. Fending off the government's encroachments, and fear of the government, were virtually national characteristics. With greater political stability in Taiwan today, cynicism and evasion are perhaps less evident, and it is extremely difficult to judge how widespread these attitudes are. The one certainty is that they do exist.

47. David Easton and Jack Dennis, "The Child's Image of Government," *Annals of the American Academy of Political and Social Science,* vol. 361 (Sept. 1965), pp. 52–55, found that American children generally have a highly favorable view of government leaders.

and the speaker. In the home scene most children felt the authority figure had rather negative feelings for the nonauthority figures. Conversely, positive feelings toward the authority figure increased with the ages of the children. Many of the children in the upper grades wrote stories that included some expressions by the nonauthority figures of gratitude or praise for the adult in the picture. Not unexpectedly, perhaps, the policeman-vendor scene was viewed by many children as one of negative feelings on both sides, with no significant differences by age. The coercive role of the policeman is evidently understood very early and is not associated, as the father in the home scene evidently is, with any positive affective sentiments to counterbalance the negative feelings arising in the coercive situation.[48] Most interesting, however, were the responses of the children in the schoolroom scene. In the early years the children wrote stories in which the teacher was pictured as having considerable positive feeling toward the children. The children in the picture, in like manner, were made to respond with equally warm feelings toward the teacher. By the upper grades, however, the pattern had virtually reversed itself, with the authority figure being pictured as having quite negative feelings and the nonauthority figures showing a marked drop in positive feelings and a rise in neutral or unknown sentiments. Figure 3–1 shows this clearly.

To generalize from such scant data has its obvious hazards. However, I believe that these results indicate a growing withdrawal of positive affect from the teacher as an authority figure. This is in marked contrast to the affect directed toward the authority figure in the family scene, where positive feelings remain very high. Very possibly the change in feeling toward the teacher is due to the influence of the cramming sessions. What is most significant, I feel, is that the responses do not reveal the children in the schoolroom scene as developing marked negative feelings. Rather, there is simply a withdrawal of positive support, and it is just this type of behavior, I would hypothesize, that accompanies political cynicism, for neutrality will allow one to maintain the outer

48. Attitudes toward the police are extremely important, I believe, for the police are authority figures the children know intimately, yet, unlike parents and teachers, the police are the ones with whom generally no personal relationship exists. How children see the police, as upright or corrupt, not only may affect their attitude toward other impersonal authority figures but may also affect their attitude toward the government after they reach the age to understand the link between the police and the government.

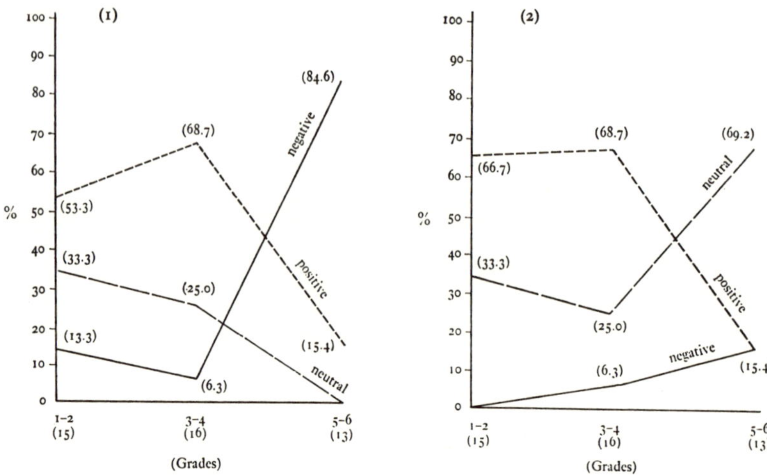

Figure 3–1
Schoolroom Scene

1. Affect of Authority Figure for Nonauthority Figure (Significant at .01 level)
2. Affect of Nonauthority Figure for Authority Figure (Significant at .05 level)

The numbers in parentheses below grades refers to the number responding (city private school).

forms of loyalty even though the positive affective sentiment is gone.[49]

If, as I suppose, one crucial aspect of cynicism is an awareness that authority figures cannot prevent corruption (or that they themselves are corrupt), then one might begin to find evidence of this awareness among school children. At that age an awareness of corruption in the society could exist along with generally favorable impressions of national authority figures, for an understanding of the system as a whole is still quite rudimentary in the primary school years. The withdrawal of positive affect from national authority figures would not take place until such an integration was firmly established, probably in the late teens.

49. Lucien W. Pye, *The Dynamics of Hostility and Hate in Chinese Political Culture*, Center for International Studies, Masachusetts Institute of Technology (C/64–23), June 1964, pp. 30–31, 48–49. Pye stresses how seriously, during socialization, the Chinese emphasize the difference in doing things the right way and the wrong way and how correct form means everything. Moreover, "correct conduct is large-ly affectively neutral." Relationships with superiors and inferiors should be according to the proper ritual despite one's personal feelings.

Evidence that children are aware of improper behavior in the society was not extensive in my survey. Nevertheless, there were some responses indicating awareness, such as those of a first-grade Taiwanese girl (city public school). The child and an interviewer were talking of the public meeting scene, and the child had just named the speaker in the picture as a military man.

Question: "Do you think that everything this person does is right?"

Response: "Not necessarily."

Question: "Will everybody do as he says?"

Response: "Not necessarily."

Question: "Why?"

Response: "Because sometimes he'll say bad things."

Question: "Do we usually need to obey him?"

Response: "No."

Question: "Why?"

Response: "Because sometimes he deceives people."

Question: "Do you think he will deceive people?"

Response: (Pause) "Sometimes he will, sometimes he won't."

Question: "When will he?"

Response: "Sometimes he'll knock on the door, and when people aren't home, he'll steal things."

In discussing the policeman-vendor scene a few children revealed a knowledge of deviant behavior. A sixth-grade mainland boy at the city public school, for instance, spoke rather matter-of-factly of this in an interview:

Child: "Should I first talk about this picture?"

Interviewer: "As you wish."

Child: "A policeman is telling a vendor at the side of the road not to block the entrance to the street."

Interviewer: "Do you think the vendor will do as he is told?"

Child: "He will leave temporarily, but after a little while he will come back and sell some more."

A sixth-grade Taiwanese girl at the country public school wrote that this scene was bad "because the vendor has pushed his cart onto the street in order to sell and the policeman has advised him to go. But the vendor has taken out a piece of fruit and offered it to the policeman, asking him not to hinder his business." At the city private school a fifth-grade mainland boy revealed a none-too-flattering image of the police. In describing the policeman-vendor scene he wrote: "There are a policeman and a vendor, and the policeman is trying to put the squeeze on the vendor and make him give him an apple. This is because the policeman is on duty and is thirsty. He knows that he's a policeman and thinks he's pretty great, and so he is trying to put the squeeze on the vendor."

Chapter 4
Conclusion

Problems of Hostility

In Chinese political culture the sanctions against open questioning of leadership and the emphasis on proper behavior put great pressure on leaders and followers alike. Any deviance by the leadership from rather rigidly prescribed norms of behavior may result in a defection of loyalty by followers. Formalistic expressions of loyalty by followers may mask a growing cynicism and a maximization of primary group goals at the expense of the larger group. Yet with no sanctioned way of expressing disagreement there is little that can be done, short of open disobedience, to influence the patterns of leadership. In moments of crisis it is very likely that extremist opposition will manifest itself. One observes an explosive quality in Chinese political behavior, passive acceptance (or the appearance of passivity) alternating with less frequent moments of violent outburst.

All societies have norms of loyalty to leadership which are openly flaunted only by the particularly adventuresome. In China, however, the transition from passivity to outburst appears more sudden than in many other political cultures. Hostility prior to an outburst is less easy to detect because of very strong emphasis on forms of loyalty.

Almond and Verba, in their study of the civic culture, concluded that, "Everything being equal, the sense of ability to participate in politics appears to increase the legitimacy of a system and to lead to political stability."[1] One crucial component of an ability to participate is a sanctioned way to express disagreement, without which the legitimacy of a political system (or a hierarchy of leaders who represent a system) may vanish when the intensity of hostility against political leaders begins to rise.

Outgroup targets of hostility are an outlet for feelings which it is

1. Gabriel A. Almond and Sidney Verba, *The Civic Culture* (Boston: Little, Brown and Company, 1965), p. 204.

taboo to express within the group. The role of outgroups as targets is justified because the outsiders do not understand the "proper" order of things. If they did understand, they would accept the ingroups' way of life and leadership. Enemies fill an extremely important role in Chinese political culture. In a sense one might almost say that if there were no such despised group, they would have to be invented in order for any emotional balance to be maintained.[2]

Defense against Group Pressure

Release of hostility against defined targets is only one of the ways in which the tensions of social existence are reduced. There are, in addition, other ways whereby friction among group members is lessened. Cynicism is one such defensive device. Social mechanisms of this nature are enormously important both for maintaining the cohesiveness of the group and as an explanation for observed incongruities of behavior which do not seem to generate open hostility yet appear inconsistent with ideal group norms. In no society is it more important to investigate such mechanisms than among the Chinese in Taiwan, for, as has been pointed out, considerable emphasis there in education is placed upon "correct" behavior. The price for noncompliance with behavioral norms is loss of face or stigmatization as a target of hostility. These sanctions are severe enough to suggest a society analogous to a colony of fearful ants, each busily photocopying the others. Such a characterization, however, is far from the truth.

One explanation for the control of tension in Chinese society in Taiwan is related to the level of deviance which seems to be tolerated within group life. Tsung-yi Lin, as has been previously noted, has found a comparative tolerance for deviant behavior in Chinese families.[3] Certain incidents pointed out earlier are also illustrative of this tolerance. Recognizing that a person may break into a bus line and stand with a friend, or that differential shop prices, varying according to one's familiarity with the proprietor, are an aspect of "the system," are indications of tacit ingroup tolerance. In the schools one notes such tolerance, in its simplest

2. See Lucien W. Pye, *The Dynamics of Hostility and Hate in Chinese Political Culture,* Center for International Studies, Massachusetts Institute of Technology (C/64–23), Cambridge, Mass., June 1964.

3. Tsung-yi Lin, "A Study of the Incidence of Mental Disorder in Chinese and Other Cultures," *Psychiatry: Journal for the Study of Interpersonal Processes,* vol. 16, no. 4 (Nov. 1953), p. 333.

form, with regard to the matter of discipline among the children. If the ideal is order, then the actual pattern is often disorder. Particularly in the lower grades the shouting out of answers whenever one feels one is correct is sometimes observed, particularly by boys, with no disapproval by the teacher. At one assembly older children with long sticks were supposed to keep charge by tapping unruly children on the head. But the sticks were passed to friends, and eventually all semblance of order broke down. The principal, standing at the back, twice told a child to go forward and sit down. The child, however, ignored him, and the principal did nothing. Unless the situation is one where authority is prescribed, there is frequently no order at all. Children quickly learn that the responses appropriate in a prescribed authority situation can be safely ignored elsewhere because there will be no threat of punishment.

When children were asked what they would do if their mother wanted them to go to bed but they did not wish to, almost a third (30.6 percent) of the 695 children who answered said they would not go. Somewhat fewer children, 28.2 percent, replied that they would go to bed, while 41.2 percent did not know what they would do. Toward school authority figures the children express greater compliance. In response to a question as to what they would do if the teacher wanted them to erase the blackboard but they did not want to, only 16.6 percent of the same children responded that they would not, 28.7 percent said they would, while again a curiously large percentage, 54.9 percent, answered Don't Know.

In many societies parents, as a source of ultimate authority, are questioned earlier than teachers. The children were asked who they felt was correct if what the teacher said and what the parents said disagreed. The results are indicated in Table 4–1.

Although the teacher is early picked as being more correct than parents (quite definitely so in the first and second grades), the data show that both teacher and parent responses decline with age, while

Table 4–1

Choice of Who Is Correct in a Conflict between Home and School: Percent

Choice/Grade	1	2	3	4	5	6
Don't Know, Unknown	33	36.8	68	78.7	66.0	77.9
Parents	24	18.9	12.8	8.7	18.9	11.0
Teacher	43	44.1	19.2	12.6	15.1	11.0
No. Responding	100	95	125	127	53	127

Significant at the .01 level.

there is a precipitous rise in Don't Know responses. In other words, while parents as a source of ultimate authority are questioned quite early, neither parents nor teachers are assumed to be infallible by the time the child reaches third grade. Although this pattern would seem to reflect the children's actual attitudes, when asked directly, first if they thought their parents were always correct and next if they felt that what the teacher said was always correct, it was not until fifth and sixth grade that an appreciable change in the ideal notion of infallibility could be detected. (See Table 4–2.) The latter two questions were scored jointly, with a double positive or double negative response being considered a definite indicator of a behavioral trait. It will be noted that a pattern of increasing double negative responses emerges, indicating again a growing disinclination to accept the mandates of these authority figures as final. This disinclination to accord infallibility to authority figures, however, should not imply any lack of positive feelings toward the same individuals, nor does such an attitude give any indication of the intensity of loyalty toward a particular leader or group.

Table 4–2
Whether Parents and Teachers Are Always Correct: Percent

Category/Grade	1	2	3	4	5	6
Both Yes	83	80.9	71.2	66.9	52.8	43.3
Both No	2	5.4	4.0	11.0	20.8	30.7
Both Don't Know	2	2.1	8.0	5.5	5.7	5.5
Mixed	13	11.6	16.8	16.5	20.7	20.5
No. Responding	100	95	125	127	53	127

Significant at the .01 level.

While examples of disobedience can be observed in school and while some of the children themselves claim that they would question or defy authority, there is reason to believe that such attitudes are normally translated into action only when prescribed forms of loyalty are not violated. It is my observation that group pressure on the indivudal is minimized less by outspoken advancement of one's own viewpoint, with a possibility of damaging the face of oneself or another, than by avoidance of potentially conflictual situations.

"Only sweep the snow away from your own door" says an old Chinese proverb. If you sweep the snow from your neighbor's door, he may think you are doing it with some ulterior purpose in mind and give you trouble.

Therefore, mind your own business; do not get involved in a situation, and you will not have to fear the consequences. The head of a large Taipei firm told of the reluctance of city officials to take initiative even on petty matters. They are afraid, he said, that if anything goes wrong, they will be blamed. This is in accordance with the old saying, "The more you do something, the more you can be wrong. Do nothing, and you cannot be wrong."

Sometimes, however, an individual becomes caught in a web of circumstances from which he cannot be extricated. Most societies have expressions which verbalize the helplessness of such a situation, expressions which serve to rationalize the tension an individual may feel. For the Chinese the appropriate expressions are "Mei-yu Kuan-hsi," meaning "It is of no consequence," and the more helpless "Mei-yu Pan-fa," literally meaning that there is no way to do something, but coming closest in spirit to the French "C'est la vie." These two expressions are used frequently, from the pettiest of annoyances to the greatest of catastrophes. They imply that a situation is beyond being corrected and the individual must simply live with the consequences.

Some observers have pointed out that the Chinese show a control of impulse and a pliant but reserved role in interpersonal relationships.[4] Others have noted how "the first reaction of a Chinese to a potentially conflictual situation is one of avoidance; only when constrained in the situation does he exhibit 'seeming compliance' or resort to the necessary lie."[5] The Chinese will often respond in a particular situation (or on a questionnaire), according to the way they conceive they are expected to respond. Yet such outward compliance and conformity are not necessarily accompanied by any internal shift of attitude. This is quite contrary to what one would expect from dissonance theory, as Hiniker has shown. A strict dichotomy between attitude and action is explicable, I think, on the basis of very deep-felt needs to exhibit loyalty or, as Richard H. Solomon phrases it, in terms of anxiety about the hostility that would be released if the established role relationships broke down.

4. Theodora M. Abel and Francis L. K. Hsu, "Some Aspects of Chinese as Revealed by the Rorschach Test," *Journal of Projective Techniques,* vol. 13, no. 3 (Sept. 1949), p. 299.

5. Paul Hiniker, *Chinese Attitudinal Reactions to Forced Compliance: A Cross-Cultural Experiment in the Theory of Cognitive Dissonance,* Research Program on Problems of International Communication and Security, Center for International Studies, Massachusetts Institute of Technology, Cambridge, Mass., 1965.

These defenses against group pressure have their obvious political implications. Outward conformity by citizens may mask real sources of latent or actual instability within a political system. Particularly in times of rapid change leadership might well be unable to gauge the actual extent of support for its policies. Not only might this incapacity increase the suspicions of political leaders, but it could also derivatively lead to policies of overcontrol, wasteful in terms of human resources and potentially self-defeating in terms of objectives.

Conversely, a sanctioning by political authorities of the mechanisms for reducing group pressure may be essential for maintaining social stability. Whether, in fact, the best way to mobilize the Chinese toward modernization goals is to make attempts to enforce a congruence between group members' inner attitudes and their actions or to permit the individual some means for escaping group pressure is one of the crucial questions of our time.

Social Change

It may be true, as Almond and Coleman have postulated, that "One of the most important factors making for resistance to social and political change is the conservatism of primary groups and the early family socialization process."[6] Yet, paradoxically, certain aspects of conservatism may prevent excessive social disruption and loss of morale that could accompany wholesale social change. The maintenance of traditional values in some areas of life may, if widely shared and of sufficient import, nullify a cleavage within the society by preventing a polarization among members of shared goals and cognitive orientations.[7] Almond has pointed out how delicately balanced is the modernization process, how changes in such things as rules pertaining to the family, if originating from the government, could result in loss of morale or disobedience, which might markedly alter the way people interact with other sectors of the society.[8]

The critical problem for any modernizing political leader is how to institute change (and the conflict which may accompany it) without

6. Gabriel A. Almond and James S. Coleman, eds., *The Politics of the Developing Areas* (Princeton, N.J.: Princeton University Press, 1960), p. 27.

7. Marion J. Levy, Jr., *The Structure of Society* (Princeton, N.J.: Princeton University Press, 1952), pp. 168–182.

8. Gabriel A. Almond, "A Developmental Approach to Political Systems," *World Politics,* vol. 17, no. 2 (Jan. 1965), pp. 205–211.

destroying political stability, upon which the permanence of much of the change itself may depend. A maintenance, even a strengthening, of certain traditional interpersonal ties may provide sufficient mutual trust and predictability for change without excessive instability. Yet the danger always remains that the continuance of certain attitudes and patterns could greatly reduce or make impossible the development of new attitudes and relationships better suited to the modernizing goals of the leaders.[9]

In any modernizing society there must be an effective direction and mobilization of the aspirations of large groups of people. Whether such direction comes from a centralized political authority or is diffused in the hands of many independent operators is secondary to the need for direction and mobilization itself. The mobilization of aspiration to obtain nontraditional ends, however, may well require patterns of behavior at variance with those that are characteristic of other and more traditional roles. There is no need to belabor this oft-repeated point, but it may be worthwhile to reemphasize the personal tension to which many individuals may be subjected because of a lack of congruity in role patterns, and to point out how important such tension may be in a politically unstable situation where such individuals are fair game for those who wish to exploit latent sources of emotional energy.

Once modernization has begun, individual attempts to reduce "role strain" and achieve new goals simultaneously may be two of the critical variables for modernization. Yet the transitional time period involved is not likely to be short. Traditional patterns of behavior will persist for several generations despite the fact that other and newer patterns of behavior govern the individual's actions in certain areas of life.[10] Child-training practices, particularly in the home, are especially likely to be highly persistent either in their original or in some related form and to continue to foster a cultural identity linked with the past. Such child-rearing patterns exist because they are part of the parent's identity, to be shattered only at a risk to the parent's emotional stability.[11]

9. Lucian W. Pye, *Politics, Personality, and Nation Building: Burma's Search for Identity* (New Haven, Conn.: Yale University Press, 1962), pp. 52–55.

10. John W. M. Whiting and Irvin L. Child, *Child Training and Personality: A Cross-Cultural Study* (New Haven, Conn.: Yale University Press, 1953), p. 38; and Albert Bandura and Richard H. Walters, *Social Learning and Personality Development* (New York: Holt, Rinehart & Winston, Inc., 1963), p. 72.

11. Erik H. Erikson, *Childhood and Society* (New York: W. W. Norton & Company, Inc., 1950), pp. 116–117, 121.

The absence of excessive political instability[12] is essential, I believe, for economic growth and social change. Such absence depends, to a very large extent, on the degree of legitimacy accorded to political leaders (and the political system) by the members of the society. Assumptions developed in early childhood about the benignity of political leaders are among the most important factors favoring the development of a sense of legitimacy. The persistence of these learned predispositions toward leadership into adult life serve as a powerful counterweight against the possible later development of attitudes of cynicism or other forms of political deviance.[13]

"Political authority is likely to be more stable when it is obeyed automatically because citizens have learned to accept certain institutions and leaders as legitimate than when sanctions have to be threatened or employed."[14] I believe that automatic responses to government authority are far more likely to occur where the pattern of such responses is reinforced in crucial areas of one's life. The essential reinforcement is a congruence between styles of primary group and governmental authority, for it is the relationships in primary groups that are most immediate and emotionally charged for the individual. As has just been pointed out, however, it is exactly in these primary groups, and especially in the family, that traditional child-training practices (which include traditional social authority relationships) are likely to persist. Because of the tension an individual may experience when there is a lack of congruity in authority role relationships between primary and secondary groups, I would hypothesize that an analysis of the political system of any successfully modernizing society (implying one where excessive political instability does not occur) will reveal very strong similarities between styles of authority in the secondary environment and the style of authority in primary groups. This inherent conservatism will exist despite the name or type of the political system. The congruence of authority patterns between home and government provides an affective link with the past for all members of society, at the same time that the political leaders themselves are a focus and a mechanism whereby

12. Despite the awkwardness of this phrase I prefer it to the more positive term, political stability, which carries connotations of lack of change.

13. Herbert H. Hyman, *Political Socialization: A Study in Political Behavior* (Glencoe, Ill.: The Free Press, 1959), p. 17, and Fred I. Greenstein, *Children and Politics* (New Haven, Conn.: Yale University Press, 1965), pp. 157–158.

14. Greenstein, *Children and Politics,* p. 2.

loyalties may be developed toward the national group as a whole.[15]

The phrase "reinforcing dualism" has been used to describe a situation where an institution toward which affect was directed in traditional society is used in modified form as a focus for loyalty and cohesion during a period of rapid and often disruptive change. Such an institution was the emperor system during the early period of Japan's modernization. Analysts of Japan have pointed out how the principles of unquestioning loyalty directed in traditional times toward the feudal lord were transferred to the Meiji emperor. The emperor was both a symbolic link with the past and the keystone of a new, unified national state.[16] It is less important that the emperor system itself survived, however, than that the patterns of loyalty associated with the emperor were highly congruent with those already existing in other social units in the society.[17] Energy, time, and resources that might have been spent establishing an unfamiliar political system were able to be devoted to other areas.

In modern China there are two competing political systems, both claiming to be the most valid model for China's modernization. Political leaders on the Mainland of China have placed less emphasis on a direct relationship between primary group authority patterns and citizen-political leader patterns. Indeed, there has been a conscious effort at certain times to weaken the affect directed toward primary groups and to change the pattern of authority relations within these groups. Ideology, and particularly "the thought of Mao Tse-tung," have been used as weapons to break the persistence of traditional patterns of thought and action.[18] Much effort has been expended to eradicate traditional

15. For an interesting exposition of concepts concerning congruence of authority patterns see Harry Eckstein, *A Theory of Stable Democracy*, research monograph no. 10, Center of International Studies, Princeton, N.J., 1961.

16. E. E. Hagen, "How Economic Growth Begins: A General Theory Applied to Japan," *Public Opinion Quarterly*, vol. 22, no. 3 (Fall 1958), p. 388, and Herbert Passin, "Japan," in *Education and Political Development*, James S. Coleman, ed. (Princeton, N.J.: Princeton University Press, 1965). p. 307.

17. Japan specialists might take exception to this but I see no real reason why the shogunate could not have survived in modified form rather than the emperor system.

18. Howard L. Boorman, "The Men Who Rule China," *Diplomat*, vol. 17, no. 196 (Sept. 1966), p. 101. These campaigns have not been uniformly successful, however. We hear repeatedly about the necessity to abolish "feudalistic" ideas and conventions, a necessity which betokens the resistance that is being met. The Communists, no less than the Nationalists, understand the importance of

defenses against group pressure. Great social changes have taken place but at a continuing political cost which often dismays outside observers. Erratic economic growth seems at least partly to be explained by repeated crises of political instability.

In Taiwan considerable effort has successfully been expended through the educational system to reinforce a congruence between styles of authority in primary groups and those that exist between citizens and political leaders. Knowingly, or unknowingly, the patterns of authority that have been taught have been conducive to political stability. Intersocietal cleavage has been minimized, and there is little display of excessively overt forms of control. Educational development has been characterized by a great mass of teachers cooperating effectively in inculcating in children support of the government. Avoidance of undue group pressure is sanctioned in accordance with traditional norms. Whether in the long view these authority patterns will be supportive of further change remains to be seen; at the moment, however, economic growth and social change in Taiwan are among the most rapid for any society in the world.

---

controlling the socialization process. Unlike the latter, however, they will tolerate no potential deviance from the patterns of training they employ and no alternate source of authority. In their conception, change is more important than even an unequal entente with the family.

Appendixes

The political atmosphere in Taiwan is not conducive to open analysis of all subject matters. A secret police watches for purity of attitude and guards against the intrusion of what are considered hostile ideas (mainly Marxist). These political controls are usually not clumsily obvious. It is far easier, in fact, to observe the effect of such controls than to observe the agent of control himself. But one is reminded of the controls, nevertheless, by police checks at home and by the need for special permission to read certain materials and special passes to go certain places.

Friends who speak on tabooed subjects will unconsciously lower their voices or look over their shoulders. They sometimes feel the need to remind listeners of their doctrinal purity and that what they discuss has no bearing on their loyalty. People are cautious. The principal of the country school I visited was extremely reluctant, to the point of demanding a letter of approval from a superior in the Ministry of Education, to allow me to do research at his school. He became visibly agitated when told I was a political scientist. Afterward, I could not have been treated more politely. But one morning I asked the principal and assistant principal if I could watch a fourth-grade citizenship class. Instead of agreeing, the assistant principal repeated the question to the principal. I waited for an answer, but none came; the conversation slipped into another channel, and I did not go.

It would be a mistake, however, to believe that it is only the Chinese who become concerned when they know their attitudes are to be studied. I have watched American school officials become equally cautious under similar circumstances. And the truth is that officials in the Ministry of Education were very helpful and encouraging. So also were most teachers and school officials. These people went out of their way to make the climate for research as compatible with my desires as possible.

Discretion, however, stayed with me, and my American friends constantly cautioned me. Whether their advice was correct or not I will never know. Certainly it was belied by the actions of most of the Chinese educational authorities and teachers that I knew, yet I was always aware that I was examining an area of great sensitivity to the government and that caution was not merely prudent but necessary. One result of this was that I purposely refrained from asking any direct questions about two crucial aspects of political socialization in Taiwan—evaluative questions relating to the President and to communism. For information in these two areas I relied on indirect questions and on observation.

Such was the general atmosphere in which this research took place. The actual observations and questionnaires were given at three different elementary schools in the Taipei area. The first was a large urban public school, located in the middle of the city, with an enrollment of approximately 8600 students. The second was a private school, also in the city, with an enrollment of about 1000 students. Last was a public school located in the countryside several miles from Taipei with an enrollment of approximately 3000.

At each school I attended class with the students, doing everything they did and participating in class activities. In this way I progressed three times from first to sixth grade, sometimes being with more than one class at any grade level. Each class in all three schools contained from about 65 to 70 students, and it was these children that I observed and questioned. In each school the school authorities assigned me to a class, but, except for the country school, they did not object to my observing other classes and often invited me to observe special functions. I stayed at the city public school for approximately four months and at each of the other two schools for about one month each. This aspect of the research was carried out during the year 1966.

The following three appendixes cover data related to this research. The first is a detailed description of the children themselves and their personal data. The second involves data related to school materials; this includes an analysis of textbook content and educational philosophy. The third is a discussion and evaluation of the tests which I used and the methods I employed in conducting my research.

Appendix 1

Children's Background Data

The following selected data by schools is based exclusively on information obtained from the personal data section (Section I) of the open-ended questionnaire (Appendix 3). There were a total of 695 responses from all three schools, divided between schools as follows:

City Public School—330 responses (156 boys; 169 girls; 5 responses no indication which sex)

City Private School—172 responses (95 boys; 77 girls)

Country Public School—193 responses (106 boys; 87 girls)

It will be noted that only very broad categories are used to describe the general socioeconomic status of the children at each school. The children were asked to state the occupation of their father and mother, but many responses tended to be of the form "in the army" or "in business." For this reason no very definite delineation of categories was possible. The status classification given is based upon the answers which were available, plus my own subjective estimate. They should, therefore, be viewed with some caution.

I. City Public School (330 responses)

    A. Family Origin

Mainland Father	148
Taiwanese Father	164
Father's Origin Unknown	18
Mainland Mother	117
Taiwanese Mother	196
Mother's Origin Unknown	17

Mainland Father (148) with:

Mainland Wife	104
Taiwanese Wife	42
Don't Know	2

Taiwanese Father (164) with
    Mainland Wife   10
    Taiwanese Wife   153
    Don't Know   1

B. Socioeconomic Status
Fathers of these children would generally hold medium-to-low occupational status positions with corresponding incomes.

C. Religion (family place of origin is based on father)
    No Religion Indicated   120
    Buddhist   118 (41 Mainland; 71 Taiwanese; 6 origin unknown)
    Catholic   25 (20 Mainland; 3 Taiwanese; 2 origin unknown)
    Protestant   67 (40 Mainland; 25 Taiwanese; 2 origin unknown)

D. Family Size
Fifty-one children have grandfather, grandmother, or both living with them, as follows:

Grandfather living with family   26
Grandmother living with family   39
Grandfather and Grandmother both
living with family   14

Number of responses indicating
a brother in the family   284
Number of responses indicating
a sister in the family   262
Number of only children   21

II. City Private School (172 responses)
    A. Family Origin
        Mainland Father   155
        Taiwanese Father   14
        Father's Origin Unknown 3

        Mainland Mother   151
        Taiwanese Mother   16
        Mother's Origin Unknown 5

Mainland Father (155) with:
    Mainland Wife   146
    Taiwanese Wife   8
    Don't Know   1

Taiwanese Father (14) with:
    Mainland Wife   4
    Taiwanese Wife   8
    Don't Know   2

B. Socioeconomic Status
    Fathers of these children would generally hold medium-to-high occupational status positions with corresponding incomes.

C. Religion (family place of origin is based on father)
    No Religion Indicated   69
    Buddhist   21 (17 Mainland; 4 Taiwanese)
    Catholic   29 (28 Mainland; 1 Taiwanese)
    Protestant   53 (49 Mainland; 3 Taiwanese;
                                 1 origin unknown)

D. Family Size
    Thirty-eight children have grandfather, grandmother, or both living with them, as follows:

    Grandfather living with family   17
    Grandmother living with family   35
    Grandfather and Grandmother
    both living with family   14

    Number of responses indicating a brother
    in the family   125
    Number of responses indicating a sister
    in the family   112
    Number of only children   18

III. Country Public School (193 responses)

  A. Family Origin
      Mainland Father   72
      Taiwanese Father   108
      Father's Origin Unknown 13

      Mainland Mother   56

Taiwanese Mother   121
Mother's Origin Unknown   16

Mainland Father (72) with:
   Mainland Wife   53
   Taiwanese Wife   16
   Don't Know   3

Taiwanese Father (108) with:
   Mainland Wife   3
   Taiwanese Wife   104
   Don't Know   1

B. Socioeconomic Status

Fathers of these children would generally hold low-to-medium occupational status positions with corresponding incomes. (The assistant principal at this school estimated that one third of the children's fathers were in industry and the rest in farming. Agricultural incomes are reputed to be relatively high in Taiwan. My estimate is perhaps too low, therefore, and may be a reflection more of appearances than actuality.)

C. Religion (family place of origin is based on father)

No Religion Indicated   124
Buddhist   33 (12 Mainland; 21 Taiwanese)
Catholic   35 (26 Mainland; 8 Taiwanese;
                     1 origin unknown)
Protestant   1 (1 Taiwanese)

D. Family Size

Twenty-two children have a grandfather, grandmother or both living with them, as follows:

Grandfather living with family   11
Grandmother living with family   17
Grandfather and Grandmother
both living with family   6

Number of responses indicating
a brother in the family   136
Number of responses indicating
a sister in the family   139
Number of only children   34

Appendix 2
Educational Materials

Many years ago William Owen Jones of the *Nebraska State Journal* wrote: "I received more inspiration from McGuffey's Readers than from any other books in my experience. I can still quote pages from their selections. I asked the people around a dinner table last night what books had influenced them most in early life. A majority declared for McGuffey's Reader, the Fifth."[1] John H. Clarke, a justice of the Supreme Court, 1916–1922, gave decisions based on the readers. He wrote: "The selections in these Readers were for the most part serious and of real worth. Oftentimes expressions, even yet, come into my mind, which very certainly are derived from them."[2]

McGuffey's Readers were first published in 1836 and were still sold in 1927. They were what Mark Sullivan called "a kind of American Confucius," taking sayings from the lore of the race. Several generations of Americans grew to adulthood learning, often by rote, such values as pride of country and of "integrity, honesty, industry, temperance, true patriotism, courage, politeness, and all other moral and intellectual virtues. . . ."[3] The writers of these textbooks were concerned about the key position textbooks occupy in the formation of the national spirit. They wrote also of filial respect of teachers and of the value of unquestioning obedience to one's father. Moreover, Sullivan tells us that "The children of that generation were not permitted to speak their minds openly, were required to act as if they believed."[4]

There is a curious similarity between the values the young of industrializing America were taught and the values the young of industrializing Taiwan learn. There are, of course, differences, one of the greatest being that all schools in America were not required to use

1. Mark Sullivan, *Our Times,* vol. 2 (New York: Charles Scribner's Sons, 1927), p. 13.
2. *Ibid.,* p. 13.
3. *Ibid.,* p. 7.
4. *Ibid.,* p. 111.

McGuffey and all teachers were not required to give the same interpretation of the Readers; this is not true of the materials used in Taiwan.

It may be true, as Greenstein has pointed out, that there is in America "little formal adult effort to shape the political information and attitudes of grade school children,"[5] yet any analysis of McGuffey's Readers will reveal how important our immediate ancestors considered the learning of proper attitudes toward authority to be. We are not less concerned today although our efforts (and perhaps our need) are less bald and uncompromising, for specific political learning is the icing on the cake, so to speak. The styles and goals of formal political education will be meaningless to most people unless they are reinforced in other areas of one's life. Crucial political attitudes are only partially acquired as a function of some specific textbook learning task. Total political attitudes are actually a composite of values acquired in many disparate situations.

Frequency of themes in a textbook is an unreliable guide for determining what values are widely held by children.[6] The frequency gives an indication of what values adults believe to be important, but with regard to the education of children, such a tabulation is nothing more or less than a statistic revealing frequency of exposure. The effectiveness of such value training can be understood only after an examination of many facets of children's lives.

Chiang Kai-shek is the unchallenged authority on the direction education should take in Taiwan. His directives have the following ring: "Let me indicate the subject matters to be taught in respect to the different aspects of the Min Sheng type of education. It is hoped that Chinese educators will make further detailed studies on the basis of the few comments which I shall offer. . . ."[7] Acknowledging that the family is the cornerstone of the nation, Chiang states that in school

the promotion of civic education must pay special attention to the teaching of "Chinese History" and "Chinese Geography," for it is only through them that the student's patriotic fervor and national pride can be really aroused, that he can be made to realize the fundamental significance of the basic virtues of loyalty,

5. Fred I. Greenstein, "The Benevolent Leader: Children's Images of Political Authority," *American Political Science Review*, vol. 54 (Dec. 1960), p. 940.

6. Milton C. Albrecht, "Does Literature Reflect Common Values?" *American Sociological Review*, vol. 21, no. 6 (Dec. 1956), p. 729.

7. Chiang Kai-shek, "Chapters on National Fecundity, Social Welfare, Education, and Health and Happiness," as supplements to Sun Yat-sen, *San Min Chu I* (Taipei, Taiwan: China Publishing Co., n. d.), p. 271.

filial piety, humanity, love, honesty, justice, peace and harmony as well as those of propriety, righteousness, incorruptibility and honor, and that he can be taught to become a citizen who loves his country more than his own life.[8]

The Minister of Education, Yen Cheng-hsin, has pointed out that education must emphasize the development of morals, learning, health, and groupness. These goals, he said, are based upon the constitution (Art. 158) and the writings of Chiang—two sources which are completely sufficient in themselves to show the direction to be taken. Based on them, education must emphasize the development of national consciousness, the spirit of self-control, national morals, good health, science, and wisdom and ability for living.[9]

Chiang Kai-shek has repeatedly addressed himself to education and bases himself, whether right or wrong, on his concept of the notion of political tutelage handed him by Sun Yat-sen. Chiang sees education as a force for change, and it is not surprising, therefore, that educational doctrine should stress that family education be brought into line with school education and that, as one educator puts it, "School and society ought not to take a stand-off attitude but ought to change opinions and intimately cooperate."[10] Chiang's concepts, however, do not simply give the state an active role in changing opinion—the direction of change is also specified. Traditionalist in outlook, these concepts emphasize

8. *Ibid.*, p. 276.

9. Editional, *Chung-yang Jih-pao* 中央日報 [Central Daily News], no. 13702 (April 15, 1966), p. 2. It is interesting to compare these goals with the code of conduct for elementary school pupils issued by the Ministry of Education of the Chinese Communist Government in 1955. The first three (of twenty) rules are as follows:

1. Strive to be a good student—good in health, good in studies, and good in character. Prepare to serve the Fatherland of the people.
2. Respect the national flag. Respect and love the leader of the people.
3. Obey the instructions of the principal and teachers. Protect and promote the reputation of the school and of the class.

Shades of leader loyalty, group emphasis, and "proper" conduct! Rules 14 and 15 stress respect and love of parents and respect for the aged. (It is not known whether these rules were ranked in an order of priority.) From Theodore H. E. Chen, "Elementary Education in Communist China," *The China Quarterly*, no. 10 (April–June 1962).

10. Kung Pao-shan 龔寶善, *Tao-te Chiao-yü Shih-shih Luen* 道德教育實施論 [A Discussion of the Practical Application of Morals Education], (Taipei, Taiwan, 1962), p. 70. 國立敎育資料館.

inculcating a pride in the past, a return to Confucian virtues, and a restoration of the traditional system of group responsibility as a basis for national reconstruction and economic development. The child must learn, Chiang says, "The position and responsibilities of the family in relation to society and the nation; an ethical view based upon the assumption that the family is the foundation of the state."[11] He must learn "The family organization and the student's relationship with his kith and kin; the importance to the student of the 'six rules of conduct' —filial piety, fraternal affection, neighborliness, love of kindred, sense of duty, and philanthropy."[12]

Chiang's viewpoint reflects a tradition as old as Mencius that objective circumstances are all important and that the duty of families to educate children in a proper way and in a proper environment is imperative because the child's nature will become vicious without proper training.[13] The value of ideology as an instrument of control has also been recognized through much of Chinese history. Wilhelm quotes a K'ang-hsi edict of 1670 as saying: "In my endeavor to bring about supreme control in the world, laws and regulations are not my only concern, but I put transformation through indoctrination first."[14] All of this is still clearly evident today. In an interview with Professor Wu Ting, chairman of the committee in charge of compiling textbooks for elementary education in the Ministry of Education, he said that the goals of education, beset though they had been by the disorders of thirty years of strife, were still Confucian in nature and emphasized a progression from rule-the-family to govern-the-state to peace-in-the-world.

Professor Wu Ting went on to say that the emphasis today, however, was on shifting prime loyalty from small groups to large groups, from the family to the state. The mechanism for doing this is morals training, as was clearly outlined by the Minister of Education in an editorial in the *Central Daily News*.[15] There Minister Yen Cheng-hsin, emphasizing

11. Chiang Kai-shek, "Chapters on National Fecundity," p. 273.

12. *Ibid.*

13. Meng Mu San Ch'ien 孟母三遷 is an old proverb about how Mencius's mother moved three times in order to find the most suitable environment for her son's education.

14. Helmut Wilhelm, "Chinese Confucianism on the Eve of the Great Encounter," in *Changing Japanese Attitudes toward Modernization*, Marius B. Jansen, ed. (Princeton, N.J.: Princeton University Press, 1965), p. 285.

15. *Chung-yang Jih-pao* 中央日報 [Central Daily News], no. 13702 (April 15, 1966), p. 2.

that the goals of education were based on two main sources—the constitution and the works of Chiang Kai-shek—stated that the first of the basic principles of education was to stress equally the development of morals, learning, health, and group consciousness. Morals, says one educational source, are an integral part of group consciousness, and therefore "morals are the most important part of school educational content."[16] Indeed, says another source, while the goal in America is merely to "enlarge the child's experience of social life in order to create a good citizen of the country," China's goal is "to follow practical citizenship morals, loving and protecting the country and its people, bringing to light the inherent culture, creating and establishing the state, promoting common trust and confidence."[17]

Japanese Influences

These educational concepts, fortuitously for the mainland leaders, were promulgated to a population already familiar with many of these same values. As a colony of Japan for fifty years, most Taiwanese were conditioned to Japanese educational goals under which morals courses dealing with family and state ethics were mandatory and indeed "were worked into the curriculum and into school life in any way the ingenuity of the educators could devise. . . ."[18] Children were left under no illusion that the education they received was for the "sake of the country."[19]

Training was carried out, we are told, with the utmost gravity. Children were told that they were Japanese living in a part of Japan (they had no knowledge of China) and many of them took Japanese names in school. Discipline was rigorous—as it still is—with the children made to sit straight, to bow when required, and to submit to corporal punishment if necessary. The teachers for their part were subservient to the principal, serving him as necessary and bowing as etiquette required. The habits of violence and student action, so characteristic

16. Kung Pao-shan, *Tao-te Chiao-yü Shih-shih Luen*, pp. 5–6, 29.

17. Wu Yuan-chieh, ed., *Hsiao-hsueh She-hui-k'o Chiao-hsueh-fa* [Teaching Methods for Elementary School Social Studies] (Taipai, Taiwan, 1961), p. 16.

18. Herbert Passin, "Japan," in *Education and Political Development*, James S. Coleman, ed. (Princeton, N.J.: Princeton University Press, 1965). p. 308.

19. Herbert Passin, "Modernization and the Japanese Intellectual: Some Comparative Observations," in *Changing Japanese Attitudes toward Modernization*, Marius B. Jansen, ed. (Princeton, N.J.: Princeton University Press, 1965), p. 467.

of this period on the Mainland, were lacking, and this discipline should contribute in no small measure to an explanation of why the Taiwanese accepted a new and, as it developed, distasteful change of fortune with such stoicism.[20]

The Ministry of Education and Educational Budgets

In implementing its educational policies the government has developed one of the most centralized educational systems in the world. This does not imply simplicity of administrative structure, however, for the presence on the island of both a national and provincial government complicates and obscures the lines of control. It is perhaps for this reason that many people feel the Ministry of Education exists only to carry out the will of the President. This, of course, is not strictly true, although as the remarks of Minister Yen Cheng-hsin would indicate, people in the ministry base their policies and objectives on the broad directives and outlines that come from above.

The Central Ministry of Education, under the Executive Yuan, has the power to make broad educational policies, select textbooks, set the standards for both educational content and the hiring of teachers, and generally supervise national education. In practice its administrative control is far more direct. The Minister of Education is the chief educational administrative officer; under him, in a staff position, is a political Vice Minister responsible for political matters, and below both are the various departments of the ministry. One of these is the Department of Elementary Education, which has the responsibility for all training through grade six. There are parent-teacher associations, and parents are encouraged to take an interest in educational matters (some of these groups are reasonably influential), but they do not have the power to challenge the directives of the ministry. In any case there is no precedence for this since education in China was traditionally left in the hands of the school master. This does not exempt parents from

20. Although I believe Japanese influence was distinctly beneficial to the Kuomintang in many ways, this influence is often used today as a catch-all for explaining the ills of society. For instance, a Taiwanese professor and student told me they cared nothing about the Kuomintang regime's goals for recovery of the Mainland. When I mentioned this to a mainland friend, he was shocked, declaring it to be a minority viewpoint that might have been prevalent several years ago. Education has been so effective, he went on, that these traces of "Japanese influence" have largely disappeared.

being dunned, however, if the funds allocated by the government to the schools are insufficient.

Budgeting for education is a major problem, aggravated by the decision at the highest levels to emphasize defense-related expenditures over other sectors, with the result that allocations to education in the central government budget are often not met, leaving the provincial and country-city government levels to carry most of the financial burden. With a large relative increase in population and the necessity to build new schools to meet the increased number of students, the shortage of teachers and the need for more school space are acutely felt and vocally and editorially expressed.[21] The problem, as much as anything, is that even if the educational sector received its total budgeted amount (15 percent of the central government budget, 25 percent of the provincial government budget, and 35 percent of the country-city government budgets according to exhibit data of the Ministry of Education), many officials feel the percentage allotted education is still far too small.

Some realization of the scope of education comes out when one notes there are approximately 2,200,000 elementary students attending roughly 2100 schools.[22] Education is compulsory through the first six years. It is financial pressure, more than any other factor, that limits the number of students who go on to middle school to 54 percent of those who graduate from elementary school.[23]

Control in the Schools

In the National Ministry there is one subsection that has authority for composing textbooks. The National Ministry authorizes the textbooks, and the provincial government has the responsibility for publishing

21. Ministry of Education data estimate a 91.7 percent increase in the number of elementary schools since 1945. The figure seems questionable, based on my personal observations, but there has undoubtedly been a great effort made to alleviate the shortage.

22. Ministry of Education exhibit data. Of students in general 2 percent are in kindergarten, 76 percent are in elementary school, 20 percent in secondary school and 2 percent at higher educational levels.

23. *Ibid.* The percentage who go on to middle school varies in different parts of the island. In Taipei, according to the ministry, 70 percent continue their education, although there is 100 percent capacity for them to do so. This indicates that other factors, such as the need in families for more income earners or a disbelief in the value of education beyond the elementary level for females, are contributing factors to the dropout rate.

them, the stories having first to be submitted to, and passed on, by a committee of educational scholars. In most Asian countries the central government compiles and authorizes the publication of a list of textbooks. Among non-Communist Asian nations, however, it is only in Afghanistan, Korea, Viet Nam, Nepal, and Taiwan that local people have no right to choose books they might wish to use from an approved general list.[24] Control of educational materials in these countries is rigidly enforced for all types and levels of schools.

Control is exercised not simply over publications, however. A corresponding check is kept upon the principals and teachers themselves. There are frequent visits by the authorities to the schools, and principals are held responsible for infractions that are discovered. Inspectors from the national, provincial, and local levels come regularly to both public and private schools to see that the proper materials are being used and that teaching is being carried out according to the texts.

Elementary schools in Taiwan have a more complex internal hierarchy than American schools. The principal is at the top of an elaborate administrative structure (necessitated to some degree by the size of the schools), at the bottom of which are the teachers. These latter receive a starting salary of roughly $20 per month, in addition to which they receive benefits that frequently include free lodging and food rations. Teachers are graduated from normal schools and are generally appointed by the ministry to their jobs based on their previous performance in school.[25] A principal sometimes has the power to hire and fire his staff and faculty, but the more normal method is for this function to be carried out by the educational authorities at the local level. While male teachers at all levels of education outnumber females by two to one, the ratio is slightly in favor of females at the elementary level. Men, however, monopolize the administrative positions and are generally used in the upper grades (five and six) because they can obtain more money for their

24. *Education in Asia*, Ministry of Education, Tokyo, Japan, 1964, pp. 140–142. Such tight control was not always so. According to one middle school teacher, schools could select their own textbooks until seven to eight years ago.

25. One very harmful effect of this is that most good prospective teachers apply to work in the cities. Country children have teachers of considerably less quality. The ministry encourages new teachers to work in the countryside but does not order them there if their standing is high and a city position is vacant for which they have applied.

families at that level by giving private supplementary lessons to pre-pare children for the admission exams to middle school.

According to my observation, most teachers are highly dedicated people. Their conformity to the system is less a matter of external pressure than a sincere desire to do their job well. It must be remembered, after all, that most of the young teachers are products of the same system. While the individual teaching styles I observed differed markedly, conformity in educational content was maintained not simply by the teacher's desire to do his job well. Competitive tests between classes, based on centrally set exams, are run by the principals to maintain quality and at these tests—three per term—teachers must exchange classrooms. This, according to one teacher, is the most effective check that correct use is being made of the textbooks. But parents also will exert pressure on the teacher if he does not sufficiently emphasize the materials that will help children do well on their examinations, for despite what parents may think of the materials themselves (and many adults voice quite negative opinions), they must, for the sake of their children's future (which depends critically on educational level and performance), encourage the learning of these materials.

School Plant and Educational Content

Schools in Taiwan are quite large, many of them having been designed by the Japanese to be used as barracks in case of emergency. Almost all schools are "national" (public), although they may be financed by local funds, but there are some private schools, and a very few provincial schools, which were established very early to meet the needs of children from the Mainland whose education might have suffered when the language of education was changed from Japanese to Mandarin.[26] Certain private schools are generally considered the best, in that their students do comparatively better on the middle school entrance exams. All children receive free textbooks, and at the public schools subsidies for poor families and free lunches may also be offered. Some schools serve as centers for training and disseminating information (on farming techniques, for instance) to the people in the local area.

26. The change to Mandarin was not made radically. Japanese and Taiwanese continued to be used in most schools during a transitional period while children learned the new language. Many Taiwanese children, I found, cannot speak Mandarin when they first attend school—they may be able to understand—and it takes about two months for them to adjust.

Children are not divided into classes on the basis of intellect, but they may be divided on the basis of sex, often at the fifth-grade level. An effort is made to keep the treatment of the sexes as equal as possible, and the division reflects an acknowledgment by the school authorities of the growing assertiveness of the boys. In any case classes for both sexes are conducted in the same way. (In the teachers' normal school girls are also required to have military training and participate in drill and rifle practice.) Starting in the first grade the children wear uniforms of a military type and have their number, by which they are sometimes identified, sewed on the front. Because of the pressure on classroom space[27] children from the first to as high as the fourth grade may be at school only half a day.

It may be that most developing countries have not pursued politicization of school curricula very rigorously, as Coleman says, but this is not true of Taiwan.[28] Citizenship and morals are highly emphasized. Civic training, in fact, actually permeates many of the other subjects. All levels of education receive instruction in this area, conveyed by the words and actions of the teachers, by slogans on the walls, by the textbooks, and by a variety of teaching aids.

Politically relevant training begins in Taiwan the moment children go to school. While the political content is rudimentary at first, children learn immediately about the President, who is held up for them as a model to be emulated. From the beginning stress is also put on those areas which the government considers important, such as anticommunism, the value of industrialism and science, and the value of education itself. It is true that the Nationalist leaders have a commitment to the values of traditional society but it is not true, as some analysts seem to imply, that such commitment has prevented them from emphasizing the excitement of learning, the role of education in increasing production, or the value of social acts outside the kinship group.[29] Indeed, in this sense both Nationalist and Communist Chinese educational patterns show very little similarity to the educational material used thrity years ago. Both are attempting to redefine the traditional bases of society.

27. The city public school I visited with 8600 students had approximately 2000 students fifteen to twenty years ago.

28. James S. Coleman, "Introduction: Education and Political Development" in *Education and Political Development*, Coleman, ed.

29. Richard H. Solomon, "Educational Themes in China's Changing Culture," *The China Quarterly*, no. 22 (April-June 1965), pp. 156–159, 162–164.

There is constant review and revising in order to bring educational content into line with government policy.

There is, in fact, probably no other topic in Taiwan which receives as much attention as education. Editorials are constantly written on the subject. Much of this comment, it is true, is criticism of the educational system. There are stories of children being punished too harshly, expressions of concern over the high dropout rate, worry about whether enough encouragement is being given to student participation, and, most of all, there are articles crying out against the long hours children must spend in school and against the pressure of the cramming sessions when children begin to prepare for the middle school exams. But the underlying thread is always the desire to see education better serve the needs of a rapidly changing society.

The following few sections give an analysis of educational materials and schedules. Teachers' manuals, civic education, and a frequency count of topics in the textbooks are included.

I. Actual Minutes per Week Children Spend on a Given Subject (City Public School)

There is a discrepancy between what the school teaches the children and what is required by the Ministry of Education regulations. The discrepancy occurs because of overcrowding, with the result that many children cannot spend all day in school. An effort is made to give all children the regulation amount of training in reading and arithmetic.

A. First and Second Grade

Subject Matter	Minutes per Week
Citizenship and Morals	120
Singing, Dancing, etc.	150
Work (making toys, etc.)	90
Reading, Writing	390
Arithmetic	60
Common Sense (learning about fruits, health, trees, seasons, inks, pencils, occupations, etc.)	120
Group Activities (exercising, how to march, get in line, etc.)	90

B. Third and Fourth Grade

Subject Matter	Minutes per Week
Citizenship and Morals	120
Music	60
Gym	90
Art	60
Project Work	60
Speaking (telling stories)	30
Reading, Characters	270
Composition	60
Brush Work	30
Arithmetic	180
Social Studies	60
Natural Studies	90
Group Activities	90

C. Fifth and Sixth Grade

Citizenship and Morals	180
Music	90
Gym	150
Speaking	30
Reading	270
Composition	90
Brushwork	60
Arithmetic	180
Abacus	30
Geography	60
History	60
Natural Studies	120
Art	60
Project Work	90
Group Activity	120
Weekend Group Activity	60
Self-Criticism and Group Criticism	30

II. Citizenship Training

While citizenship (as noted in Section I) is a separate category of learning, it is also included in much of the subject matter of other areas.

Educators are very specific about this. It has been stated, for instance, that social studies is important precisely because it includes citizenship training and is the basis of citizenship.[30] An attempt is made to integrate lessons in various categories of learning so that at any particular time a certain theme will be stressed and reinforced in several areas. Such disparate areas of learning as citizenship, literature, art, and nature studies are coordinated. Certain materials, because of their relative complexity, must be introduced gradually, but citizenship training, according to educators, can and should start in the first grade.[31] The goal of citizenship and morals training is, among other things, the "nurturing of a happy group spirit of cooperation."[32]

The lesson standard for citizenship and morals itself is broken down into three parts: (1) building character (thought); (2) having good daily habits (action); (3) being a good citizen and contributing. In outlines for course presentation, materials for (1) and (3) are usually combined, while (2) is treated separately. All materials are broken into sections which individually constitute about two weeks' training material. The sections themselves are subdivided into finer subheadings which serve as the lesson topics for the various levels of grades—lower (first and second grade), middle (third and fourth grade), and upper (fifth and sixth grade). The morning orations which the principal gives frequently have relevance to a section which the classes can later individually discuss according to their grade level. The topics include such items as honesty, hard work, creativity, filiality, brotherly love, neighborliness, cooperation, benevolence, what is shameful, responsibility, guarding the laws, patriotism, and peace. There is, it is believed, a natural progression in these items which is usually followed in the talks, although this is up to the discretion of the school authorities.[33]

Under the section "patriotism" the topics for lower grades are: "I respect the flag," "I respect the President," and "I like to use the products of my country." Topics for middle grades are: "I am not

30. Wu Yuan-chieh, ed., *Hsiao-hsueh She-hui-k'o Chiao-hsueh-fa*, p. 12.

31. Suen Pang-cheng, ed., 孫邦正編著 *Hsiao-hsueh Tu-shu Chiao-hsueh-fa* 小學讀書教學法 [Methods for Teaching, Reading in Elementary School], (Taiwan, 1961) 國立教育資料館.

32. Wu Yuan-chieh, ed., *Hsiao-hsueh She-hui-k'o Chiao-hsueh-fa*, p. 8.

33. *Kuo-min Hsueh hsiao, K'o-ch'eng Piao-chun* [Curriculum Standards for National (Elementary) Schools] (Taipei, Taiwan: Cheng Chung Book Co., 1962), pp. 13–23.

frightened when a crisis occurs" and "I respect the great people in my country's history." Upper-grade children discuss topics such as: "I wish to use my full strength to serve the country," "I give special attention to guarding defense secrets," "I wish to join in the activities of the glorious and respected military," and "I deeply believe that the Three Principles of the People is the ideology for saving the country."

Under the section "guarding the laws" little children study "I respect and guard the school's regulations." Middle grades cover "I want to respect and guard the regulations of public places," while upper grades study "I know the duty the people have to pay taxes and serve in the military."

Under "cooperation" lower grades study "I enthusiastically join in the group activities of the school," middle grades cover "I carry out the wishes of the group," while upper grades learn "We want to have public feelings and forget private feelings."

Under "honesty" the topic for upper grades is "I can frankly recognize my own failings and moreover can conceive of ways to correct them."

Citizenship books, which children begin to use in the upper grades, have their lessons divided into distinct categories. Here again one can note a steadily increasing emphasis on the society and nation rather than on the individual and family.[34]

Table A2–1
Citizenship Lessons by Category

Grade	Individual	Family	School	Society	Nation	World
5	3	3	5	4	0	0
6	0	0	2	3	7	4

Most authorities state that one goal of citizenship is to teach the children democracy (including free speech, free elections, etc.) as the ideal political system for the modern society they envision. The full implementation of democratic practices, they say, is impeded now only by the special circumstances and necessities associated with the civil war with the Communists. There is considerable emphasis in the citizenship courses on elections and citizen rights.

Yet far more than an emphasis on rights and freedoms in the citizenship courses is the emphasis on duties and obligations—the duty to serve one's country and to pay taxes, and the obligation to be loyal and un-

---

34. Wu Yuan-chieh, ed., *Hsiao-hsueh She-hui-k'o Chiao-hseuh-fa,* pp. 19–20.

questioning. This latter type of emphasis is explicit in much course work and implicit in the educational process itself. Children's responses to the various questionnaires all show conclusively, I believe, how responses emphasizing duty, obligation, and proper behavior have been internalized and generally override notions of individual rights or freedom.

In *The Civic Culture* Gabriel Almond and Sidney Verba came to the cautious conclusion that "If an individual has had an opportunity to participate in the family, in school, or at work, he is more likely than someone who did not have the same opportunities to consider himself competent to influence the government."[35] In all the societies they studied they found "that a family that is open to reciprocal discussion of political issues provides a type of political socialization that enables children to develop *within the family itself* a sense of political competence and obligation, and to learn to tolerate the ambiguities of politics and political controversy."[36] The authors discuss two types of political competence—citizen competence and subject competence. Citizen competence is where the "competent citizen has a role in the formation of general policy. Furthermore, he plays an *influential* role in this decision-making process. . . ."[37] In subject competence, however, the individual "does not participate in making rules, nor does his participation involve the use of political influence"; his competence "is more a matter of being aware of his rights under the rules than of participating in the making of the rules."[38] While there is some training in citizen competence in Taiwan, the major thrust of citizenship training is the development of competent subjects.

III. Teachers' Manuals

The lessons in the primers are designed so that one theme will serve as a central focal point for several lessons and subject materials. The object is to take similar subject material and, by putting it together, give the children a deeper understanding of one question and a means for

35. Gabriel A. Almond and Sidney Verba, *The Civic Culture* (Boston: Little, Brown and Company, 1965), p. 300.

36. *Ibid.*, p. 334 (italics in original).

37. *Ibid.*, p. 168 (italics in original).

38. *Ibid.*, pp. 168–169. For a discussion in this general vein see also Robert Le Vine, "Political Socialization and Cultural Change," in *Old Societies and New States*, Clifford Geertz, ed. (New York: Free Press of Glencoe, 1963), p. 296.

heightening comparative awareness of the merits of each lesson.[39] In order to facilitate these objectives a teacher's guide book has been compiled. Each lesson is discussed and the teacher instructed on how to teach the relevant theme. Emphasis is placed on the points of stress, the goal of the lesson, how much time to use, how to prepare, and what teaching aids to employ. All teachers are expected to use these guides.

Following are some suggested teaching aids and hints, plus capsule comments on the themes of the stories as the educational authorities see them, for the reading primer, book 5, which is used in the first term of third grade:[40]

A.   Lessons 1 and 2: The main theme is diligence.
B.   Lessons 3 and 4: The main themes are cooperation and guarding the law. Children are to learn the spirit of orderliness, discipline, and the strength of group life.
C.   Lessons 5 through 8: The main themes are tactfulness and taking heed. Children learn not to be discouraged over difficulty but to think of a way to solve the problem. They learn to observe carefully, industriously study and plan before doing.
D.   Lessons 9 through 12: The main theme is to liberate and save our compatriots on the Mainland. The central morals are bravery, benevolence, faithfulness, reverence, and uprightness. Oppression on the Mainland and the brutality of the Communists should be stressed. This is to be contrasted with life in Taiwan and with the helpfulness of the Nationalist military. An attempt should be made to increase the children's sympathy for the Mainlanders and to develop a determination to oppose the Chinese Communists and resist the Russians. Visual aids should be used, including pictures of Chiang Kai-shek's life.
E.   Lessons 13 through 16: The main theme is great love. Stress is put on the love between parents and children and between brothers. Posters should be used saying: "I want to follow the teachings of my parents," "I want to work industriously to be a good child and not make my parents angry," and "There is mutual love between brothers."[41]

39.   Suen Pang-cheng, ed., *Hsiao-hsueh Tu-shu Chiao-hsueh-fa*, p. 29.

40.   Taiwan-sheng Cheng-fu Chiao-yu-t'ing Chu-pien, *Kuo-yu Chiao-hsueh Chih-yin, Ch'u-chi Ti-wu-ts'e*, 臺灣省政府教育廳主編, 國語教學指引, 初級第五冊 [Office of Education of the Taiwan provincial government, ed., A guide for Teaching Mandarin, Beginner's book 5] (Taiwan n.d.) 臺灣書店印行.

41.   *Ibid.*, p. 174.

F. Lessons 17 through 20: The theme is industry and learning to stick to a task until the obstacles are overcome. Use your brain and you will succeed. Posters to be used should say: "I am happy to serve my country and society," "When I meet trouble I don't lose heart but industriously work to overcome it," and "Industry is the mother of invention."[42]

G. Lessons 21 through 24: The central theme is exercising the body. Suitable posters would be; "Exercise every day," "Failure is the mother of success. If you fear to fail, then you will never have the opportunity to succeed," and "Everyone's body must always work and then it can have strong health; bodies with strong health can then work for the country."[43]

H. Lessons 25 and 26: The main theme is the New Year's holiday.

I. Lessons 27 through 30: The main theme is to love the country loyally and bravely. Children are to be taught that they are an important part of society and cannot, "even from when they are little, prevent themselves from being of use to all. [They are urged] not to fear difficulty but to have the spirit for laborious struggle and brave sacrifice. Everyone must be willing to sacrifice everything in order to fulfill that which is of use to the country and the people."[44] This spirit must be developed from the time children are small so that they will manifest it as adults. But children can have the same goals in their own age group and organizations. Teaching aids should include stories of Sun Yat-sen and Chiang Kai-shek.

IV. Textbook Themes

Parents sometimes mention how uninteresting children find the content of the elementary school texts, a matter of some importance, since lack of interest may affect the internalization of the themes of the educational materials. While one cannot assume any direct relationship between educational content and children's attitudes—the latter must be determined by separate analysis—an analysis of educational materials can reveal some insight into the values of the adults who control the educational system.

Elementary texts are constantly revised. The following analysis is

42. *Ibid.*, p. 224.
43. *Ibid.*, p. 260.
44. *Ibid.*, p. 315.

based upon those editions published just prior to the latest revised texts, some volumes of which were being sold to the children beginning in 1965. Changes in the revisions were relatively few in number and the style of presentation remained virtually unchanged.

A committee of roughly twenty members compiles the textbooks on the basis of broad guidelines set down in Ministry of Education directives. These directives state that a certain percentage of stories at any grade level must deal with specific themes. The committee follows this directive, but the order of the stories, as well as the particular stories that are used, is based on the choices of the individual committee members. However, if a revision is made, the new story or altered story is submitted to the entire committee. If other members disapprove of the change, then the story will go back to the author for rewriting.

The lessons, with their moral injunctions, are consciously selected. Book 5, for instance, starts with two lessons on diligence (time and its value) because the children are just returning after vacation. The next two lessons continue with a stress on cooperation and orderliness. Even the cover receives attention. The flag on the cover of the first through fourth grade reading textbooks is put there purposely to draw a connection between children's groups and the flag. Another aim of the stories is to introduce the most commonly used Chinese characters.

The analysis of the elementary school reading textbooks which follows is based upon categories which I myself determined. A story was listed as having this or that particular attribute if, in my subjective opinion, its theme or presentation corresponded with a particular category. Percentages may not add up to 100 percent in any section because the lesson material (1) may have been listed under more than one category or (2) may not have been listed at all if the lesson's theme did not coincide with a subcategory in any section. Percentages indicate only what percent of total stories in any particular year contain a particular theme or orientation. Under the category of Main Moral Themes I used the following subheadings to help me define the theme of a story:

Respect—obedience, deference, politeness, filiality
Self-discipline—responsibleness, orderliness, value of time
Achievement—value of learning, competitiveness, perseverance,
    willingness to work
Value of Intelligence—using one's head to solve problems
Affect—kindness, love, forgiveness
Patriotism—love of country or culture

Group—helpfulness, loyalty, cohesiveness
Hostility—revenge, defiance, hatred of outsiders
Bravery—courage
Other

Table A2-2
Analysis of the Content of the Elementary School Reading Textbooks: Percent

Category	Precharacter Reader	Grade 1	2	3	4	5	6	Total*
A. Type of Story								
Political Symbols and Institutions	0	9	2	0	8	2	8	5 (16)
Policy Oriented								
Anticommunism	0	0	5	10	12	10	13	8 (27)
Praise Nationalist Army	0	0	2	2	5	0	4	3 (9)
Leader Cult—Chiang Kai-shek or Sun Yat-sen	0	0	8	10	10	4	4	3 (9)
Government Reforms	0	0	0	0	5	2	0	1 (4)
Mainland Recovery	0	0	0	0	7	10	6	3 (12)
Health and Safety	0	15	10	5	2	0	2	6 (19)
Practical Knowledge	90	2	2	8	5	8	2	5 (16)+
Science and Industry	0	0	0	8	10	10	13	6 (22)
Moralistic	5	69	78	61	63	64	67	63 (218)
Other	5	9	0	7	2	8	2	5 (16)
B. Main Participant(s)								
Individual	15	9	28	32	32	25	27	25 (87)
Family	35	41	23	32	20	8	0	22 (75)
Group (not family)	45	48	52	42	38	54	60	48 (165)
Other	0	0	0	2	18	13	17	8 (27)
C. Main Moral Themes								
Respect	0	11	7	8	7	2	13	7 (25)
Self-discipline	0	13	7	7	2	17	4	8 (26)
Achievement	0	17	23	23	28	40	17	23 (80)
Value of Intelligence	0	0	13	17	0	2	4	6 (21)
Affect	0	11	2	10	5	15	10	8 (27)
Patriotism	0	7	10	20	15	21	27	15 (53)
Group	0	26	28	20	35	15	33	25 (85)
Hostility	5	2	5	18	7	21	19	11 (39)
Bravery	0	0	10	18	10	31	27	15 (51)
Other	0	0	17	5	2	6	6	6 (20)

Table A2–2 (Continued)
Analysis of the Content of the Elementary School Reading Textbooks: Percent

Category	Precharacter Reader	Grade						Total*
		1	2	3	4	5	6	
D. Contemporary Setting	100	100	75	80	78	79	63	79(274)
E. Hierarchical Social Order	55	30	26	33	32	33	48	45(154)
F. Authority Figure Stressed								
Father	0	9	7	17	13	10	2	9 (32)
Mother	30	22	7	8	10	4	4	10 (35)
Other Family	5	0	2	0	0	2	2	1 (4)
Educational	20	9	12	2	5	13	0	8 (26)
Peer	0	0	0	0	0	0	2	.3 (1)
Political	0	0	0	7	8	10	33	9 (30)
Other	0	0	2	0	2	2	4	1 (5)
G. Attitude of Authority Figure								
Benevolent	55	30	26	25	28	23	40	30(103)
Nonbenevolent	0	0	0	8	2	6	6	4 (13)
Neutral	0	0	0	0	0	2	2	1 (2)
H. Total No. of Stories	20	46	60	60	60	48	48	(342)

* Numbers in Parentheses following total percentages refer to the actual number of stories having such content.

+ Not including Precharacter reader.

V. Proverbs

Under the assumption that much everyday educational content at home and among peers is condensed into shorthand expressions of high meaning and often high emotional content, an analysis was made of commonly used Chinese proverbs. I asked two Chinese friends to examine independently a book of commonly used proverbs and select those which, in their opinion, were most frequently used.[45] By this method I obtained a list of 250 proverbs (from an original selection of 440) and analyzed them according to five general categories: (1) stress on means

45. Kao Mo-yeh and Chou Lo-shan, eds. 高莫野, 周樂山 *Ch'eng-yu Ku-shih,* 成語故事 [Proverb Stories] (Kaohsiung, Taiwan, 1964) 正言出版社印行 [Cheng Yen Publishing Co.].

to achieve some goal; (2) stress on limits for obtaining some goal; (3) stress on praising some type of behavior; (4) stress on condemning some type of behavior; and (5) other.

The results of this analysis, given in Table A2–3 indicated that no content category was of outstanding significance.

Table A2–3
Analysis of the Content of Commonly Used Chinese Proverbs

Category	Percent	Number
A. Means to Achieve Some Goal		
Careful Preparation	4	10
Perseverance	3	8
Possession of Intelligence and Ability	6	15
Other	0.4	1
B. Limits on Obtaining Some Goal		
Failure	2	5
Lack of Perseverance	2	5
There Is a Natural Limit for Everything— Don't Go beyond	2	6
Objective Circumstances Are Greater than One's Subjective Viewpoint	3	7
Changeability of Human Fortune	6	14
Luck	2	6
Omnipotence of the Leader	2	4
Other	0	0
C. Praise of Some Type of Behavior		
Loyalty to the Country	3	7
Loyalty to Friends or Family	6	14
Other—Goodness, Bravery, etc.	8	19
D. Condemnation of Some Type of Behavior		
Stupidity	6	16
Fear of Outsiders	1	3
Worthlessness	3	8
Other—Treachery, Suspicion, Pomposity, Arrogance (particularly about knowledge), etc.	19	48
E. Other	22	54

Questionnaire and Research Techniques

One of the difficulties associated with the field approach is that one observes the simultaneous influence of many variables and it is often difficult to identify, let alone isolate, which variables are crucial. Part of the difficulty can be alleviated by approaching the problem with sets of well-developed hypotheses concerning which are, and which are not, the crucial factors. Another method is through the use of several testing devices, by means of which consistent patterns of thought or action can be more readily isolated. Despite such precautions, however, some ambiguity is always likely to be present at this stage of our knowledge and development.

In addition to the problems associated with isolating crucial variables, there are those difficulties associated with administering questionnaires. These problems have been the subject of considerable investigation, and it is not my intention to repeat the findings of those who have worked in this area. Suffice it to say that the presence of an observer may alter certain behavior patterns and there may be biases introduced into responses (oral or written) through the subject's knowledge of being tested. Chinese psychologists have noted the particular tendency of Chinese subjects to mask the way they feel and to conform to what they believe are, in the opinion of the interviewer, approved responses. It is generally assumed by such specialists that these defense mechanisms are not strongly developed in children. Undoubtedly they exist to some degree, however. One of the best ways to overcome this difficulty is to utilize several testing techniques. In this way it is hoped that contradictions can be discovered and accounted for.

In addition to extensive observation both in and out of school, I utilized four different types of testing techniques. After adequate pretesting, these questionnaires were administered at the three schools where I conducted my main observations. In each class I attempted to familiarize the children with me by being with them for several days in advance of any tests. During this period I joined in all their activities and attempted to be as good a comrade as possible, doing magic shows, singing American songs, playing games, etc. Shortly before I departed from the class, I utilized approximately one hour of class time to give the tests. School authorities were somewhat reluctant to give me more time than this because of the study time that would be lost.

At the city public school, which I attended first, I administered during my first stay only the open-ended questionnaire. This was given to all the children in one class at each grade level. At the city private school and country public school I varied this procedure by asking two rows in a class to answer the open-ended questionnaire. The children in the remaining two rows wrote stories for me based on two large poster pictures (the projective test pictures) which I hung on the blackboard at the front of each row. Each row of children answering the projective test utilized one picture. This means that two pictures were responded to by first graders, two different pictures by second graders, while third graders responded to the same two as the first graders, and so on. When analyzing projective responses by age I divided the children into lower-, middle-, and upper-grade categories. This method proved to be both practical and satisfactory.

Several months later I returned to each of the three schools with the ten-picture cognitive association quiz (p. 185.). This was administered on a random basis to fifteen boys and fifteen girls in each grade in the classes I had previously attended. Several months later I again returned to the city public school for interviews utilizing the projective test picture posters. Interviews were held with four children each from grades one through six (24 students in all) selected on a random number basis. The interviews were conducted by two Chinese (male and female) child guidance experts.

There was a noticeable difference in the response patterns between the country public school children and the children of the city schools, children from the country public school being generally less articulate and also more prone to answer Don't Know. The children from the city private school were the most articulate, a result which conforms to findings about American children. Greenstein has pointed out that higher-status children in the United States tend to have superior verbal and scholastic capacity and a greater ability to express feelings and ideas.[1]

---

1. Fred I. Greenstein, *Children and Politics* (New Haven, Conn.: Yale University Press, 1965), pp. 90–91.

In administering the various tests, one major problem was that first- and second-grade children were too deficient in a knowledge of Chinese characters to read and respond to the open-ended questionnaire and the projective test. To surmount this difficulty I utilized fifth- and sixth-grade girls to sit with the smaller children, read the questions to them, and write down the spoken response. The girls were instructed to read only the question and in no way to suggest a response. Generally I felt these little assistants carried out their tasks conscientiously. However, either because my instructions were imperfectly carried out or because the oral responses tended to differ from the written ones, it will be noticed that younger children's responses (and particularly those of second graders) tend to show some shifts in the direction of upper grades. These differences are by no means consistent. In any case I did not feel they were large enough to invalidate either the testing method or the data.

With the exception of first and second grades and the interviews, all testing was supervised by myself (even in first and second grade I gave the instructions and generally supervised). The one exception was a fifth-grade class at the city public school. There a teacher insisted on "helping" me and in doing so suggested many responses. It was interesting to note the very considerable effect this "help" had on the data. Unfortunately, however, the responses were so biased that I had to eliminate city public school fifth-grade data from the analysis.

In analyzing differences between Mainlanders and Taiwanese, all data from the city private school was omitted. The inclusion of this school, composed almost entirely of Mainland children, tended to misrepresent the data by creating apparent ethnic differences out of what in fact were socioeconomic differences. Therefore, only the data from the two public schools was used when analyzing for this factor.

The various questionnaires that were used follow.

I. Open-Ended Questionnaire (translated from the Chinese)

A Questionnaire for Students

The questions written below are not a test. There is no wrong answer and no right answer. Answer just as you wish to. (Children were instructed not to write their names on the questionnaire.)

If your answer is a person, write who this person is but do not write his name. If you do not know the answer to any question, write "I don't know."

A. You and Your Family
   1. How old are you?   Are you a boy or a girl?
      What grade are you in?
   2. Who lives at your home?
   3. Is your father Taiwanese or a Mainlander?
      What is his occupation?
   4. Is your mother Taiwanese or a Mainlander?
      What is her occupation?
   5. Does your family believe in a religion?   Which religion?
   6. Are you a member of a school activity?
      Are you a member of the Scouts or a sports team?
      What is the name of the activity you participate in?

B. Who Decides
   At Home
   1. If you wanted to change schools, who in your family would
      you ask?   Why?
   2. In a family discussion about whether to buy a new radio, who
      would decide?   Why?
   At School
   3. Who in your school decides when your school will have an
      assembly?   Why?
   In Your Town
   4. Who in Taipei decides whether a new park ought to be built?
      Why?

C. When Something Is Wrong
   At Home
   1. Do you think what your father and mother say is always right?
      If they said something you thought was wrong, what would
      you do?
   At School
   2. Do you think your teachers are always right?
      If they said something you thought was wrong, what would
      you do?

D. Your Opinion
   1. When you grow up, what kind of person do you want to be like?
   2. When you grow up what job would you like to do?
   3. Who is your favorite Chinese hero?

Who is the kindest person?
Who is the worst person?
Who is the smartest person?

E. Who Comes First

At Home

1. Between boys and girls, who in your house always get new clothes first? Who always eats an apple first?

2. Between younger and older people, who always first get the best things to eat?   Who sits in the most comfortable seat?

School and Home

3. If your teachers told you something at school and your parents told you the opposite at home, who would you think was usually right?

In Your Town

4. In your town, which people ride in the best and nicest cars? Which people live in the best and nicest homes?

F. Whose Job

At Home

1. Who is the head of your home?   What do you feel about this person?

At School

2. Who is the head of your school?   What do you feel about this person?

In Your Town

3. Who is the head of the Taipei City government? What do you feel about this person?

G. Why You Do Things

At Home

1. If you didn't want to go to bed but your mother told you to go to bed, what would you do?   Why?

At School

2. If the teacher asked you to clean the blackboard but you didn't want to, what would you do?   Why?

H. You and Others

At Home

1. If all the family wants to buy oranges but one child wants to buy bananas, how should the family be toward the one child? What do you think of the opinion of the child who wants to buy bananas?

At School

2. If cleaning the blackboard is your work but you have forgotten, do you feel the other students should also be blamed? Why?

In Your Town

3. If a group of people have decided to go together to a park and one of them knows of a shortcut, do you think that person ought to tell the others?   Why?

I.   Why People Do Things

At Home

1. Why do parents punish children?

In Your Town

2. Sometimes people who drive cars go through red lights. Why do you think they do this? How do you feel the police should react to this?

J.   Why People Have the Responsibility

1. A little boy grew up to be a famous man in the government. What do you think the reason for this was?

2. A person in the military could not become an officer. What do you think the reason for this was?

3. A child was not elected to be the class leader. What do you think the reason for this was?

K.   When You Play Games

1. When you and your schoolmates are wondering what games to play, are you the one who usually decides? Do you like to be the one who decides?

2. Do you think a basketball team should have a captain? Why?

II. Projective Questionnaire

The accompanying four pictures (in large poster size) were used to obtain projective responses.

When writing stories about the events in the pictures the children were asked to use the following special form. As with the open-ended questionnaire, the children were asked not to write their names on the questionnaire form.

The Schoolroom

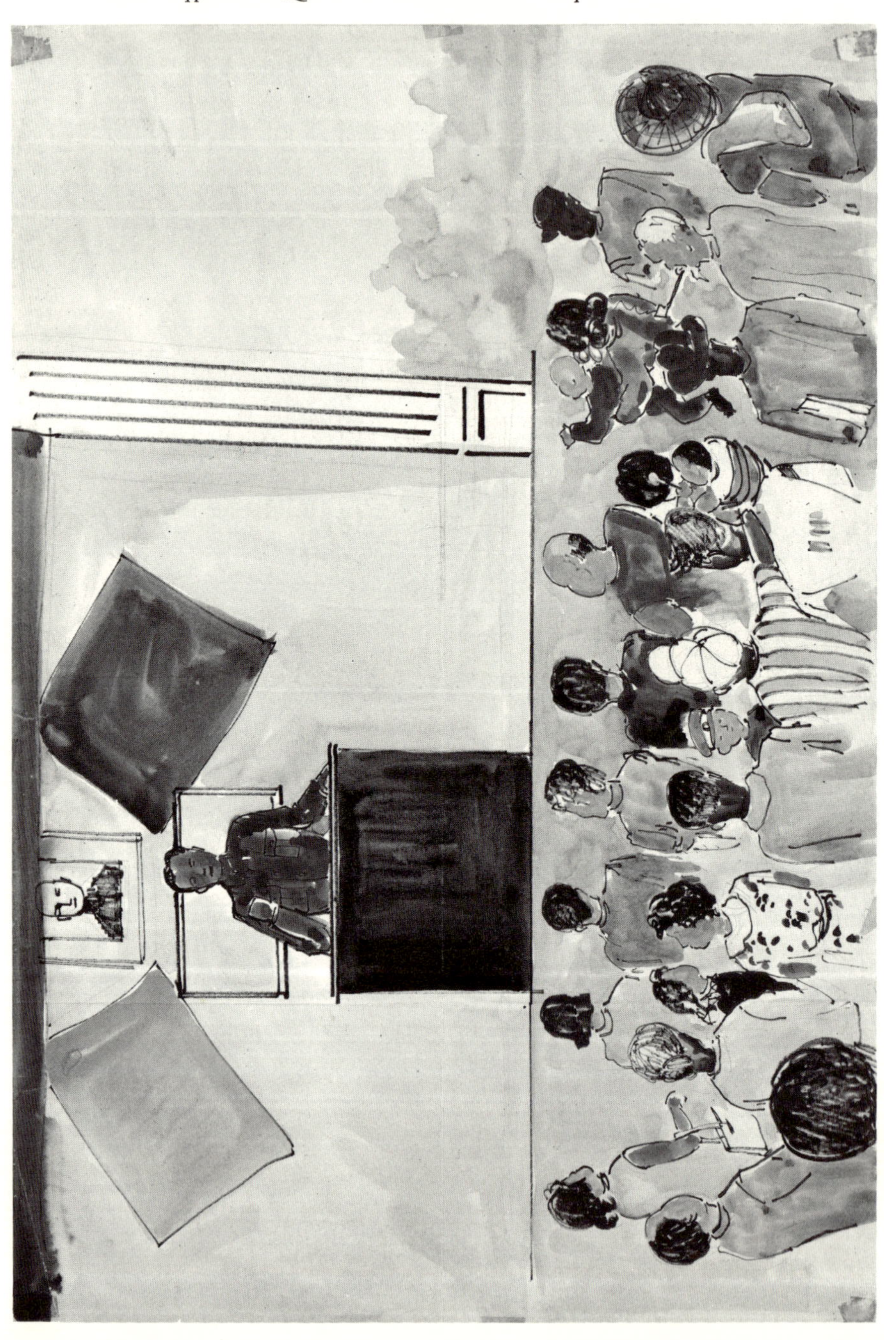

Public Meeting

Family

Policeman/Vendor

Speaking of Your Impressions
(translated from the Chinese)

A. You and Your Family
   1. What school do you go to?
   2. How old are you?
   3. Are you a boy or a girl?
   4. Are your father and mother Taiwanese or Mainlanders?
   5. What is your father's occupation?
B. The questions written below are not a test. There is no right or wrong answer to these questions. First look at the picture and then write what you think below each of the questions. Write down whatever pleases you.

   Please first write down the number of the picture you are using. Afterward answer the questions below. (Each of the four pictures had a number which I wrote on the blackboard beneath the picture when hanging them. This was done to distinguish the responses. On the forms there was considerable spacing between the questions so that the children could develop their responses. This spacing has been omitted here.)
   1. Who are these people? What are they doing?
   2. How did this situation occur?
   3. What are the people thinking? What do they want to do?
   4. What will happen after this situation takes place?
      Please write down what you think is likely to happen.
   5. After this situation occurs, what kind of feelings will they have?
   6. Do you think the situation in the picture is good or bad? Please discuss your opinion.

III. Cognitive Images of Government Questionnaire

   The accompanying form was administered to grades one through six. On this questionnaire older children were not requested to assist first and second graders. The children were requested to check the appropriate boxes in Section A and in Section C to put the numbers of two pictures in the boxes provided beneath each question.

   The questions under Section A read as follows: (1) Name of School; (2) Grade Level (one through six); (3) Boy or Girl; (4) Taiwanese or Mainlander.

A.

1. 學校名稱：
2. ☐一年級　☐二年級　☐三年級　☐四年級　☐五年級　☐六年級
3. ☐男　生　☐女　生
4. ☐外省人　☐本省人

B.

（1）

警　察

（2）

國　父

（3）

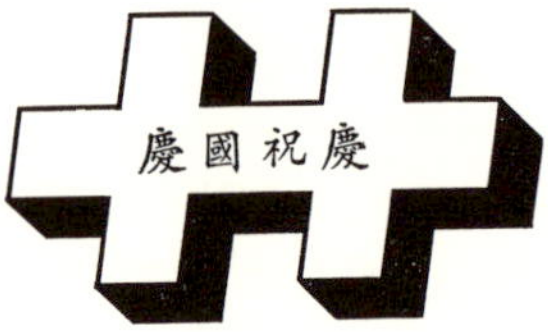

慶國祝慶

雙　十　節

（4）

選　舉

（5）

法　院

（6）

總　統　府

（7）

立　法　院

（8）

國　旗

（9）

三民主義

三　民　主　義

（10）

蔣　總　統

（11）

我
不
知
道

C. 問　答

1. 當你想到政府的時候最先想到的是什麼？

☐　　☐

2. 法律是誰規定（作成）的？

☐　　☐

Chinese questionnaire

Each picture in Section B was labeled as follows: (1) Police; (2) Father of the Country; (3) Double Ten (The Nationalist Chinese "Fourth of July"); (4) Voting; (5) Law Courts; (6) Presidential Palace; (7) Legislative Yuan; (8) National Flag; (9) Three Principles of the People; and (10) President Chiang. The lettering in box (11) reads "I Don't Know." In picture (3) the lettering on the symbol reads "Congratulatory Wishes to the National Celebration." The inscription on the book in picture (9) says "Three Principles of the People."

In Section C are two questions. The first reads "When you think of government, what is the first thing you think of?" The second question is "Who makes the laws?"

IV. Interview Questions

Each of the interviewers was given a set of questions. The interview was to be allowed to develop as naturally as possible, using the projective test posters (and particularly the public meeting scene) as a basis for discussion. All the questions were to be asked, if possible, but there was no set pattern and interesting sidelines were to be explored, if appropriate. In general, each interview covered the following questions:

A. What responsibility does the leader have for followers?
B. What responsibility do followers have toward leaders?
C. What are the characteristics of a leader?
D. Is a leader necessary? Why do we have leaders? What is the job of leaders? Is the leader's job to tell us what we should be like?
E. Are leaders always right? Should we follow leaders if they are not right?
F. Can a leader be criticized? When can a leader be criticized? Which leaders can be criticized?
G. Can a leader do something that everybody does not want done?
H. How is a leader selected?
I. How can a leader be gotten rid of?
J. How should we feel about people who don't agree with a leader?
K. Should a person go against the group and try to lead himself if he thinks he is right?

Bibliography

Abel, Theodora M., and Hsu, Francis L. K. "Some Aspects of Chinese as Revealed by the Rorschach Test," *Journal of Projective Techniques*, vol. 13, no. 3 (Sept. 1949).

Abernethy, David B., and Coombe, Trevor. "Education and Politics in Developing Countries," *Harvard Educational Review*, vol. 35, no. 3 (Summer 1965).

Albrecht, Milton C. "Does Literature Reflect Common Values?" *American Sociological Review*, vol. 21, no. 6 (Dec. 1956).

Almond, Gabriel A. "A Developmental Approach to Political Systems," *World Politics*, vol. 17, no. 2 (Jan. 1965).

Almond, Gabriel A., and Verba, Sidney. *The Civic Culture: Political Attitudes and Democracy in Five Nations*. Boston: Little, Brown and Company, 1965.

Apter, David. E. "Non-Western Government and Politics," in *Comparative Politics*, Harry Eckstein and David E. Apter, eds. New York: Free Press of Glencoe, 1963.

Arendt, Hannah. *Between Past and Future: Six Exercises in Political Thought*. New York: The World Publishing Company, Meridian Books, 1963.

Axelbank, Albert. "Chiang Kai-shek's Silent Enemies," *Harper's Magazine*, Sept. 1963.

Azrael, Jeremy R. "Soviet Union," in *Education and Political Development*, James S. Coleman, ed. Princeton, N.J.: Princeton University Press, 1965.

Bandura, Albert, and Walters, Richard H. *Social Larning and Personality Development*. New York: Holt, Rinehart & Winston, Inc., 1963.

Bates, F. L. "A Conceptual Analysis of Group Structure," *Social Forces*, vol. 36, no. 2 (Dec. 1957).

Benedict, Ruth. *The Chrysanthemum and the Sword*. Tokyo: Charles E. Tuttle Co., 1954.

Berger, Peter L. *Invitation to Sociology: A Humanistic Perspective*. Garden City, N.Y.: Doubleday & Company, Inc., Anchor Books, 1963.

Boorman, Howard L. "The Men Who Rule China," *Diplomat*, vol. 27, no. 196 (Sept. 1966).

Bredemeier, Harry C., and Stephenson, Richard M. *The Analysis of Social Systems*. New York: Holt, Rinehart & Winston, Inc., 1962.

Brim, Orville G., Jr., and Wheeler, Stanton. *Socialization after Childhood: Two Essays*. New York: John Wiley & Sons, Inc., 1966.

Chang, David W. "U.S. Aid and Economic Progress in Taiwan," *Asian Survey*, vol. 5, no. 3 (March 1965).

Chang, Jen-Chi. *Pre-Communist China's Rural School and Community*. Boston: The Christopher Publishing House, 1960.

Chen, Theodore H. E. "Elementary Education in Communist China," *The China Quarterly*, no. 10 (April-June 1962).

Chiang Kai-shek. "Chapters on National Fecundity, Social Welfare, Education, and Health and Happiness," in Sun Yat-sen, *San Min Chu I* [The Three Principles of the People]. Taipei, Taiwan: China Publishing Co., n.d.

———. *China's Destiny*. New York: Roy Publishers, 1947.

———. "On the Birthday Centennial of Dr. Sun Yat-sen," *China Post*, vol. 14, no. 4773 (Nov. 12, 1965).

Child, Irvin L. "Socialization," in *Handbook of Social Psychology*, vol. 2, Gardner Lindzey, ed. Cambridge, Mass.: Addison-Wesley Publishing Co., Inc., 1954.

Chu, Godwin Chien. *Culture, Personality, and Persuasibility*. Unpublished doctoral dissertation (Mass Communications Research), Stanford University, 1963.

Ch'u, T'ung-tsu. *Law and Society in Traditional China*. Paris and The Hague: Mouton and Co., 1961.

Clubb, O. Edmund. "Sino-American Relations and the Future of Formosa," *Political Science Quarterly*, vol. 80, no. 1 (March 1965).

Coleman, James S., ed. *Education and Political Development*. Princeton, N.J.: Princeton University Press, 1965.

Coleman, James S., and Almond, Gabriel A. *The Politics of the Developing Areas*. Princeton, N.J.: Princeton University Press, 1960.

Coser, Lewis A. *The Functions of Social Conflict* Glencoe, Ill.: The Free Press, 1956.

Cox, F. N. "An Assessment of Children's Attitudes towards Parent Figures," *Child Development*, vol. 33, no. 4 (Dec. 1962).

Davies, James C. "The Family's Role in Political Socialization," *Annals of the American Academy of Political and Social Science*, vol. 361 (Sept. 1965).

De Bary, William Theodore; Chan, Wing Tsit; and Watson, Burton. *Sources of Chinese Tradition*. New York: Columbia University Press, 1960.

Deese, James. *The Psychology of Learning*. New York: McGraw-Hill Book Co., Inc., 1952.

Dollard, John. "Hostility and Fear in Social Life," *Social Forces*, vol. 17, no. 1 (Oct. 1938).

Dubin, Elisabeth Ruch and Robert. "The Authority Inception Period in Socialization," *Child Development*, vol. 34, no. 4 (Dec. 1963).

Easton, David, and Dennis, Jack. "The Child's Image of Government," *Annals of the American Academy of Political and Social Science*, vol. 361 (Sept. 1965).

Eckstein, Harry. *A Theory of Stable Democracy*, research monograph no. 10. Princeton, N.J.: Center of International Studies, 1961.

Eckstein, Harry, and Apter, David. E., eds. *Comparative Politics*. New York: Free Press of Glencoe, 1963.

Economic, Social, and Political Change in the Underdeveloped Countries and Its Implications for U.S. Policy, Center for International Studies, Massachusetts Institute of Technology, report prepared for Senate Foreign Relations Committee, pursuant to S.R. 336, 85th Congress, and S.R. 31, 86th Congress. Washington, D.C.: Government Printing Office, 1960.

Education and Development: The Role of Educational Planning in the Economic Development of the Republic of China, vol. 2 (prepared for the Minister of Education, Government of the Republic of China, Taipei, Taiwan). Menlo Park, Calif.: Stanford Research Institute, 1962.

Education in Asia. Tokyo: Ministry of Education, 1964.

Educational Statistics of the Republic of China. Taiwan: Ministry of Education, 1964.

Erikson, Erik H. *Childhood and Society.* New York: W. W. Norton & Company, Inc., 1950.

————. "Growth and Crises of the Healthy Personality," in *Personality in Nature, Society, and Culture,* 2nd edition, Clyde Kluckhohn and Henry A. Murray, eds., with the collaboration of David M. Schneider. New York: Alfred A. Knopf, 1954.

————. *Young Man Luther.* New York: W. W. Norton & Company, Inc. (The Norton Library), 1962.

Fairbank, John K. "How to Deal with the Chinese Revolution," *The New York Review of Books,* vol. 6, no. 2 (Feb. 17, 1966).

Fei, Hsiao-tung. *Peasantry and Gentry: An Interpretation of Chinese Social Structure and Its Changes,* reprinted from *The American Journal of Sociology,* vol. 52, no. 1 (July 1946). New York: International Secretariat, Institute of Pacific Relations, [1946?].

Froman, Lewis A., Jr. "Learning Political Attitudes," *The Western Political Quarterly,* vol. 15, no. 2 (June 1962).

————. "Personality and Political Socialization," *Journal of Politics,* vol. 23 (1961).

Fung Yu-Lan. *A Short History of Chinese Philosophy,* Derk Bodde, ed. New York: The Macmillan Company, 1962.

Geertz, Clifford, ed. *Old Societies and New States.* New York: Free Press of Glencoe, 1963.

Gibb, Cecil A. "Leadership," in *Handbook of Social Psychology,* vol. 2, Gardner Lindzey, ed. Cambridge, Mass.: Addison-Wesley Publishing Co., Inc., 1954.

Greenstein, Fred I. "The Benevolent Leader: Children's Images of Political Authority," *American Political Science Review,* vol. 54 (Dec. 1960).

————. *Children and Politics.* New Haven, Conn.: Yale University Press, 1965.

————. "More on Children's Images of the President," *Public Opinion Quarterly,* vol. 25 (Winter 1961).

Hagen, E. E. "How Economic Growth Begins: A General Theory Applied to Japan," *Public Opinion Quarterly,* vol. 22, no. 3 (Fall 1958).

Henry, Jules, and Boggs, Joan Whitehorn. "Child Rearing, Culture, and the Natural World," *Psychiatry,* vol. 15, no. 3 (Aug. 1952).

Hess, Robert D., and Easton, David. "The Child's Changing Image of the President," *Public Opinion Quarterly*, vol. 24, no. 4 (Winter 1960).

Hiniker, Paul. *Chinese Attitudinal Reactions to Forced Compliance: A Cross-Cultural Experiment in the Theory of Cognitive Dissonance*. Cambridge, Mass.: Research Program on Problems of International Communication and Security, Center for International Studies, Massachusetts Institute of Technology, 1965.

Hoselitz, Bert F. "Investment in Education and Its Political Impact," in *Education and Political Development*, James S. Coleman, ed. Princeton, N.J.: Princeton University Press, 1965.

Hsu, Francis L. K. *Americans and Chinese: Two Ways of Life*. New York: Henry Schuman, 1953.

Hsu, Leonard S. *Study of a Typical Chinese Town*. Peiping, China: The Leader Press, 1929.

Hu, Hsien Chin. "The Chinese Concepts of Face," *American Anthropologist*, vol. 46. no. 1, pt. 1 (Jan.-March 1944).

Hyman, Herbert H. *Political Socialization: A Study in Political Behavior*. Glencoe, Ill.: The Free Press, 1959.

Inkeles, Alex, and Levinson, Daniel J. "National Character: The Study of Modal Personality and Sociocultural Systems," in *Handbook of Social Psychology*, vol. 2, Gardner Lindzey, ed. Cambridge, Mass.: Addison-Wesley Publishing Co., Inc., 1954.

Jansen, Marius B., ed. *Changing Japanese Attitudes toward Modernization*. Princeton, N.J.: Princeton University Press, 1965.

Kahin, George McT.; Pauker, Guy J.; and Pye, Lucian W. "Comparative Politics of Non-Western Countries," *American Political Science Review*, Dec. 1955.

Kluckhohn, Clyde, and Murray, Henry A., eds. *Personality in Nature, Society, and Culture*. New York: Alfred A. Knopf, 1954.

Kulp, Harrison D. *Phenix Village: Kwangtung, China*. Country Life in South China: The Sociology of Familism, vol. 1. New York: Bureau of Publications, Teachers' College, Columbia University, 1925.

La Barre, Weston. "Some Observations on Character Structure in the Orient: The Chinese," *Psychiatry*, vol. 9, no. 3, pt. 1 (Aug. 1946), and vol. 9, no. 4, pt. 3 (Nov. 1946).

Larson, William R., and Myerhoff, Barbara G. "Primary and Formal Family Organization and Adolescent Socialization," *Sociology and Social Research*, vol. 50, no. 1 (Oct. 1965).

Latourette, Kenneth Scott. *The Chinese: Their History and Culture*. New York: The Macmillan Company, 1950.

Leites, Nathan. "Psycho-Cultural Hypotheses about Political Acts," *World Politics*, vol. 1 (Oct. 1948).

LeVine, Robert. "Political Socialization and Culture Change," in *Old Societies and New States*, Clifford Geertz, ed. New York: Free Press of Glencoe, 1963.

Levinson, Daniel J. "The Relevance of Personality for Political Participation," *Public Opinion Quarterly*, vol. 22, no. 1 (Spring 1958).

Levy, Marion J., Jr. *Some Problems of Modernization in China.* New York: Institute of Pacific Relations, 1949.

———. *The Structure of Society.* Princeton, N.J.: Princeton University Press, 1952.

Levy, Marion J., Jr., and Shih, Kuo-heng. *The Rise of the Modern Chinese Business Class.* New York: Institute of Pacific Relations, 1949.

Lifton, Robert J. *Thought Reform and the Psychology of Totalism.* New York: W. W. Norton and Company, 1961.

———. "Youth and History: Individual Change in Postwar Japan," *Daedalus,* vol. 91 (Winter 1962).

Lin, Tsung-yi. "A Study of the Incidence of Mental Disorder in Chinese and Other Cultures," *Psychiatry: Journal for the Study of Interpersonal Processes,* vol. 16, no. 4 (Nov. 1953).

Lindzey, Gardner, ed. *Handbook of Social Psychology.* Cambridge, Mass.: Addison-Wesley Publishing Co., Inc., 1954.

Loh, Pichon P. Y. "The Politics of Chiang Kai-shek: A Reappraisal," *The Journal of Asian Studies,* vol. 25, no. 3 (May 1966).

McClelland, David C. *The Achieving Society.* Princeton, N.J.: D. Van Nostrand Co., Inc., 1961.

———. *Personality.* New York: The Dryden Press, 1951.

McGowan, Rev. John. *Sidelights on Chinese Life.* London: Kegan, Paul, Trench, Trübuer and Co., Ltd., 1907.

March, James G. "Group Autonomy and Internal Group Control," *Social Forces,* vol. 33, no. 4 (May 1955).

Marcus, Philip M. "Expressive and Instrumental Groups: Toward a Theory of Group Structure," *The American Journal of Sociology,* vol. 66, no. 1 (July 1960).

Meisner, Maurice. "The Development of Formosan Nationalism," *The China Quarterly,* no. 15 (July-Sept. 1963).

Merelman, Richard M. "Learning and Legitimacy," *The American Political Science Review,* vol. 60, no. 3 (Sept. 1966).

Merton, Robert K.; Broom, Leonard; and Cottrell, Leonard S., Jr., eds. *Sociology Today.* New York: Basic Books, Inc., 1959.

Myrdal, Jan. *Report From a Chinese Village.* London: William Heinemann Ltd., 1965.

Neff, Kenneth L. *National Development through Social Progress: The Role of Education.* Washington, D.C.: Department of Health, Education, and Welfare, OE-10027, Bulletin 8, 1963.

Newcomb, T. M. "Communicative Behavior," in *Approaches to the Study of Politics,* Roland Young, ed. Evanston, Ill.: Northwestern University Press, 1958.

Osgood, Charles E. "Behavior Theory and the Social Sciences," in *Approaches to the Study of Politics,* Roland Young, ed. Evanston, Ill.: Northwestern University Press, 1958.

Parsons, Talcott. "General Theory in Sociology," in *Sociology Today,* Robert K. Merton, Leonard Broom, and Leonard S. Cottrell, Jr., eds. New York: Basic Books, 1959.

Parsons, Talcott, and Bales, Robert F. *Family, Socialization, and Interaction Process.* Glencoe, Ill.: The Free Press, 1955.

Passin, Herbert. "Japan," in *Education and Political Development,* James S. Coleman, ed. Princeton, N.J.: Princeton University Press, 1965.

―――. "Modernization and the Japanese Intellectual: Some Comparative Observations," in *Changing Japanese Attitudes toward Modernization,* Marius B. Jansen, ed. Princeton, N.J.: Princeton University Press, 1965.

Piaget, Jean. *The Moral Judgment of the Child.* New York: Collier Books, 1962.

Pinner, Frank A. "Parental Overprotection and Political Distrust," *Annals of the American Academy of Political and Social Science,* vol. 361 (Sept. 1965).

Pye, Lucian W. *The Dynamics of Hostility and Hate in Chinese Political Culture,* Center for International Studies, Massachusetts Institute of Technology (C/64–23), June 1964.

―――. *Politics, Personality, and Nation Building: Burma's Search for Identity.* New Haven, Conn.: Yale University Press, 1962.

Pye, Lucian W., and Verba, Sidney, eds. *Political Culture and Political Development.* Princeton, N.J.: Princeton University Press, 1965.

Queener, Llewellyn. "The Development of Internationalist Attitudes," *Journal of Social Psychology,* vols. 29–30 (1949).

Riecken, Henry W., and Homans, George C. "Psychological Aspects of Social Structure," in *Handbook of Social Psychology,* Gardner Lindzey, ed. Cambridge, Mass.: Addison-Wesley Publishing Co., Inc., 1954.

Riggs, Fred. W. *Formosa under Chinese Nationalist Rule.* New York: The Macmillan Company, 1952.

Rodd, William G. "A Cross-Cultural Study of Taiwan's Schools," *The Journal of Social Psychology,* vol. 50, 1st half (Aug. 1959).

Scofield, Robert W., and Sun, Chin-wan. "A Comparative Study of the Differential Effect upon Personality of Chinese and American Child Training Practices," *The Journal of Social Psychology,* vol. 52, 2nd half (Nov. 1960).

Sebald, Hans. "Studying National Character through Comparative Content Analysis," *Social Forces,* vol. 40, no. 4 (May 1962).

Sigel, Roberta. "Assumptions about the Learning of Political Values," *Annals of the American Academy of Political and Social Science,* vol. 361 (Sept. 1965).

Smith, Arthur H. *Chinese Characteristics.* New York: Fleming H. Revell Co., 1894.

―――. *Village Life in China.* New York: Fleming H. Revell Co., 1899.

Solomon, Richard H. *The Chinese Political Culture and Problems of Modernization,* Center for International Studies, Massachusetts Institute of Technology (C/64–38), n.d.

―――. "Educational Themes in China's Changing Culture," *The China Quarterly,* no. 22 (April-June 1965).

Sullivan, Mark. *Our Times,* vol. 2. New York: Charles Scribner's Sons, 1927.

Sun Yat-sen. *San Min Chu I* [The Three Principles of the People]. Taipei, Taiwan: China Publishing Co., n.d.

Sutton, Francis X. "Education and the Making of Modern Nations," in *Educations and Political Development*, James S. Coleman, ed. Princeton, N.J.: Princeton University Press, 1965.

Theodorson, George A. "The Function of Hostility in Small Groups," *The Journal of Social Psychology*, vol. 56, 1st half (Feb. 1962).

Tung, Chi-ping, and Evans, Humphrey. *The Thought Revolution*. New York: Coward-McCann, Inc., 1966.

Verba, Sidney. "Organizational Membership and Democratic Consensus," *The Journal of Politics*, vol. 27, no. 3 (Aug. 1965).

Weakland, John H. "Family Imagery in a Passage by Mao Tse-tung," *World Politics*, vol. 10, no. 3 (April 1958).

Webb, Eugene J., Campbell, Donald T., and Schwartz, Richard D. *Other Measures: A Survey of Unconventional and Cooperation-Free Measures for Social Science*. (This research was supported, in part, by the U.S. Office of Education, project C-998, contract 3–20–001, under provisions of Title VII of the National Defense Education Act, n.d.).

Weinstein, Eugene A. "Development of the Concept of Flag and the Sense of National Identity," *Child Development*, vol. 28, no. 2 (June 1957).

Whiting, John W. M., and Child, Irvin L. *Child Training and Personality: A Cross-Cultural Study*. New Haven, Conn.: Yale University Press, 1953.

Wilhelm, Helmut. "Chinese Confucianism on the Eve of the Great Encounter," in *Changing Japanese Attitudes toward Modernization*, Marius B. Jansen, ed. Princeton, N.J.: Princeton University Press, 1965.

Wright, Arthur F. "Struggle vs. Harmony: Symbols of Competing Values in Modern China," *World Politics*, vol. 6, no. 1 (Oct. 1953).

Wylie, Margaret. *Children of China*. Hong Kong: Dragonfly Books, 1962.

Yang, Martin C. *A Chinese Village: Taitou, Shantung Province*. New York: Columbia University Press, 1945.

Young, Roland, ed. *Approaches to the Study of Politics*. Evanston, Ill.: Northwestern University Press, 1958.

Chinese Bibliography

Chang Chin-hung and Wu Wen-kuei, eds. 張錦鴻, 吳文貴. *Yin-yüeh K'e-pen* 音樂課本 [Music Primer], books 1–8. Taipei, Taiwan, 1961 臺灣書店 [Taiwan Bookstore].

Ch'en Tao-sheng, ed. 陳道生. *Hsiao-hsueh Tzu-jan-k'o Chiao-hsueh-fa* 小學自然科教學法 [Teaching Methods for Elementary School Natural Science]. Taiwan, 1960 國立教育資料館 [National Educational Materials Office].

Cheng Ying, ed. 鄭嬰. *Yu-erh K'e-pen* 幼兒課本 [Beginner's Primer], books 1–3, Taipei, Taiwan, 1963 童年書店 [T'ung Nien Bookstore].

Chiang Kai-shek. *Chiao-yu Yu Ke-ming Chien Kuo ti Kuan-hsi* 教育與革命建國的關係 [The Relevance of Education to the Revolutionary Establishment of the Nation], Taiwan, 1958 中央文物供應社印行 [Central Educational Materials Supply House].

Ch'uang-tsao Shih-tai ti Chu-jen 創造時代的巨人 [Great Men Who Create an Age]. Taipei, Taiwan, 1965, 文儒出版社 [Wen Ju Publishing Co.].

Chung-kuo Ming-jen Yu-nien Ku-shih 中國名人幼年故事 [Stories of the Early Years of Famous Chinese Children]. Taipei, Taiwan, 1964 童年書店 [T'ung Nien Bookstore].

Chung-kuo Wei-jen Chuan 中國偉人傳 [Biographies of Notable Chinese]. Kaohsiung, Taiwan, 1966, prepared by the editorial department 正言出版社 [Cheng Yen Publishing Co.].

Chung-kuo Ying-hsiung Chuan 中國英雄傳 [Biographies of Chinese Heroes], Kaohsiung, Taiwan, 1966, prepared by the editorial department, 正言出版社 [Cheng Yen Publishing Co.].

Chung-kuo Ying-hsiung Chuan 中國英雄傳 [Biographies of Chinese Heroes]. Taipei, Taiwan, 1963 亞洲出版社有限公司 [Asia Publishing Co., Ltd.].

Chung-yang Jih-pao 中央日報 [Central Daily News]. Taipei, Taiwan.

Erh-nien Tzu-hsi 二年自習 [Second Grade Self-Study]. Taipei, Taiwan, 1965, prepared by the editorial department, 光大圖書出版社 [Kuang Ta Book Publishing Co.].

Hou Fan 侯璠, *Chiao-yu T'ung-chi-fa* 教育統計法 [Educational Statistical Methods], vol. 2. Taipei, Taiwan, 1957 中華文化出版事業社 [Chinese Cultural Affairs Publishing Co.].

Hsieh Ping ying *et al.* 謝冰瑩. *Ch'uan-chih Shao-nien Wen-k'u* 全知少年文庫 [A Literary Treasurehouse of Complete Knowledge for Young People], collection 7 (9 vols.). Taipei, Taiwan, 1964 華國出版社 [Hua Kuo Publishing Co.].

Hsieh T'ing-sen, Chang Jung-kung, and Chu Hsueh-tien 謝廷森, 張榮恭, 朱學典, *Wo-men Yung-yuan shih i Chia* 我們永遠是一家 [We Are Perpetually One Family]. Taichung, Taiwan, 1961 臺灣通訊社 [Taiwan News Agency].

Hsu Fu-kuan 徐復觀. *Hsueh-shu yu Cheng-chih chih Chien* 學術與政治之間 [Scholarship and Politics], vols. 1–2, Taichung, Taiwan, 1957 and 1963 中央書局 [Central Book Co.].

Kao Mo-yeh and Chou Lo-shan, eds. 高莫野 and 周樂山. *Ch'eng-yu Ku-shih* 成語故事 [Proverb Stories]. Kaohsiung, Taiwan, 1964 正言出版社 [Cheng Yen Publishing Co.].

Kung Pao-shan 龔寶善. *Tao-te Chiao-yu Shih-shih Luen* 道德教育實施論 [A Discussion of the Practical Application of Morals Education]. Taipei, Taiwan, 1962 國立教育資料館 [National Educational Materials Office].

Kuo-li Pien I Kuan 國立編譯館 [National Compilation and Translation Office]. *Kung-min Yu Tao-te* 公民與道德 [Citizenship and Morals], upper grades, book 1, *Tao-te K'o-pen* 道德課本 [Morals Primer], upper grades, books 2–4. Taiwan, 1964 臺灣省政府教育廳 [Office of Education, Taiwan provincial government].

———. *Kuo-yu K'e-pen* 國語課本 [Mandarin Primer], precharacter reader, lower and middle grades, books 1–8; upper grades, books 1–4. Taiwan, 1964 臺灣省政府教育廳 [Office of Education, Taiwan provincial government].

———. *Li-shih K'e-pen* 歷史課本 [History Primer], upper grades, books 1–4. Taiwan, 1964 臺灣省政府教育廳 [Office of Education, Taiwan provincial government].

———. *She-hui K'e-pen* 社會課本 [Social Studies Primer], books 1–4. Taiwan, 1964 臺灣省政府教育廳 [Office of Education, Taiwan provincial government].

———. *Suan-shu K'e-pen* 算術課本 [Arithmetic Primer], books 1–12. Taiwan, 1964 臺灣省政府教育廳 [Office of Education, Taiwan provincial government].

———. *Ti-li K'e-Pen* 地理課本 [Geography Primer], upper grades, books 1–4. Taiwan, 1964 臺灣省政府教育廳 [Office of Education, Taiwan provincial government].

———. *Tsu-jan K'e-Pen* 自然課本 [Nature Studies Primer], books 1–8. Taiwan, 1964 臺灣省政府教育廳 [Office of Education, Taiwan provincial government].

Kuo-min Hsueh-hsiao K'o-ch'eng Piao-chun 國民學校課程標準 [Curriculum Standards for National (Elementary) Schools]. Department of National (Elementary) Education, Ministry of Education. Taipei, Taiwan, 1962 正中書局 [Cheng Chung Book Co.].

Liu Hung-hsiang, ed. 劉鴻香. *Erh-t'ung Yen-chiu* 兒童研究 [A Study of Children], 21–23. Taipei, Taiwan, 1966 臺北師範專科學校兒童發展研究中心 [Taipei Normal College Child Development Research Center].

Liu Nien Tzu-hsiu 六年自修 [Sixth-Grade Homework], books 1, 2. Taiwan, 1964 臺灣圖書出版社 [Taiwan Book Publishing Co.].

Shih Chien-sheng *et al.* 施建生. *Chung-kuo Chiao-yu Hsien-k'uang* 中國教育現況 [The Present Nature of Chinese Education], 3 vols. Taipei, Taiwan, 1958

中華文化出版事業委員會 [Chinese Cultural Affairs and Publishing Commission].

Shih Hsiao-wen, ed. 施孝文. *Chung-kuo Ming-jen Yu-nien Ku-shih* 中國名人幼年故事 [Stories of Famous Chinese Children], book 2. Taipei, Taiwan, 1964 童年書店 [T'ung Nien Bookstore].

Suen Pang-cheng, ed. 孫邦正. *Hsiao-hsueh Tu-shu Chiao-hsueh-fa* 小學讀書教學法 [Methods for Teaching Reading in Elementary School]. Taiwan, 1961 國立教育資料館 [National Educational Materials Office].

Taiwan-sheng Cheng-fu Chiao-yu-t'ing Chu-pien, *Kuo-yu Chiao-hsueh Chih-yin, Ch'u-chi Ti-wu-ts'e*, 臺灣省政府教育廳主編, 國語教學指引, 初級第五冊 [Office of Education of the Taiwan Provincial Government, ed., A Guide for Teaching Mandarin, Beginner's book 5] Taiwan n.d., 臺灣書店印行 [Taiwan Bookstore Printing Co.].

Taiwan Tu-shu, Ch'u-pan-sheh 臺灣圖書出版社 [Taiwan Book Publishing Co.,]. *Erh-nien, San-nien, Szu-nien, Wu-nien, Chia-t'ing Lien-syi* 二年, 三年, 四年, 五年, 家庭練習 [Second-, Third-, Fourth- and Fifth-Grade Homework]. Taiwan, 1965.

Ts'ui Hsu Yuan-hui 崔徐遠暉. *Huo-shen—I-chih Lao-ying ti Ku-shih* 火神—一隻老鷹的故事 [The God of Fire—The Story of a Hawk]. Taiwan, 1958 臺灣商務印書館 [Taiwan Commercial Book Printing Office].

Tzu-hsiu Hsueh-yu 自修學友 [The Self-Study Fellow Student]. Taipei, Taiwan, 1964 學友圖書出版社 second grade [Hsueh-Yu Book Publishing Co.].

Tzu-hsiu Liang-yu 自修良友 [The Self-Study Companion], grades 2, 3. Taipei, Taiwan, 1965 良友書局 [Liang Yu Book Co.].

Wo-men ti Kuo-fu 我們的國父 [The Father of Our Country]. Taiwan, 1965, 文昌出版有限公司. [Wen Ch'ang Publishing Co., Ltd.].

Wo-men ti Tsung-t'ung 我們的總統 [Our President]. Taiwan, 1965, 文昌出版有限公司 [Wen Ch'ang Publishing Co. Ltd.].

Wu Yen-ho 吳燕和. "Ts'ung Jen-lei-hsueh Kuan-tien K'an Mu-ch'ien Chung-kuo Erh-t'ung ti" 從人類學觀點看目前中國兒童的 [An Anthropologist Looks at Chinese Child Training Methods], *Szu yu Yen* 思與言 [Thought and Word], vol. 3, no. 6 (March 1966). Taipei, Taiwan.

Wu Yuan-chieh, ed. 吳元杰. *Hsiao-hsueh She-hui-k'o Chiao-hsueh-fa* 小學社會科教學法 [Teaching Methods for Elementary School Social Studies]. Taipei, Taiwan, 1961 國立教育資料館 [National Educational Materials Office].

Yang Kuo-shu 楊國樞. "Hsien-tai Hsin-li-hsueh-chung Yu Kuan Chung-kuo Kuo-min-hsing ti Yen-chiu" 現代心理學中有關中國國民性的研究 [Modern Psychological Studies of the Chinese National Character], in *Szu yu Yen* 思與言 [Thought and Word], vol. 2, no. 5 (Jan. 1965). Taipei, Taiwan.

Yu-chih-yüan Ch'ang-shih 幼稚園常識 [Kindergarten Common Sense], books 1, 4. Taiwan, 1964 現代教育出版社 [Modern Education Publishing Co.].